ART
as therapy with children

ART
as therapy with children
second edition

EDITH KRAMER
introduction by Laurie Wilson

Magnolia Street Publishers — Chicago

© 1993 2nd edition
Published by
MAGNOLIA STREET PUBLISHERS
1250 W. Victoria
Chicago, Illinois 60660

Original © 1971 Schocken Books

ISBN: 0-9613309-4-5
Library of Congress Catalog Card No. xxxxxxxxxxx
Cover Design: Sarah Reinken
Printed in the USA

To Friedl

Contents

FOREWORD

INTRODUCTION TO THE SECOND EDITION *by Laurie Wilson*

INTRODUCTION *by Muriel M. Gardiner*

PREFACE

ACKNOWLEDGMENTS

I. *Art, Art Therapy, and Society*   1
   The Influence of Modern Psychology   4
   Art Therapy and Art Education   6
   Art and the Problem of Emptiness   9
      THE SCRIBBLE   10
      STEREOTYPED CHAOS   11
   The Underprivileged Spoiled Child   15
   New Defenses   17
   Emptiness and the Affluent Society   20

II. *Art, Art Therapy, and the Therapeutic Milieu*   25
   Art and Play   26
   Projection and Confrontation   29
   Confrontation in Art and in Psychotherapy   32
   Art and Craft   33
   The Function of the Art Therapist   34
   Interpretation of Reality and of Functioning   37
   Transference and Counter-Transference   38
   Practical Suggestions   43

III. *Art Therapy and the Problem of Quality in Art*   47
   Artistic Failure and Success   51
   Different Ways of Using Art Materials   54
      PRECURSORY ACTIVITIES   55
      EMOTIONAL DISCHARGE   55
      COMPULSIVE DEFENSES   56
      PICTOGRAPHS   59
      FORMED EXPRESSION   63

Contents

IV. *Sublimation*   67
The Concept of Sublimation   67
Displacement and Sublimation   70
Symptom and Sublimation   73
Sublimation in Process   80

V. *The Art Therapist's Role in Sublimation*   92
The Art Therapist's Function as an Extension of the Ego   93
The Talented Child and the Group   103
Support and Dependency   111
Approaches and Detours—For the Art Therapist   114

VI. *Art in the Service of Defense*   121
Art Education and Defense   123
Repetition and Stereotype   127
Examples of Stereotyped Art   130
Defense and Deadlock   143
Various Stereotyped Ways of Using Art Materials   147
Talent in the Service of Defense   149
Adolescent Art and Defense   156

VII. *Art Therapy and Aggression*   158
Dammed-Up Aggression   160
Aggression and Control   162
The Ego Ideal and Identification with the Aggressor   172
Aspects of Aggression   178
Ambivalence   194
    AMBIVALENCE AND IDENTIFICATION WITH
      THE AGGRESSOR   194
    AMBIVALENCE AND FORM   202
    AMBIVALENT FEELINGS TOWARD THE PRODUCT   203
Limitations of Art Therapy   205
Aggression Channeled, Reduced, and Transformed   208
Closing Remarks   220

EPILOGUE   225

BIBLIOGRAPHY   229

INDEX   235

Illustrations

In each instance where a child gave a name to his work, it has been used in this list. To help the reader's memory, descriptive titles have been given to work that was left unnamed.

1.	*Kenneth*: Giant	31
2.	*Bob*: Champion	31
3.	*Max*: Black and White	53
4.	*Robert*: Sneaker	58
5.	*Kramer*: Benign Trap	61
6.	*Angel*: Benign Trap	61
7.	*Robert*: Reconciliation Picture	62
8.	*Robert*: Dog with Blood and Caca	63
9.	*Christopher*: Spring Tree	78
10.	*Christopher*: Great Blue Heron	78
11.	*Christopher*: Man with Dog and Bird	78
12.	*Tonio*: Man, detail	101
13.	*Tonio*: Man	101
14.	*Allan*: Portrait of Clyde	105
15.	*Clyde and Stanley*: Horse in Eclipse	107
16.	*Helen*: Santa Claus	126
17.	*Helen*: Pink Monster	126
18.	*Ralph*: Portrait of Eddie	128
19.	*Ann*: Birds	131
20.	*Henry*: Stars of David	132
21.	*Angel*: Superman	136
22.	*Angel*: The Occupational Therapist	136
23.	*Angel*: Portrait of the Art Therapist	136
24.	*Angel*: Hercules Fighting a Centaur	137
25.	*Angel*: Gemsbok	137
26.	*Frank*: Angry Indian	141
27.	*Larry*: Grinning Witch Doctor	151
28.	*Larry*: Brooding Witch Doctor	151
29.	*Larry*: Indian Chief	151

30.	*Larry:* Man with Bible	151
31.	*Larry:* Winter Night	153
32.	*Larry:* Christ	153
33.	*Alice:* Angry Girl	161
34.	*Margaret:* Caged Lion	166
35.	*Michael:* Father Dragon and Baby Dragon	169
36a.	*Walter:* Young Man with Switchblade	173
36b.	*Walter:* Boxer	176
37.	*Willie:* Rabbit Pursued by a Vulture	177
38.	*Willie:* Dragon	177
39.	*Leon:* Sea Battle	181
40.	*Leon:* Brown Horse and White Horse	183
41.	*Harry:* Giant Squid	187
42.	*Harry:* Protection Coat	190
43.	*Harry:* All-Purpose Animal	191
44.	*Gordon:* Egyptian Princess	199
45.	*Gordon:* Egyptian Princess, detail	199
46.	*Gordon:* Cyclops	201
47.	*Gordon:* Mexican Rider	201
48.	*Martin:* Burlesque Dancer	213
49.	*Martin:* City Street	217

PLATES

I. *Herman:* Fairies

II. *Herman:* Angel with Harp Pursued by a Devil

III. *Herman:* Family of Horses

IV. *Mary:* The Mountains of New Hampshire

V. *Lillian:* Tree Struck by Lightning

VI. *Gordon:* Moby Dick

VII. *Andrew:* Design with Indian's Head

VIII. *Andrew:* Portrait of a Friend

IX. *Frank:* Indian Chief

X. *Frank:* Mexican

XI. *Mrs. Smith:* Angry Cottage Parent

XII. *Willie:* Suspicious Devil

XIII. *Leon:* Horse Against Master

XIV. *Carl:* Lucifer and Angel

XV. *Carl:* Speedboat

XVI. *Martin:* Mad Santa Claus

Foreword

I am gratified to find that the ideas presented in "Art as Therapy with Children" have endured over more than twenty years. Thus, Sara Reinken and Kathryn Stern, publishers of Magnolia Street Press were able to venture a new edition. In its new guise the book will be read by a generation of art therapists as well as other individuals interested in the ideas presented, who live and work under conditions that differ in many ways from the situations I had encountered when I completed this book's manuscript in 1969.

I have therefore asked my friend, colleague and collaborator Dr. Laurie Wilson to introduce my book to the new readership, a request to which she gracefully consented.

Introduction to the
Second Edition

Art as Therapy with Children has been an invaluable text for
students of art therapy since its original printing in 1971. Though
the settings and populations about which Edith Kramer wrote have
changed considerably in the past two decades, the human condition
and the need to understand and assist children in trouble remains
unaltered. Edith Kramer's description of her methods and theories
hold up as well as the methods and theories themselves.

Two of the three places in which her work with children was
done have closed, Wiltwyck School and 9 West, the child psychiatric inpatient unit at Jacobi Hospital–Albert Einstein College of
Medicine. Longterm inpatient treatment for children is unfortunately rare and becoming rarer as economic pressures and the idea
of medication as a cure-all supersedes the expectation that long,
slow, careful therapeutic work with children can and will make a
substantial difference in their lives. Contemporary pressures for
quick results and behavioral solutions often outweigh a deeper
psychodynamic approach to pathology and treatment. Furthermore,
the kinds of children now seen in clinical and educational settings
are often more damaged and in deeper trouble than even those
seriously disturbed children seen by Edith Kramer twenty years
ago.

Today's children not only have to deal with the constant passive experience of continuous television watching, they are now assaulted by a vastly increased amount of graphic violence and raw sexual material in the visual media through movies and television. They are offered fewer opportunities to be active and creative than ever before as the family structures which were crumbling in the sixties and seventies have collapsed entirely for many of our present child populations. Families are now decimated by illness and death through AIDs and tuberculosis, as well as other diseases once thought cured. The dissolution of families along with economic hard times has been accompanied by a huge increase in abuse of children, sexual, physical and mental, usually in combination with familial substance abuse. The actual world of childhood is more dangerous than it has been in centuries, with guns in the streets, homes, and the schools, and with the options for escape into productive work rapidly diminishing.

Finally, the position of art in children's lives has continued to diminish since this book's first publication. Academic and economic pressures have made the arts seem increasingly irrelevant to educational establishments, which have seen their task grow from education to provision of societal structure and even daily nurturance, as children come to school unfed, unwashed, and exhausted from sleepless nights in chaotic homes. On a more positive note, we now know much more about the complications of learning disabilities and such conditions as hyperactivity.

In the face of all of these changes, Edith Kramer's profoundly wise volume offers inspiration and genuine assistance to the fledgling clinician as well as to anyone else working with children who wishes to understand how and why art can have such a profound effect. Clinicians working now in the face of such obstacles are in even greater need of the insights and observations in this book. They will be led to understand why the art in art therapy can be so effective. An example is Kramer's comments about the potential value of art therapy with Leon, a bright delinquent African-American boy functioning well under his potential.

"Art can absorb and contain more raw affect than most other

equally complex and civilized endeavors. In art, a child such as Leon, still deeply engrossed in his conflicts, can make the transition from fantasy to imagination, exercise his faculty for creating images that contain and express his feelings, and learn what it is like to function successfully. This can reduce the inclination to withdraw and may even help to stave off a break with reality."

Atheoretical approaches to treatment have become the norm, and many therapists now do not understand why their techniques work, only that if they follow this or that regimen, this or that result will unfold.

As Director of Art Therapy training at New York University and a clinician who has worked with children in urban and suburban settings for over twenty years, I know the value of this book. I have seen it open the eyes of students to the range of meanings decipherable in children's art and behavior they had not imagined. Miss Kramer's eloquent words capture the vital interplay between child, artwork and therapist, bringing to life the fast-moving events in an artroom peopled by emotionally disturbed children. I have also repeatedly heard how many people have been inspired to enter the field of art therapy as a result of reading this book.

Kramer's humility in the daunting task of seeking psychological change, coupled with her willingness to expose her own technical errors, are as good lessons as I can imagine of the value of honesty in writing about clinical work.

Eminently readable, yet sacrificing no complexity in its discussion of theory, *Art as Therapy with Children* is an ideal volume to be used for acquainting students of art therapy with some of the fundamental ideas in the field. Kramer's discussions of sublimation, art and defense, aggression, and the role of the art therapist have not been surpassed by later volumes or by other authors.

New material written for this edition informs the reader of the fate of several children with whom the author had worked, demonstrating both the extraordinary predictive powers of art and the potential and limits to which it can be put.

LAURIE WILSON, PH.D., ATR

Introduction

Art as Therapy with Children is more than its title indicates. Not only is it a stimulating study of a method of working with disturbed children, but, just as important, it rests on principles basically true for the education of all children.

Edith Kramer has worked as art therapist in a variety of settings with children suffering from just about every known emotional or social disorder: neurosis, psychosis, delinquency, the problems resulting from extreme deprivation, and the frustrations attending blindness and other handicaps. Her true and practical understanding stems from a deep knowledge of psychoanalysis combined with the skill and intuition of an artist and the humane love of a born teacher.

The book deals with such subjects—important for every human being—as sense of identity, feelings of emptiness, interpretation of reality, ambivalence, aggression, defenses, sublimation. It is organized around these ideas, and richly documented with case material. This book is not a collection of case histories, but the reader becomes intimately acquainted with a number of children as they appear and reappear in the various chapters which deal with one problem or another. Sublimation receives the thoughtful study it deserves (and so often fails to get) in any book having to do with therapy or education.

Awareness of the unconscious is essential in the art therapist's approach, the author tells us in her preface, but "art therapy is conceived of primarily as a means of supporting the ego, fostering the development of a sense of identity, and promoting maturation in general." These aims are never lost sight of throughout the book. Thus, in discussing nine-year-old Lillian who, fearful of a storm and of her own stormy fantasies, was nevertheless able to paint a dramatic picture of a storm, Miss Kramer writes: "Unconscious material could come close to the surface and find symbolic expression without endangering her necessary defenses. . . . She had transformed a potentially upsetting experience into creative adventure." The author emphasizes the importance of serenity in the actual act of painting, no matter how disturbing or negative may be the emotions the picture contains.

The children Miss Kramer describes come to life in a few well-chosen words. It is fascinating to glimpse, through these descriptions and the carefully selected illustrations, the development of their art and, through this, the growth of the children themselves. The reader need not be an artist or a teacher to follow the children's problems, their conflicts, ambitions, and successes or failures as they are presented in the brief but convincing portrayals of Martin, Gordon, Larry, and the many others. Perhaps the most moving story of all is that of the blind boy, Christopher, with his remarkably beautiful sculpture.

Edith Kramer understands the children's needs as well as the inner laws that govern the creative process in art, and realizes that the art therapist's role is determined by both of these. Concentrating on the specific, she allows general principles to emerge, alive and convincing.

Although the author has an excellent knowledge of psychoanalysis, she never attempts to be a psychotherapist—indeed, she purposely avoids this, remaining purely the art therapist. This should be heartening to every teacher, who can learn from Edith Kramer's insights and methods, even if working in a quite different field. For every child has creative drives which, if encouraged in an atmosphere of controlled freedom, can mean growth and satisfaction and joy, and a gain in self-esteem. To do something active and creative in this world of increasing mechanization and passivity is in itself therapeutic. Our children have become too used to looking and listening and taking in, rather than expressing in constructive form their thoughts, feelings, and dreams. Watching television, listening to the radio or record-player, cannot possibly take the place of doing, of making, in a child's development, nor can it offer half the satisfaction that creation gives. Miss Kramer shows us this by example and illustration.

I have seen the great success of a similar attitude in general teaching by a man who might well be called a "teaching therapist." A. J. Hill, formerly Inspector of East London Schools, gets every child he teaches, no matter what age or in what subject, to write a book. His belief is that the good teacher must draw on the unconscious of every child and give him the opportunity to express his thoughts and feelings in organized form, in an atmosphere of serenity. This is what Edith Kramer practices in her teaching of art, and describes simply and vividly in this well-written book.

As a psychoanalyst serving as psychiatric consultant in our public schools, and working daily with both normal and disturbed children and their teachers, I feel certain that *Art as Therapy with Children* will be of value not only to art therapists and art teachers but also to every teacher who is aware of the emotionally disturbed children in his classroom and is mindful of the conflicts and frustrations of even the "average" child. This is a book no person interested in therapy or education should miss.

MURIEL M. GARDINER, M.D.

Preface

This book presents ideas that have developed in the course of working with children in the field of art for more than thirty years.

My point of view is that of a practicing artist and educator who combines professional skills in the field of art with general knowledge of normality and pathology in childhood. The theoretical framework of my understanding of child psychology is based in the main on Freudian psychoanalytic thought. The emphasis, however, is on the idea of *art as therapy* rather than on psychotherapy which uses art as a tool. Thus, while the *therapeutic approach* is based on the *awareness* of psychic processes that include the unconscious, the *therapeutic maneuvers* described in this book do not depend on the uncovering of unconscious material or interpretation of unconscious meaning. Instead art therapy is conceived of primarily as a means of supporting the ego, fostering the development of a sense of identity, and promoting maturation in general. Its main function is seen in the power of art to contribute to the development of psychic organization that is able to function under pressure without breakdown or the need to resort to stultifying defensive measures. So conceived, art therapy becomes both an essential component of the therapeutic milieu and a form of therapy which complements or supports psychotherapy but does not replace it.

Insofar as philosophical thinking enters my concepts of art in general, they have been influenced by the work of Susanne

Langer, the one modern philosopher who has a concrete under-standing of the making of works of art and of the indivisible unity of form and content which it implies.

My understanding of child development in art and of methods of teaching art to children owes much to Viktor Lowen-feld, particularly to his ideas about work with the blind and the visually handicapped.

The first chapter, being confined to a discussion of the rise of art therapy as a profession and its relationship to art educa-tion, contains no case material. The rest of the book, on the other hand, depends on numerous vignettes as well as longer case histories that illustrate and document my ideas. These have been collected in a great many different situations. My earliest observations on the value of art for children under stress go back to the late 1930's, when I conducted art classes for the children of refugees from Nazi Germany in Prague.

It was among those traumatized children that I first observed the different responses to stress as they manifested themselves in children's art, responses that would later become so very familiar to me. I saw regression; repetition that told of unresolved con-flict; I first observed identification with the aggressor in children who identified with Hitler, who had proved his power by the very damage he had done to them; I saw withdrawal into frozen rigidity, and, finally, the capacity for creative expression surviv-ing under difficulties.

The artist who organized the classes that gave me my first taste of art as therapy, Friedl Dicker-Brandeis, remained in Czechoslovakia after its occupation by Nazi Germany. Eventu-ally she was confined in Terezin, where she continued to work with children. Their surviving art, which was salvaged after World War II and widely exhibited in Europe, testifies to the power of art in preserving and fostering children's capacity for growth and self-expression under hardship.

In 1939–41, I taught art at the Little Red Schoolhouse in New York, a progressive school for normal children. Later I worked in various neighborhood houses and other after-school programs. Thus I became acquainted with the art of children whose lives are rich in cultural and intellectual stimulation as well as of those who are deprived of it. Some of the lessons learned in these early years are incorporated in this book. One piece of case material on sublimation, for instance, is based on an experience that occurred at the Little Red Schoolhouse in 1941.

Most of my examples, however, were gathered between 1950 and the present, when I was working as a specialist. Some of my case material was collected in private practice. A few examples are taken from a therapeutically oriented art program which I conducted at the Leake and Watts Children's Home in Yonkers in 1960–63. The bulk of my case material derives from three art therapy programs which I initiated and conducted in three different settings: in a residential treatment home, in a hospital's child psychiatric ward, and at a day school for disturbed blind children.

Since this book is organized to present various aspects of art therapy rather than to describe methods of working in specific settings, my stories are selected to illustrate different ideas without regard to their sequence in time. Thus the same children appear and reappear throughout the book. The reader will become well acquainted with those children who figure on several occasions, but he will not learn much about the art programs in which they functioned. A brief description of these three settings therefore seems desirable.

I had my first sustained experience in art therapy at Wiltwyck School for Boys where I initiated and conducted a program from 1950 to 1957. I have described this experience in my book, *Art Therapy in a Children's Community.* Readers who are interested in a detailed account will find it in this book.

Wiltwyck School is a residential treatment home devoted to the rehabilitation of emotionally disturbed boys from the slums of New York City. The home is equipped to care for one hundred children of normal intelligence, aged eight to twelve. Although ready to deal with severe emotional disorders, Wiltwyck does not admit boys who require the safety of a hospital setting. The majority of the children show aggressive, delinquent behavior, although severely neurotic or withdrawn boys are also treated. In the eleven years since I left the agency, Wiltwyck has continued to grow, and the reader should remember that the conditions described in this book refer to the period between 1950 and 1957 only.

At this time one of the agency's weaknesses was a lack of funds and facilities for working with the children's families and for providing sufficient aftercare. At present a great deal is being done to rehabilitate the children's families. Family therapy sessions, for instance, are an important feature of the treatment program. In addition, the Floyd Patterson Home, a halfway house for adolescent boys, provides shelter and continued treatment for children who have outgrown Wiltwyck School but are still unready to return to the community.

A number of case histories presented in this book tell of difficulties that remained unresolved partly because the parents' pathology had not changed during the child's residence at the school, or show boys who had improved but were not ready at the age of thirteen to face a return to the slums. At present there are more resources at hand for meeting such problems than were available ten years ago.

In my story about "the Cobra," I have told of an episode in which a counselor's malign personality proved destructive to the boys in his charge. Had this counselor risen to a position of power in the administration (and such things are not unheard of), this would indeed have been an indictment of the agency's integrity. Since the counselor was discharged in due time, the episode only illustrates the hazards of hiring and firing child-care personnel. Unfortunate mistakes, such as the admission of a "Cobra" to a child-care staff, can never be totally safeguarded against. All an administration can do is recognize a destructive situation and see to it that it is soon terminated.

Another source of many examples has been a pilot program conducted under the auspices of the Albert Einstein Medical

College at the Jacobi Hospital in the Bronx, N.Y., which functions as a teaching hospital to the college. The program served a thirteen-bed psychiatric ward for children between three and nine years of age.

Most of the participating children were between five and nine years old, and had been diagnosed as borderline rather than acutely psychotic. On the whole, the children in the hospital ward were younger and more severely disturbed than the Wiltwyck boys.

Treatment facilities included individual psychotherapy, art and dance therapy, and occupational therapy, a nursery school program geared to the needs of severely disturbed children, and an elementary school staffed by trained teachers.

Since many of the children remained in the ward for a year or longer, it was possible to study in depth the function of art therapy for such a group.

Although professional standards were high and the therapeutic team, including nurses, nurse's aides, and orderlies, was enlightened and devoted, the treatment program's effectiveness was seriously curtailed by the inadequate physical setup. The children's ward was located on the ninth floor, not fully separated from the adolescent and adult psychiatric wards. Taking the children to playgrounds or on trips entailed engineering their departure through a general hospital entrance which inevitably exposed them to the sight of ambulances, stretchers, and sick and maimed patients.

The children's ward lacked adequate play areas or space for constructive activities. Art therapy sessions were held in a converted utility room, which provided running water and tile floor and walls, but lacked storage space or space in which to move around. (The program has since been continued in another ward, in a converted linen closet still smaller and without running water.) I mention these conditions because some of my examples show the children's response to the mazelike institutional environment in which they were confined.

Again it seems that this particular cause of trouble may be

alleviated by the time this book is published, for the construction of a 200-bed children's psychiatric hospital is now under way, and this will provide a carefully planned architectural setting for their care and treatment.

My work with the visually handicapped children at the day school maintained by the Jewish Guild for the Blind in New York has been another source of case material which is used repeatedly. The Guild School is the therapeutic arm of the Guild's psychiatric clinic. It provides an educational setting for blind and visually limited children who have learning and behavioral difficulties. The art program was initiated in 1964 and is still operating. Children are seen once a week, individually or in small groups never exceeding three at a time.

Ceramic clay, wire, wax, and other materials that lend themselves to three-dimensional representation are used. Every effort is made to counteract the restrictions that blindness imposes upon the child in attaining control of his own person and of his environment, to develop the child's body image and foster his sense of identity.

We see that this book is based on a wide range of experiences, but naturally they do not cover the whole field of art therapy with children. I believe that the principles developed in it are also applicable to situations of which I have no personal experience. The methods of implementing them, however, will vary according to both the necessities of the situation and the personality of the art therapist.

Acknowledgments

A great many people have helped me in the making of this book. As I acknowledge my indebtedness I regret that I cannot name them all.

Foremost I am grateful to the New Land Foundation for the grant which freed my time for writing. In particular I am grateful to Dr. Kurt Eissler and Dr. Muriel Gardiner for their confidence in my capacities as art therapist and writer.

For creating the position of art therapist at the child psychiatric ward at Jacobi Hospital and for the full freedom he gave me to use case material from this ward I thank Dr. Joseph Cramer, formerly director of child psychiatry at the Albert Einstein Medical College.

I also give thanks to the entire staff of the child psychiatric ward of Jacobi Hospital, in particular the nurses, nurse's aides, and teachers who respected and supported the art therapy program and graciously endured the disorder and disruption of routines caused by the children's work with art materials.

I thank Mrs. Marie Anchel, principal of the school conducted by the Jewish Guild for the Blind, and her staff of teachers for guidance in my work with the visually handicapped. Mr. Yasha Lisenco, sculptor, and director of the adults' activities program, supplied expert advice and help in the many technical problems one encounters in teaching sculpture to the blind.

The Wiltwyck School for Boys generously gave me access to

the agency's files so that I could refresh my memory of former pupils and inform myself of their later fate.

For her highly skilled editorial help I am deeply indebted to Elinor Ulman, editor of the *American Journal of Art Therapy*, who never tired of reading and rereading the manuscript as it took shape over three years.

I thank Mrs. Elizabeth Rosshandler, who managed to decipher my handwriting and transform it into typed manuscript.

To Dr. Annie Reich, who read this book in many stages, I am grateful for constructive criticism concerning psychoanalytic theory; I also owe much thanks to Dr. Viola Bernard for valuable criticisms and suggestions.

In giving this book its final shape I have had the invaluable help of Bertha Bornstein, who gave most generously of her time, her great wisdom as a child analyst, and her sense of clarity and economy in writing. I cannot thank her enough.

Finally I give thanks to all the many children with whom I have worked throughout the years, who have taught me more than books and have given me joy in my work.

I

Art, Art Therapy,
and Society

THE IDEA THAT self-expression through art is good for people and especially for unhappy people has been widely accepted. Social workers, family doctors, psychiatrists, and psychologists advise their troubled clients to find solace and satisfaction in art. Art programs are being established in prisons, training schools, and hospitals, in homes for disturbed children and homes for the aged, in neighborhood houses and clubs. This quest for salvation through art is gaining ascendancy at a time when art has all but disappeared as a normal ingredient of daily life.

Before the advent of industrialism there always existed, beyond the rise and fall of styles and schools of art, art as one of the natural by-products of the business of making things by hand. Not only decorative folk art, which constitutes a kind of overflow of the joy of making and possessing things, but the very style of the total environment made by man inevitably expressed and reflected the character of the people who made it. In this way, a certain measure of self-expression and self-recognition was woven into the fabric of daily life, satisfying the needs of the average man, so that it was natural that only the artists among the population were driven to wrestle with art in its more severe, undiluted form.

When most things are produced by machine the average person misses the sense of well-being that comes about when the pattern of life is reflected and confirmed by the physical appearance of the environment. It is no longer possible to contribute

1

to these forms simply by working with one's hands on tasks that are part of everyday life.

I believe that this deficiency has created a hidden hunger, a feeling of emptiness, and a fear of loss of identity that drive people to seek out art experiences where they can still be found. Their need, often vaguely described as a desire for "self-expression," contributes, along with the increase of leisure time, to the influx of mediocre students to art schools, to the proliferation of art programs for amateurs, to the popularity even of such travesties of art as number-painting kits. It is disconcerting that a basically sound desire should so often result in deplorably inept attempts that lead to anti-art rather than to art.

Inasmuch as art therapy constitutes an organized attempt to bring art into the lives of troubled people, it is also a response to this unfulfilled need. Because it has been recognized that art is somehow good for people, we try to introduce it into the artificial environments that society provides for its sick members, and because art is no longer a normal ingredient of life, specialists must be found who know how to make this mysterious matter palatable.

The goal of art therapy and the skills that are brought to it go beyond the aims of recreation or of art education. However, if we want to understand how art therapy actually functions, we must recognize how profoundly both the absence of a living tradition in the fine arts and the lack of art in everyday life influence the work of the art therapist.

Often it seems that the attempts to introduce artistic experience as a remedy for emotional suffering are comparable to the reintroduction of vitamins into foods that have lost their innate vitality through excessive processing. The dangers are even greater. Our vitamin-enriched bread, for instance, remains inferior in taste and quality to the bread that was baked before the original flavor was lost and before vitamins were discovered. Artificial art programs in hospitals, prisons, or treatment homes are frequently just as flavorless and dull as the boiled cotton that goes by the name of bread, but while even tasteless bread can provide nourishment, insipid art programs are totally useless, for the nourishment of the soul cannot be divorced from the vitality and flavor of the spiritual food which is offered.

But how does one go about awakening and nourishing the creative spirit in an artificial community of damaged and troubled people? The problem reaches beyond the art therapist's area of competence. Nevertheless, because the art therapist works with art in its most raw and simple form, because he is in a position where it is possible to experiment, art therapy can contribute to the understanding and even in a modest way to the solution of the problem. We can learn about the conditions that bring forth art that has truth and vitality and about those that produce saccharine rubbish, vulgar monstrosities, and other forms of anti-art. This knowledge may help us to wrestle more successfully with the forces that destroy art where it is sensible to combat them, and to learn to accept them where this is unavoidable.

When a system fails to function smoothly we are forced to learn about the many interlocking factors that are necessary for its maintenance. In the void left by the decline of traditional forms we have encountered art in the raw.

For instance, the special character of the art of children and the regularity of its development could not easily be discerned in an environment where folk art was practiced. The naïve representational style of folk art is readily understood by the average eight- to twelve-year-old child. Children who grow up in such traditions begin to imitate the work of their elders successfully from an early age. Therefore, the particularly childlike characteristics of those children's art tend to remain unnoticed by the observer. When, on the other hand, strong traditions of highly evolved art prevail, children's products are overlooked or stifled because they are by such standards unacceptable. It is only when folk art was on the wane and when established artistic traditions had lost their vitality that the art of children began to attract attention.[1] The unusual and bizarre products of the insane, the

1. Cf. Franz Cižek, *Children's Colored Paper Work.*

work of retarded persons and the blind became a matter of interest for much the same reasons.[2]

We see that the state of art in our society has had a profound and contradictory effect on the development of art therapy. The decline of tradition in the fine arts and the disappearance of folk art was one of the causes for the discovery of those art forms which develop beyond the pale of tradition and are the art therapist's chief interest. The widespread unfulfilled need for art has contributed to the rise of art therapy as a profession. These same conditions, on the other hand, also impede the art therapist's work, for when the creative capacities of the ordinary citizen no longer have a legitimate function beyond the confines of the therapeutic milieu, it is hard to make art therapy a living experience.

THE INFLUENCE OF MODERN PSYCHOLOGY

The newly awakened interest in previously neglected forms of art would have remained purely descriptive if modern psychology had not provided new tools for their understanding.[3] Artists and educators such as Florence Cane, Margaret Naumburg, and Henry Schaefer-Simmern began to combine their own skills with the study of psychoanalytic theory and to practice remedial art activities which eventually acquired the name of art therapy.[4]

It is interesting that art therapy has—with a considerable time lag—mirrored certain patterns of the development of psychoanalysis. For example, emphasis in psychoanalysis moved from fascination with the unconscious and with interpretation of

2. Cf. L. Münz and V. Lowenfeld, *Plastische Arbeiten Blinder;* H. Prinzhorn, *Bildnerei der Geisteskranken.*
3. L. Bender, *Child Psychiatric Techniques;* Ernst Kris, *Psychoanalytic Explorations in Art.*
4. Florence Cane, *The Artist in Each of Us;* Margaret Naumburg, *Studies of the Free Art Expression of Behavior Problem Children and Adolescents;* Henry Schaefer-Simmern, *The Unfolding of Artistic Activity.*

dreams and symptoms to the investigation of developmental phases and of psychic structure, and still later to the study of the ego. Art therapists such as Margaret Naumburg likewise initially focused mainly on the interpretation of unconscious meaning and of graphic symbols in art production. When the close relationship between graphic form and character structure was noted, interest in the formal qualities of art work and in diagnosis quickened.[5] When, finally, psychoanalytic ego psychology was better understood it was recognized that inner consistency and unity of form and content in art were the work of the ego, and aesthetic qualities became phenomena worthy of observation.[6]

There are a number of reasons why art therapists have been slow to concern themselves with the problem of artistic quality. The basic rule, which applies in art therapy as it applies in psychotherapy, of accepting all products, regardless of form or content, is not conducive to posing the question of quality. Furthermore, art therapy—straddling art and therapy—has one foot in a field that is on an upward trend, the other in an area of helpless turmoil. While there have been advances in medicine and psychotherapy, the visual arts have been split into commercial pseudo-art and frantic search for meaning in the fine arts, with no remedy in sight.

It is not surprising that art therapists have been inclined to stay close to the more promising field of psychotherapy. Ultimately, however, these very conditions force the art therapist to focus upon the *art* in art therapy. There is, in my opinion, evidence that the lack of active art experiences and the concomitant saturation with pseudo-art among large segments of the population constitute a pathogenic condition. The art therapist is in a position both to contribute to the understanding of this condition and to help develop methods of dealing with it. As

5. R. H. Alschuler and L. W. Hattwick, *Painting and Personality;* E. F. Hammer, *Clinical Application of Projective Drawings;* H. Y. Kwiatkowska, "The Uses of Families' Art Productions for Psychiatric Evaluation"; E. Ulman, "A New Use of Art in Psychiatric Diagnosis."
6. E. Kramer, "The Problem of Quality in Art"; "Stereotypes."

concern over the function of the total environment in the under-standing of emotional difficulties becomes more widespread, art therapy will join forces with the new discipline of community psychiatry, which focuses on the relationship between socio-cultural conditions and the epidemic rise of specific syndromes of emotional disturbance.[7]

RAPY AND ART EDUCATION

rt therapist who works with children's groups will, as a : his program on methods developed by those educators : profoundly influenced the art education of our time, igh he may modify them considerably according to the specific needs.

:hildren, in turn, will usually have had some experience at nursery and elementary school, where the teaching is 1 on methods developed by pioneers of modern art edu-cation such as Franz Cižek, Viktor Lowenfeld, Florence Cane, and others, although their ideas may often have been squeezed into the rigid molds of the public school syllabus, watered down, and misunderstood.

Important above all was the discovery that children's art de-velops in a typical and predictable sequence. Lines and configu-rations, the representation of human figures, of objects, and of space all grow according to inner laws that should not be dis-turbed. This discovery freed children from having to attempt the impossible, to render the world according to the concepts of their adult teachers, and thus made possible the blossoming of children's art.

Even though it is common knowledge, we seldom pause to realize that there is no art form in which the interdependence

7. Cf. Stephen E. Goldstone, ed., *Concepts of Community Psychiatry;* W. Viola Bernard, Perry Ottenberg, and Fritz Redl, "Dehumanization: A Composite Psychological Defense in Relation to Modern War"; E. Ulman, "Therapy Is Not Enough."

between style, development, and personality is as all-pervading as in the visual arts. In the performing arts, conditions are less absolute. For example, schizophrenia influences body movement and therefore also the dance of schizophrenics, but the movement of psychopaths is not usually hampered by their illness and it would not be possible to draw inferences about their disturbance from their dance.

Music probably bears less relationship to general development than any other art. A normal child who is talented soon acquires the musical skills of his teachers, and nothing in his performance could tell us anything specific about his age or his emotional state. The same holds true for musical improvisation. Atypical children with inborn musical gifts often develop rapidly in music even though speech may be absent and general development impaired. Indeed, because musical functioning seems to be independent of the capacity for object relationships and for reality testing, unusual performances in music may be slightly more frequent among such children if they are talented than among equally talented normal ones. It appears that available integrative energies tend to flow into those few areas where functioning remains possible and to bring about a hypertrophic blossoming of isolated faculties.

Such entirely isolated performance is not possible in the visual arts. Although excellent work can be produced by seriously disturbed children, its style and form will, with great precision, indicate not only talent, but also mental age, personality, and above all the ego's capacity for integration and the nature of the children's relationship to the object world.

In evaluating children's art, it is helpful to separate those elements which are characteristic of mental age and those that express more enduring individual traits: a picture may be static or full of rhythm and motion, rich or impoverished; form may dominate color or color dominate form; it may be fragmented or well integrated, original or dull, and so forth. These qualities tell us of the child artist's personality. The way people are depicted or the way space is denoted will, on the other hand, be typical of an age group which of course may or may not coincide with the child's chronological age.

The enlightened art teacher will not interfere with those aspects of the child's art that are characteristic of his age, unless the child is on the verge of progressing from one level to the next and seems to need only a little encouragement to make the step. He will, on the other hand, try to increase the vitality, originality, and coherence of his student's work as best he can.

The interdependence between the vitality and evocative power of children's art and their sense of identity has been vividly described by Viktor Lowenfeld, who skillfully used art as a means of strengthening the sense of identity, particularly in handicapped children. He elicited remarkable art work by helping children to feel and know who they were, what they could do, and where they belonged.

Florence Cane was one of the first art teachers to develop techniques to combat blocking and stereotypes by setting up situations that precluded intellectual planning and facilitated the relaxation of defenses. She encouraged movements that engage the whole body in the act of drawing; projection of images; concentration on memories and inner experiences.

The acceptance of affect, mood, and private fantasies as subjects for artistic expression opened the way to work that did not portray recognizable objects.

Approaches that led toward greater self-awareness were particularly helpful in work with those emotionally disturbed individuals who are too preoccupied with their acute conflicts and obsessions, too locked up in their private world, to be receptive to impressions and stimulation from the outside.

This new knowledge and the enlightened methods that grew from it made art teaching infinitely more adaptable than it had been previously. While art therapy is not identical with art teaching, progressive art-teaching methods are indispensable tools in therapeutic art programs. How much of this enlightened art teaching actually occurs in current practice in public schools, camps, neighborhood houses, and other educational and recreational settings? How much has been corrupted and perverted as once-revolutionary insights become common coin? How well do teaching methods developed twenty years ago fulfill the needs of today's children?

ART AND THE PROBLEM OF EMPTINESS [8]

No new discovery or method is exempt from mechanical application and misuse. Sensible suggestions are sometimes transformed into inflexible rules. For instance, the observation that the earliest configurations small children are capable of are large elliptical and circular motions (while straight lines and angles appear somewhat later) led to the suggestion that children should be allowed to enjoy producing such forms without being pressured prematurely toward representational art. In New York City this suggestion has been frozen into a syllabus that limits six-year-olds to painting only circles or other simple geometrical shapes and discourages representational art in the first grade!

Lowenfeld encouraged children to depict themselves engaged in familiar actions. He happened to use an illustration of a child reaching for an apple in a tree. So now we have thousands of city children—who know apples mostly from the grocery shelves —draw pictures of themselves reaching for apples in a tree!

But this kind of pedantry is found in every age. We are more interested in those distortions that are unique symptoms of our time. For instance, techniques designed to help the individual free himself from stereotypes and find subject matter that has deep personal meaning through projection and free association were developed when psychoanalytic thinking began to influence art teachers such as Florence Cane. They could become distorted only after psychoanalytic ideas had been sufficiently popularized to be misunderstood.

8. Ideas developed in this section have been published, in another version, under the titles "Art and Emptiness" and "Art Education and Emptiness."

The Scribble

The fate of the "scribble" as developed by Florence Cane is a good example of the corruption of a sound idea. The original procedure began with "drawing" in the air with wide rhythmic movements that engaged the whole body. When a certain freedom and intensity were reached, the student drew with those movements on a large sheet of paper, working with closed eyes. The resulting "scribble" was then examined from all sides, until the student "saw" forms that suggested a picture to him. He then completed this picture, using those lines that fitted his ideas and obliterating others at will, so that the finished picture usually bore little resemblance to the initial scribble.

The procedure had several interlocking functions. At the beginning there was a radical departure from stereotyped drawing habits coupled with the exhilarating experience of body movement. The student was then encouraged to do the forbidden and childish, to produce random shapes, perhaps express a mood, but represent no specific object. The third step, finding an image in the scribble, made use of the fact that images projected into random forms invariably touch upon latent fantasies. The subject matter was therefore likely to contain very personal material. The last phase, completing the image, elaborating the idea, constituted the creative work proper. Only now was material brought forth by playful activity and projection transformed into artistic communication.

The technique is valuable for working with adults and adolescents or with mature but inhibited pre-adolescents. Younger children cannot use scribbles very well as a point of departure for their drawing. They are still bound to schematic concepts which are too rigidly defined to fit into random shapes.

Playful activities with paint and other material were originally used in a similar way. The procedure started with the breaking of taboos (getting dirty, "wasting" materials, engaging in primitive childish pleasures). In this way random configurations were produced which, via the projection of latent fantasies, were transformed into pictures by conscious effort. Those pictures often had originality and vitality which the students' more conventionally produced work lacked.

Stereotyped Chaos

If we compare this complex process with the scribble designs that now decorate many of our classrooms, we see that the idea has suffered total perversion. The procedure is simple. Either the whole class, or those children who cannot think of anything else to make, quickly draw a squiggle on a little sheet of paper, size 9″ x 12″ or at best 12″ x 18″. Then they diligently fill in the loops and random shapes with colored crayons or with paint, until the whole sheet is covered. The procedure is the same for all ages, and includes both children who would be developmentally ready to complete an image from a scribble and those who would be too young for it.

We see that the scribble is no longer adventure, but routine: no longer created by free rhythmic body movement but by random motions of the hand performed without pleasure or conviction. The second phase—projecting an image into the scribble or identifying it with a mood or feeling—is left out entirely. The third step—completion of the image—is replaced by coloring-in the mechanically produced areas. It is busy-work, comparable to the traditional coloring book except that coloring books may stimulate fantasies about the story which is depicted, while the scribble is totally meaningless. While the pictures produced via Florence Cane's method were often highly original, even though they took their departure from curved loops that tend to look similar no matter who draws them, the scribble pictures of our classrooms cannot be told apart.

Playful activities with paint and other materials are somewhat less barren than scribbles. Children are stimulated and excited by the interesting colors or textures they produce, but again the activity stops short of creative work. The children are taught to make patterns by dropping color-saturated strings on paper, by making Rorschach-type color blots, by innumerable failure-proof tricks that assure easy success even to the most unimaginative child. Evolving pictures from these experiments is not encouraged. These products differ from the scribble designs by being impersonal, chaotic, and exciting rather than being impersonal, confused, and dull.

In both instances methods invented to stimulate originality and personal expression are perverted into ways of manufacturing art work that has less individuality even than the old-fashioned standard three-pronged tulip or the bowl of fruit. These other stereotypes still survive in our schools, but are considered less enlightened than the stereotypes produced by the new methods.

The introduction of a greater variety of materials was another innovation. Using the conventional materials, the student found that the expressive possibilities of any medium are infinite (a piece of charcoal, a few colors, a lump of clay—each suffice to create a whole world). With the addition of unorthodox materials he learned that one medium can stand for another. Bits of colored tile, paper, or cloth may replace paint; sculpture can be created from cardboard, wire, stone, or wood, as well as from clay.

This education toward artistic economy and resourcefulness is now often perverted into a search for novelty. Exploration of the infinite possibilities of each medium is supplanted by superficial acquaintance with a multitude of techniques. Children become greedy for new sensations and are impoverished among a wealth of goods which they have not learned to use creatively.

What are the reasons for these changes? Certainly mechanically produced pseudo-art is easier to make than genuine art, and all good ideas are eventually corrupted. This, however, does not explain the exact nature of the corruption. Why has the copying of plaster casts been abandoned in favor of arid scribble designs? Why have the old materials such as hard pencils, soft and sprawling brushes, and rock-hard watercolor which starve creativity given way to deluges of scrap materials which drown imagination?

The specific quality of any corruption is never accidental. It is determined by the basic problems and contradictions of the culture. In the history of anti-art, which is as ancient as the history of art itself, our time has brought forth a new phenomenon. The ancient polarity between the two enemies of art, chaos and stereotype, has been replaced by a composite: "stereotyped chaos." How did it happen?

One of the causes may be found in the oversimplification of psychoanalytic theory. It seems as though the recognition of the role of unconscious processes and primitive, instinctual drives in artistic creation, which was uncovered by psychoanalytic investigations, has led to a confusion of the source of energy with its end product. Let us illustrate this by a fantasy in the Swiftian manner:

On his voyage to Laputa, Gulliver inspects the Academy of Prospectors in the land of Balnibarbi. There he meets a scientist-gardener who has come to the following conclusion: no plant life can exist above ground without being fed by roots deep in the earth. Ergo, root and flower are the same; indeed because of its dependence on the root, all growth above ground is negligible and worthless. Consequently our gardener decorates his house with roots only, and cuts all sprouting buds as they appear above ground, because their growth might deplete the all-important roots. The consequent withering of his roots he combats by ever-increasing vigilance in the destruction of any growth that might still appear in his garden. The desolation and waste he has created are to him signs of new and wondrous developments below the surface.

Like our gardener, modern art educators understand something about the inception of creative activities but inhibit their fruition. Common to all these pseudo-art activities is acceptance of primitive, playful use of art materials. Regression is accepted; it is indeed induced. This means that one of the conditions for creative work is well provided for.

Temporary regression is a necessary phase in every creative act. When the child seems to have lost touch with his own ideas and fantasies, the educator or therapist may be justified in encouraging a relaxation of defenses by the various methods we have described. However, he must be reasonably sure that the child is capable of integrating the fantasies and affects which are likely to be freed by such methods so that he will not be flooded by passions or overwhelmed by fantasies beyond his control. When such art-teaching methods were developed nobody foresaw how great those dangers were. Battling against constricting standards, teachers were intent on finding ways of overcoming inhibitions. They did not realize that the loss of control would present new problems.

Since then we have learned that it is essential to all education and to all therapy that stimulation and help toward maturation be given even while regression is encouraged or tolerated. When the adult abdicates his function as guide and helper in creative maturation, he seems to join forces with the very powers that threaten the child from within. When classroom walls are covered with images of unredeemed chaos and empty confusion, the temptation to regress replaces stimulation toward creative communication.

At this point we must remark that we are doing grave injustice to teachers and educators. What we describe may be perpetrated in the classrooms, but it does not originate there. Not just school art, but most of the pseudo-art of our time has the same quality of stereotyped chaos. Emptiness and seduction pervade large areas of our cultural life. The use of scribble designs or other foolproof ways of manufacturing products that can pass as art are often the last resort of a desperate teacher confronted with an ever-increasing number of children and adolescents who are empty, bored, and chronically dissatisfied. That these teaching methods feed the very evils that the teacher strives to overcome constitutes a vicious circle in which the teacher and students alike are caught.

The art therapist who works with children and adolescents encounters many of the same difficulties. While the traditional defenses against creative work such as stereotyped houses, trees, and flowers and copies from magazines have not completely disappeared, resistance increasingly takes the form of endlessly repeated scribbles or aimless play with paint and other materials. It almost seems as though those children who scribble and mess are even a little harder to reach than those who produce traditional stereotypes.

This is surprising. Modern art activities, even in their mechanized, stereotyped forms, are closer to art, or at least to the origins of art, than are the senseless teachings of the old school. Yet anyone who has tried to induce a resistant child of the modern school to develop a picture from a color blot or scribble knows that he is often confronted with a wall of incomprehension, a solid unwillingness to make any step in the direction of a personal statement. The resistance seems more unshakable than the old fear of abandoning the safety of the traditional houses, trees, and flowers for more adventurous work. The question arises: Are the difficulties which we encounter in the art room symptoms of some profound change in today's troubled children and adolescents? Are there some inner reasons that make them unresponsive to the challenge and appeal of the arts?

THE UNDERPRIVILEGED SPOILED CHILD

If we compare today's underprivileged disturbed children of New York City with the children of ten or fifteen years ago, we find a subtle change in the character of the disturbance. Certain qualities exist frequently among the very poor, which we used to associate rather with the emotionally deprived rich child who is brought up by indifferent paid help and offered material goods as a substitute for human relationship: distrust of the motives of adults who make friendly overtures, the conviction that all kindness has ulterior motives, a cynical readiness to exploit this situation, insatiable hunger for material goods, and a compulsion to destroy and waste such goods as soon as they are obtained.

This similarity is caused by kindred experiences. Today's neglected, unloved children, rich or poor, are brought up, comforted, instructed, and amused largely by paid help. They have in the television entertainer an ever-available slave who will help them to endure loneliness, anxiety, and isolation. In the service of his sponsors the entertainer establishes a pseudo-relationship with the child. He necessarily resorts to ingratiation and seduction, since he must please the child and stimulate his desire for more without being able to establish a genuine relationship. Even the least perceptive child soon learns to distrust the flattery of television and knows that the entertainer's statements are full of exaggeration and lies. The neglected child thus learns to depend for comfort on people whom he does not trust.

This does not mean that commercial entertainment is itself the cause of emotional disturbance, but that it influences its character. Ever-present access to escape diminishes the need for finding one's own solutions. It not only enfeebles the healthy impetus to seek out relationships or to turn passive experience into active mastery, it even diminishes the inclination to form well-defined neurotic symptoms and personal fantasies and daydreams. Rather than becoming neurotic under strain, children to whom such escape is open are apt to develop amorphous, dependent personalities lacking inner resources.

The experience of being bribed with material goods is also no longer the privilege of the wealthy. Mass bribery directed against all children includes even the destitute. A child who eats breakfast is, for example, supplied with an abundance of toys and trinkets; since these goods are not tokens of affection but bait, recognized as such by the child, they cannot give satisfaction. Instead their possession stimulates greed, which operates in the interest of the manufacturer. We see that whenever genuine satisfactions are missing, ersatz is available. As with all flattery, such offerings are based on a shrewd understanding of children's needs and their weaknesses. Often the substitute is almost indistinguishable from the real thing, so that gratification of basic needs, distrust, and disappointment become inextricably mingled.

Today's disturbed underprivileged children and adolescents in our large cities are not only deprived of love, understanding, space to live and play in, and exposed to the brutality of the streets; they have also been bribed, seduced, and left empty. They are in a sense all addicts, dependent on synthetic gratifications which destroy their capacity to seek genuine satisfactions for their emotional needs. Today's delinquent gives the impression of being both deprived and spoiled. He is not only violent and destructive but also capricious, convinced that he can get something for nothing, and that desirable experience can be had without effort.

The task of rehabilitation has changed. With the diminution of publicly condoned brutality against children, the average underprivileged child is somewhat less afraid of cruelty from the adult in authority. Instead, authority has become indifferent and impersonal. The child suspects the adult's sincerity and sees in him a salesman who will cheat and disappoint him. It no longer suffices to satisfy unfulfilled needs. We have to withdraw injurious ersatz satisfactions. We have to prove not only that we are not monsters and brutes but that we are not lying salesmen.

NEW DEFENSES

This digression into analysis of change in the character structure of contemporary city slum children was undertaken because it occurred to us that the transformation of progressive ideas in art teaching might have more than one cause. Besides the misinterpretation of psychoanalytic theory and the general tendency of all revolutionary ideas to harden into rigid systems, there is a change in the students' type of resistance to art. Stereotypes are never merely imposed by the outside; they arise to fill an ever-present need to ward off the emotional upheaval that creative work may cause. They help guard the individual's equilibrium against the emergence of unwelcome or dangerous feelings and knowledge by a system of denial, avoidance, and lies. Not every individual nor every society fears the same thing, but none is free of fears.

This need for defense was previously fulfilled by set standards that determined choice of subject matter and manner of representation. Reality was falsified and censored. Passion, conflict, hostility, ugliness, and other unwelcome facts and feelings were not permitted expression. The conventionally accepted stereotypes were intricate; their execution required time, patience, and dexterity. Such a system satisfied the needs of people accustomed to obedience, who possessed well-established inhibitions and defenses, and whose aggressions were to a great extent turned inward in the form of guilt or channeled into compulsive work.

The modern version fulfills the need for the avoidance of creative work in a simpler way. Reality is not censored or falsified but negated and overlooked. There is no false standard of perfection, but the very concept of standards is avoided in an indiscriminate acceptance of any and every product. Awareness of unwelcome feelings and facts is obliterated in incoherent expression. This solution corresponds to the character structure of the spoiled underprivileged child who is accustomed to flattery and persuasion rather than to authority and criticism. It does not help to ward off specific forbidden or dangerous ideas and emotions, but rather expresses a universal fear of reality on the part of young people who have been fed on substitutes until they have lost the capacity to respond to direct experience.

When such a child is confronted with a blank piece of paper and the invitation to make a statement on it, he becomes aware of a great and frightening emptiness. The lack of a solid self and the absence of relationships have emptied the world of substance and meaning. While such children are relatively free of anxiety caused by feelings of guilt, they are defenseless against the nameless fear of loss of identity, of being overwhelmed and annihilated by primeval impulses of rage and desire. Does producing stereotyped chaos help reduce these children's anxiety? We find that the fear of nothingness and emptiness is alleviated by producing something, however inadequate it may be, but the products remain anonymous and amorphous—they cannot serve as valid self-representation. Thus the activity is helpful for the moment, but its beneficial effect cannot endure.

It is interesting to observe how each culture as it develops specific mechanisms of defense also develops tolerance against certain weaknesses that are inherent in the defense system. Thus the Victorian age, which made excessive demands on children's control, had great tolerance of hypocrisy, indeed demanded it from children. We, who more often sin by omission, failing to help our children build sufficient ego strength, have developed tolerance toward expressions of violence both in words and deeds.

How then should we work with children who use scribbles and splashes as a defense? Certainly we must accept the scribbles and splashes as we must accept the old-fashioned stereotyped tulips or anything else the child offers. We cannot, however, expect work that is produced in such a playful way to have the liberating effect that it often has for the inhibited but well-integrated child. The stereotyped chaos is the image of the child's habitual state of being, for the modern child's emptiness is not bare, as that of the neglected child of the past, but cluttered with intense but meaningless stimuli.

We must recognize the stereotyped chaos as a tragic expression of helplessness and deadlock. To ask a pre-adolescent or adolescent of this kind to see an image in his scribbles or in his blots of paint means asking for the impossible, because he has not learned to see order in a world that is for him chaotic. Only when he has accumulated a sufficient store of well-defined mental images can he project them onto random forms.

When there is too great a vacuum the scribble or color blot remains a butterfly or an explosion or a "design," and that is as far as it goes. Such children could no more make such "designs" into abstract art by imposing deliberate form onto accidental configurations than they could develop them into representational pictures.

The children who make abstract art that is not empty are those who are also able to project representational images onto the accidental forms. The empty children we are describing here are unable to go beyond a passive surrender to chance. At best they may claim a pretty or exciting accidental configuration as their own by putting their names under it. At worst they surrender to their destructive impulses and produce an irredeemable mess. Often they are cynically aware of the fraud which is being perpetrated. As one boy put it: "You make something, it don't look like nothing, you call it a design; that's modern art."

Although usually there are also constrictions and perfectionism, the task is not so much to free the child from inhibitions as to help chaotic fantasy to become imagination and to develop the faculty for observation and self-observation.

The major obstacles to creative expression have changed. Instead of inhibitions and guilt feelings, there are fear of emptiness and fear of annihilation. Working against such difficulties is also not as immediately gratifying. When we succeed in freeing a child from inhibitions we are rewarded with an increase of available energies and a lifting of depression. When structure is built up, on the other hand, energies are bound and direct instinctual gratification is diminished. When all goes well, increased mastery and ego strength ultimately bring about feelings of victory and elation, but the process is slow and strenuous.

EMPTINESS AND THE AFFLUENT SOCIETY

Children who suffer from emptiness panic easily before a blank piece of paper or a plain lump of clay. In an effort to reduce this fear, teachers often rely on materials that already have a certain amount of form. Pictures are assembled from scraps of fabric, buttons and bottle caps, leaves and sand; sculptures are made of boxes, milk containers, cans, and so forth.

When used with restraint, such expedients can be helpful. However, in a mountain of goods, form is easily buried, and instead of stimulating inventiveness the activity may stimulate greed. The empty child is a bottomless pit ready to swallow any amount of goods without getting any fuller.

The commercial interests that have contributed to the making of the spoiled deprived child exert continuous pressure to keep him a passive consumer, living in a psychological climate that would persuade us that any new thing is a good thing. However, the trend toward using novel materials does not originate solely in the commercial world and its rage for promoting kits for making anything from jewelry to mechanically produced abstract paintings. It also has more creative sources: stimulated by the abundance of waste in our industrial age, as if in self-defense against the onslaught of indestructible garbage—dead cars, discarded washing machines, cans and containers, corrugated cardboard, leaflets, or broken bottles—modern artists try to make creative use of it. At times they succeed; sometimes they fail. Unfortunately, much of the available waste bears the indelible stamp of mass production; much of it is made of synthetic materials that lack life and character. Often old junk is used just to make new junk. Selection of discarded material for creative use demands the capacity to reject the nonessential. Deluged by goods of all descriptions, we have to learn not only to distinguish between the good and the shoddy, but to discipline ourselves to reject the superfluous even when it is in itself good.

Children who have grown up under this kind of pressure can learn with time to distrust the exaggerated claims of salesmanship and become shrewd and judicious shoppers. It is much harder for them to learn to withdraw emotional investment from the idea of acquiring goods and free those energies for the pursuit of more constructive goals.

In the battle against the superfluous which threatens to debilitate our cultural life, art has an important function. Art respects matter without being materialistic. The artist must love and understand his medium. In the act of creation, idea and medium become one. As the medium is transformed into a vehicle of expression it does not lose its specific material qualities; indeed, these qualities are enhanced.

The child of the affluent society, who is no longer taught economy by necessity, can learn about the elegance of economy and the ugliness of waste through the aesthetic experience of art.

This does not mean that we must guard against all waste. Deprived and disturbed children are notoriously wasteful, and unless waste is tolerated up to a point it is not possible to work with them at all. Only we must hold fast to the goal of helping those children to find new and different values. In general we can say that variety of media is beneficial when it demonstrates the unity of matter and creative idea. It becomes harmful when it dilutes this experience. In practice, this is a question of timing and discriminating choice.

Very young children need to explore the material world by handling things physically. Exploration of many media is therefore valuable at this age. During the period of latency, roughly between six and ten, children are able to use art materials for symbolic expression and communication. This faculty is developed best through concentration on the basic media—paper, crayons, paint, and clay. This does not mean that other materials should be avoided altogether, but they should be an occasional adventure, not a daily distraction.

In prepuberty, roughly from eleven to thirteen, there is a greater need for broadening the range of experiences. But new media should never replace the basic materials which, just because they are simple and familiar, make the greatest demands on the child's artistic initiative and inventiveness.

New materials become a real aid in adolescence when imagination falters and self-criticism is severe. If we have offered too much too early, we often find the adolescent jaded. Whatever we offer, he "already did that in first grade." Such contempt makes us suspect that the experiences in first grade were superficial and not really satisfying.

Whatever the necessary detours, ultimately there is no way to bypass the crucial moment when the making of a work of art becomes an independent act, and the young artist confronts a blank surface or an amorphous lump of matter with the will to make a statement and the moral courage to commit himself.

The emphasis on building up structure in art coincides with our general therapeutic approach. The controls of the young people we have described are but a thin veneer supported by a flimsy structure which gives way readily under stress. Rehabilitation begins by strengthening the ego, cementing relationships, fostering identification and internalization of values. Uncovering of unconscious material has to be handled cautiously and slowly.

Earlier we suggested that art therapists would be able to contribute to the understanding of the relationship between sociocultural conditions and the epidemic rise of specific kinds of emotional disturbance. Our long detour into problems of art education has indeed brought us such insights. In taking stock of existing art-teaching methods and their application in art therapy, we have come upon a number of abuses of methods which in themselves are sound and continue to be useful. Trying to understand the reasons for the specific kind of misuses which have spread in the last twenty years, we found several interlocking factors: the increase of synthetic experiences in daily life; the mechanical application of progressive teaching methods; the oversimplification and misinterpretation of psychoanalytic theory. We specified a new character type, the spoiled underprivileged child, and the syndrome of stereotyped chaos that serves as defense against the fear of emptiness and of annihilation which is part of those children's pathology. Neither condition is strictly limited to the underprivileged, young or old; they pervade our society and our art. Their further investigation, however, lies beyond the subject of this book.

If ersatz gratifications are recognized as serious threats to the mental health of deprived and unloved people, it will be possible to attempt protection where a therapeutic milieu is being created, in schools, day-care centers, treatment homes, and hospitals. The difficulty will be the same we encounter in other aspects of milieu therapy.

It is a basic rule that any disturbed person should be protected carefully from those situations that caused the initial injury. We also know that it is almost impossible to create such an environment, because every disturbed individual is under the compulsion to re-create the situation that led to his illness. Children who have been impoverished and corrupted by substitute gratifications force the environment to give in to their addiction. Attempts to replace substitutes with substance, passive consumption with active participation, meet with resistance. In a milieu that recognizes the problem and works toward its solution, art therapy can do its share to give depth and meaning to children's lives.

My own experience has taught me that art therapy can function under all sorts of difficulties. It can endure heat, cold, lack of space and facilities, disorder and violence, but it cannot well endure emptiness. When people's lives are too consistently filled with synthetic living, art does not survive easily. If the battle against emptiness seems hopeless at times, we must remember that twenty-five years ago the battle against well-entrenched academism may often have seemed equally disheartening to those who fought and won it.

II

Art, Art Therapy, and the Therapeutic Milieu

HAVING LOOKED AT art therapy in relationship to society at large and in relationship to art education, we must now take a closer look at the function of art in the therapeutic milieu. At this point a fundamental cleavage in the interpretation of art therapy must be briefly stated: some art therapists practice it as a specialized form of psychotherapy, but here we are concerned mainly with art therapy that depends on *art* as its chief therapeutic agent. Art therapy is seen as distinct from psychotherapy. Its healing potentialities depend on the psychological processes that are activated in creative work.

The art therapist functions as an artist and educator who is capable of modifying his working methods according to the patient's pathology and needs. He is trained to appraise the patient's behavior and production and to interpret his observations to the therapeutic team. He implements the team's therapeutic goals, but he does not ordinarily use his clinical insight for uncovering or interpreting to the patient deep unconscious material, nor does he encourage the development of a transference relationship.

When visual symbols are used mainly to replace or supplement the spoken word in the interchange between therapist and patient, as in the art therapy of practitioners such as Margaret Naumburg,[1] the creative act is of secondary importance and usually remains abortive. This form of art therapy must be prac-

1. Margaret Naumburg, *Schizophrenic Art: Its Meaning in Psychotherapy.*

ticed only by the professionally trained psychotherapist or by the art therapist who works under close psychiatric supervision.

Both approaches have their value in the therapeutic milieu, and the same therapist may employ either approach according to the demands of the situation. This book, however, stresses art therapy in which creative work is of central importance.

Most children like art. The making of visual images is differentiated from the playful experimentation with art materials that precedes it, roughly between the ages of three and five years. From then on, through latency and prepuberty up to eleven to thirteen years of age, art is accessible and emotionally satisfying to a far greater number of people than at any other time of life, and it seems to have special value.

Provided that certain ego functions which we will specify later are intact, art appears to have unique powers to mobilize energies that are not otherwise available to the child for a form of expression that makes considerable demands on the child's ego. Because art is compatible with a high degree of pathology, it has particular value for children whose disturbance restricts their capacity to participate in activities such as games and sports, which children normally enjoy and grow on and which make comparable demands on the ego.

What exactly is so special about art, assuming that this claim to unusual virtues is not just born of the specialist's enthusiasm for his field? How does art differ from related activities such as imaginative play or crafts? If it is true that art can be used therapeutically, what is the relationship between therapeutic art and psychotherapy?

ART AND PLAY

The freedom of art links it to imaginative play. They both constitute islands wherein the reality principle is partly suspended. Forbidden wishes and impulses can be symbolically expressed. Painful and frightening experiences that had to be endured passively can be assimilated by actively reliving them on a reduced scale. Affect can be safely discharged in play and also in art.

There are, however, essential differences. The rules of play are simple: the child must learn to distinguish play from real life, and must develop the ability to suspend play when necessary.

The understanding adult will not be unduly harsh in enforcing these demands. For example, building blocks representing castles or garages will be left standing when this is possible. A child of three or four years may be permitted to carry on with a fiction such as being the mother of a doll-child as long as it does not seriously interfere with the tasks of daily life. However, when a child seems really unable to relinquish his play at all we begin to worry.

Young children often welcome the adult's participation in their imaginative play. As children grow older the adult's role becomes that of the protector who interrupts play when it becomes dangerous to life, limb, and property and who picks up the pieces after quarrels. Usually he is supposed to stay out of the magic circle of children's play, or, if he is invited to join it, he must for the duration subordinate himself to the leadership of the children with whom he is playing. More often, the adult is seen as the intruder, the reality principle personified, and he is seldom welcome.

In art it is different. The adult visitor is greeted by a chorus of "Look what I have done!" and is rarely allowed to depart before he has admired each child's work. To be part of children's art activities the grownup need not become a child. Indeed, his adult leadership and support are essential for art to grow and flourish, if only he is able to understand children's art and knows how to help them without imposing his adult ideas.

The exclamation "Look what I have done!" epitomizes the difference between play and art. In play, objects or people assume symbolic roles by a simple act of designation, so to speak by decree; two chairs become a boat, a boy turns into a lion.

Such fictions may be supported by props or acted out with toys. A boy may put on a space helmet to be an astronaut or wrap himself in a sheet to be a ghost, or a girl may be a mother by cradling a doll, but such accessories are not essential to play. Play depends mainly on the child's capacity to sustain the fiction; it ends when imagination falters.

The aim of art is the making of a symbolic object that contains and communicates an idea. The idea depends largely on the child's wishes and fantasies, but the making of the object is a complex ego function that engages his manual, intellectual, and emotional faculties in a supreme effort.

This distinction also applies to those arts where no tangible object results. For instance, if a child *plays* at being an animal, he may sustain his fiction by appropriate noises and gestures or he may not—the play can go on either way. If the child undertakes to *play the part* of the same animal in a dramatic performance, he must make every effort to imagine the animal well and to convey his idea to the spectators—otherwise he fails as an actor.

Sometimes play and art overlap, and we can observe how play is for a moment transfigured. A little girl chanting to her doll makes music; a child building a sand castle becomes engrossed in giving exquisite form and proportions to his structure; children putting on war paint to play Indians transform themselves into beings of truly awe-inspiring ferocity. But art that is embedded in play does not prevail for long, and play goes on as art falters.

Art in its undiluted form makes infinitely greater demands on the child's faculties and on his moral courage than does play. Play is the prerogative of childhood. In adult life art supersedes it as one of the few areas of symbolic living that remain accessible.

PROJECTION AND CONFRONTATION

When material is given form without strict adherence to prescribed patterns it inevitably takes on the image of its maker. We know in particular that disturbances in feelings of identity and personal intactness invariably reveal themselves by distortions and fragmentations of the visual images the child produces. This limits the supremacy of the pleasure principle in art. While the object may be created in the service of wish fulfillment, the child's capacity to make the object fulfill his wish is limited by his pathology, the state of his ego, his manual skill, his "talent," and many other factors. The finished product never simply represents the fantasy, but rather expresses the child's relationship to his fantasy. The following example illustrates these differences.

Kenneth: Kenneth, a six-year-old abandoned child who had knocked about in many foster homes, was much given to grandiose fantasies that consoled him in his isolation and helplessness. One day he wanted to paint a picture of a giant "as tall as the art room." He climbed a high closet from which he could reach the ceiling and measured out a long strip of brown wrapping paper reaching from there to the floor. While he was measuring, Kenneth declared that he wanted all the colors because the giant would be very beautiful. Then he laid his paper on the floor. He chose a black crayon and at the top of the paper drew a life-sized head with faint features. Then he drew two lines reaching from the head down to the bottom of the paper, representing legs and body at once. In the middle of this configuration he placed a small rectangle—"the penis"—above it a tiny circle—"the bellybutton" (Fig. 1). That was all. I asked Kenneth if the giant would have arms. Kenneth did not respond. I offered him a tray full of "all the colors"; he did not take them. There was a moment of sadness. Both Kenneth and I knew that there was nothing we could do. To urge him on would only have deepened his sense of defeat. We rolled the paper up and put it away with Kenneth's other work. Maybe a time would come when he would have the inner strength to paint him.

In spite of Kenneth's grandiose fantasies his picture remained as insubstantial as Kenneth really felt, and nobody could give him the power to paint the strong, colorful giant of his dreams.

Later in the same session Kenneth modeled a little clay dog in a doghouse. He had no trouble making both dog and kennel sturdy and complete. In contrast to the giant which originated in a consolatory fantasy, this sculpture embodied Kenneth's true feelings about himself. He presents himself as an appealing and dependent domestic animal, not exactly homeless, but relegated to a lonely doghouse. The sculpture shows Kenneth's strength as well as his troubles, for although dependent and rejected he is still capable of longings and of hope.

Bob: Of course, one need not be a giant in order to paint good giants. Art is a place where fantasies can take form. Eight-year-old Bob had spent many years in hospitals for tuberculosis. He was frail and short, but his vitality was indestructible. He painted a strong man lifting a weight; the picture was simple but convincing. The man's biceps were clearly marked and he stood firmly on his platform, a broad smile on his face (Fig. 2).

No doubt Bob's desire for greater bodily strength had inspired the painting; it can be predicted that he will not grow up to be a strong man. However, his relationship to his fantasy was straightforward and secure.

Inasmuch as the strong man represents the concept of an intact, potent male in the symbolic language of an eight-year-old, the self-image has truth. Life had not destroyed Bob's feeling of intactness or interfered with his masculine identification. His inner strength enabled him to create a convincing hero.

The opposite also occurs. Husky bullies often produce fragmented and feeble art work, revealing an inner weakness which no amount of physical strength can compensate for.

Art, though it is not circumscribed by the physical laws that limit actions, has its own laws that are just as unalterable. Our examples have demonstrated one of these laws: any act of crea-

FIGURE 1. *Kenneth*: Giant (2' x 9')

FIGURE 2. *Bob*: Champion (18" x 24")

tion implies a confrontation with some aspect of the artist's personality. Kenneth, drawing a giant, confronted the full impact of his pathology. When he modeled a dog he encountered the better-integrated parts of his personality. Art always reveals truth, but not necessarily the whole truth. Different pictures may show different, sometimes contradictory facets of personality.

CONFRONTATION IN ART AND IN PSYCHOTHERAPY

The confrontation that creative work induces resembles the confrontation in psychoanalysis and in psychoanalytically oriented psychotherapy in certain respects. The amorphous condition of the art material and the lack of specific directions for forming it are analogous to the blank quality of the therapeutic relationship. This freedom induces the child to form the art material or the relationship in his own image. In both situations the child is confronted in the course of time with many aspects of himself. He learns to know who he is, how he feels, and what he can do. However, there are differences.

In psychotherapy the child's activities are varied. He may talk, play, draw, or model—do any number of things. The only constant factor is the therapist's presence. The child may remain isolated, unable to relate to him for long periods of time. Nevertheless some form of partnership between patient and therapist is bound to develop, and this relationship constitutes the core and main tool of the therapeutic process.

Art activities on the other hand invite the creation of a world that is egocentrically organized. Each element in the child's work contains part of himself. The menace that confrontation with the self and its pathology constitutes is mitigated by narcissistic gratification. This makes possible the mobilization of great energy in the service of an activity that implies risking failure and confrontation with conflict. The tale of Kenneth's giant is an example of the kind of stress that a child is apt to encounter. Like Kenneth, many children are able to sustain considerable tensions in art at a time when they are not ready to make similar efforts in other areas of life, or to risk themselves very far in psychotherapy.

Inasmuch as increased ego strength in one area leads to maturation in general, art therapy may bring about personality changes. When the disturbance was caused by a traumatic event, symbolic expression in art may help the child master the experience even without psychotherapeutic intervention. However, art therapy alone does not usually provide leverage for the resolution of more profound emotional disturbance.

On the whole, art therapy and psychotherapy reinforce and supplement one another. By opening the door to a new order of experiences wherein ideas can be told and retold in many different guises, art therapy prepares the child for the symbolic interchange of psychotherapy. In turn, children who are in treatment are apt to produce art that has much personal meaning and emotional impact because psychotherapy has made them more aware of themselves. Art then often becomes a preferred area for re-enacting the inner tensions and changes engendered by psychotherapy.

ART AND CRAFT

Inasmuch as the narcissistic investment of art work contributes to self-esteem, art is related to all productive work, in particular to the crafts. Both art and crafts develop manual skill, intelligent handling of materials, and related ego functions. Even though personality expresses itself in many ways in the crafts, the element of confrontation is much diluted.

Thus, the object produced can serve to build up self-esteem in persons who reject their art work because it contains too much evidence of pathology, or in persons who cannot endure regression and relaxation of compulsive defenses, which are inseparable from art. Even a fragmented child whose art remains disjointed can produce a whole pot holder if he is at all able to follow directions, and this may be very reassuring to him. Obsessive perfectionism that is a hindrance in art can be an asset in the crafts.

THE FUNCTION OF THE ART THERAPIST

The art therapist makes himself the ally of the child's creative venture, lending both technical assistance and emotional support. By upholding the basic requirement that the material be used to produce works of art, the art therapist counteracts the tendency toward dissipation into fantasy or play.

To perform this function well, the art therapist must recognize and respond to the hidden as well as the overt aspects of the child's production and behavior. He will not, as a rule, directly interpret unconscious meaning, but he will use his knowledge to help the child produce art work that contains and expresses emotionally loaded material. The three following examples illustrate this mode of functioning.

Clyde: Eight-year-old Clyde, an intelligent, inhibited, and depressed child, had grave doubts about the size, permanence, and intactness of his sexual organs, even though they were normally developed. Clyde was a good sculptor. One day he modeled a gorilla, standing upright with raised arms, about a foot high. He wanted to give it a penis and asked me how big he should make it. When I suggested that he show me what *he* thought, he shyly proffered a clay sausage the size of an adult penis. I made him hold the clay penis against his sculpture and pointed out that it was as big as the gorilla's legs. I asked him whether he had ever seen a person with a penis as large as his leg. Clyde smiled, and shook his head. Looking down on his lap he seemed to ponder the relative size of leg and penis. Then without further hesitation he sculptured a very lifelike sexual organ in a state of erection, complete with testicles. The proportion of body and penis corresponded to that of an eight-year-old boy like Clyde himself rather than to that of an adult man. The whole figure was very much like Clyde, big but somehow powerless and sad. Clyde, nevertheless, was very pleased with his work. He subsequently sculptured a chimpanzee and had no difficulty modeling the sexual organs.

My response to Clyde's question was both reasonable and geared to his problems. Clyde had not resolved his Oedipal conflicts. He still wanted to possess his father's penis and suffered from fears of retaliation. Clyde's penis seemed so tiny to him because he compared it to his father's, which to him seemed gigantic.

Clyde was intelligent and had, in spite of his disturbance, matured normally in many respects. He was ready to begin to accept his status as a little boy whose penis was smaller than his father's but perfectly adequate for his own age and size. A response that made him ponder the problem of relative sizes and demonstrated to him the absurdity of his first idea was, therefore, helpful both on the conscious and on the unconscious level.

Had I encouraged Clyde to stick an outsized penis onto his gorilla, this would have aggravated rather than allayed his anxieties. He would have seen me both a seductress and a fool—seductress because I catered to his wildest sexual fantasies, fool because I lacked common sense.

Bernard: While my response was right for Clyde, it might have been wrong for another child. When Bernard, six years old and mildly retarded, made a rudimentary clay figure and adorned it with an enormous penis, I accepted the figure wholeheartedly. Bernard was at a developmental stage when realistic proportions are not yet conceived of and size denotes only order of importance. He was a deeply insecure boy and making a penis at all was for him an act of supreme courage. The idea of realistic proportions would have had no meaning for him. He would have interpreted my introducing it only as a rejection. Bernard was neither psychotic nor did he lack common sense; he merely had not reached the stage where this particular kind of reasoning develops. The following story illustrates the importance of adapting one's line of argument to the child's pathology.

Judy: Seven-year-old Judy lacked a stable sense of identity. Being uncertain who she was, she was compelled to imitate other little girls constantly. Whenever Judy and Martha were both in the art room, Judy made every effort to arrange it so that they both worked at the same table and produced identical pictures. Judy was by far the better painter and therefore usually able to make Martha copy *her*. However, when Martha took it into her head to pursue her own ideas, Judy was compelled to imitate her even when Martha's primitive daubs made no sense to her. She would become terribly confused and anxious as she tried frantically to maintain her picture in an identical state.

Although it would have seemed reasonable to exhort Judy not to copy Martha, this would not have made sense to her. Judy had no concept of separateness and therefore could not understand the idea of imitation.

Instead, I had to tell Judy over and over again that she was Judy and not Martha, and that nothing bad would happen if she painted a Judy picture and Martha painted a Martha picture. This reassurance helped Judy cease anxiously watching Martha's work and concentrate on her own work instead.

In each of the three examples the art therapist supported the child's ego in an area where functioning was already possible but still precarious. I strengthened Clyde's beginning capacity for reality testing, supported Bernard's attempts at self-assertion, and helped Judy to attain a more secure sense of identity. In doing it, I responded to the unconscious as well as the conscious elements of the child's behavior, but I purposely did not uncover or interpret unconscious meaning. Instead I performed a kind of first aid that made creative functioning possible. When such help is successful it gives the child a feeling of being very deeply understood. This understanding encourages creative rather than defensive processes.

INTERPRETATION OF REALITY AND OF FUNCTIONING

The word "interpretation" is often used loosely. We must distinguish between the interpretation of reality, of functioning, and of unconscious meaning. The last belongs primarily to psychotherapy; the other two are part of all education.

Interpretation of reality is a continuous process. Children's sense of reality is tenuous; primary-process thinking and a magic interpretation of the world are more natural to them. Megalomania and ideas of reference are, to some degree, part of normal childhood. They are, of course, more marked among disturbed children, but even here they are less ominous than they would be in an adult. The following scenes are not uncommon.

Five children are ready for painting. Tommy has been given the task of distributing the paint trays to the other four. When three children have been given their paint Mark sees that he is the only child who has no paint at his table. He screams, "I have no paint, I have no paint! Who stole my paint?" I ask Mark, "Why do you have no paint? Who is giving out the paint? How many trays are left for Tommy to hand out?"—leading him toward a realistic understanding of the situation which he has interpreted in a paranoid manner.

Johnny drops a paintbrush while I am standing behind him. He turns around and says accusingly, "Look what you made me do!" To Johnny, whose emotions are on a three-year-old level, I am the source of all good and all evil that befalls him in the art room. I have to remind him that it was *he*, not I, who dropped the brush and I must reassure him that I mean no harm, by helping him find the lost brush, for instance.

Art therapy lends itself particularly well to the interpretation of functioning. For example, Clyde of the gorilla was a child who expected disaster always. He never failed to predict that his sculptures would collapse in the making, or that they would blow up in the firing. His prophecies became something of a standing joke between us, and there was no doubt that this helped Clyde to gain some insight into the way he functioned.

Eleven-year-old Brian had painted a figure on a green background. When another child messed up this background, Brian declared that the whole painting was no good. He was about to destroy it in spite of my remonstrances. Finally I wrestled the picture away from him. Later I painted out all distracting spots in the background but did not touch the figure. When I presented Brian with the restored picture he understood that there really had been nothing wrong with his work. He admitted that when I assured him that his picture was salvageable I had not tried to console him with a lie. There was a moment of illumination when he saw how ready he was to believe that anyone who tried to help him was a liar or a fool.

Whenever Allan paints his clay sculptures he starts out with many colors, but the sculpture always ends up black. We discuss this disconcerting phenomenon and agree that I will keep an eye on him whenever he is painting a sculpture, and when I foresee that the sculpture is about to turn black, I will warn Allan to stop painting. He can then choose to wait until the black mood has passed, or choose to paint his work black, but we will no longer have black accidents.

Interpretations such as these stop short of uncovering but they lead to awareness of recurring patterns of behavior. This makes the child less a victim of his habitual ways of functioning. At times it becomes possible for him to anticipate and control certain patterns or even to modify them somewhat.

TRANSFERENCE AND COUNTER-TRANSFERENCE

Deeply damaging events engender a powerful compulsion to repeat them. The individual loses the capacity to perceive new situations objectively. Instead he is inclined to interpret them in terms of past experiences, to respond to them in distorted ways, or to distort them to fit his compulsive needs. The individual whose earliest relationships have been damaging retains the inclination to transfer the emotions which these experiences engendered upon persons who become important to him in later life.

Psychoanalytic treatment makes constructive use of these phenomena. The therapeutic situation invites the transference of infantile feelings, wishes, and fears onto the therapist's person. Within the ensuing transference neurosis, the patient's original infantile conflicts are re-enacted under more favorable circumstances, and this ultimately lessens the destructive influence of early childhood tragedies.

In the therapeutic interchange the psychotherapist maintains a state of openness toward the patient's communications, allowing them to find an echo in his own inner life. The precision and subtlety of his responses depend equally on his knowledge and training and on his capacity for empathy. On occasion it may happen that a patient's affect-laden behavior touches deeply upon a vulnerable area in the therapist's psyche, causing him to react in terms of his own past, rather than according to the patient's needs. The therapist's counter-transference then interferes with the therapeutic process.

Even though the development of transference in the full sense does not occur in art therapy, the therapist must understand the phenomenon. As we have said before, the universal inclination to respond to the present in terms of the past is particularly powerful among disturbed persons. Whatever relationships the art therapist establishes will therefore inevitably be colored by the children's transference, and it is likely, too, that his own responses will occasionally be contaminated by his counter-transference.

I will present two examples: the first one of a child who responded to certain situations that were objectively safe with panic caused by an earlier traumatic event; the second, an incident of dovetailing transference and counter-transference between child and art therapist.

Henry: Henry, now six years old, had two years earlier been subject to a thinly veiled murderous attack by his psychotic mother. One of the favorite activities of the children in Henry's art therapy group was having me trace the outlines of their bodies on large sheets of wrapping paper which they used as a basis for various kinds of self-representations. They also loved it when, as a special treat, I drew their portraits. My actions seemed to reassure them and to strengthen their feelings of identity.

With Henry such methods had the opposite effect. Although he insisted on being traced and having his portrait painted like the others, whatever I did was wrong and ended in torn paper, tears, and tantrums. Nevertheless, Henry's demands did not abate, but became even more insistent and frantic.

Henry had transferred his terrifying experiences with his mother onto me. When I looked at him closely or came close to his body as I traced his outline, he sensed it as an attack. Yet he was driven to create situations that repeated the original trauma and to interpret new events in its image.

To make further art work possible, I had to avoid all activities that had become loaded with transferred meaning and somehow make Henry perceive me as distinct from his mother. We achieved this by making pictures together. At first we confined ourselves to impersonal geometric figures. Later we created animals, and eventually we even drew people. In this way I became Henry's auxiliary ego. I seemed less overpowering to him and ceased to be the object of emotions and fears that belonged to Henry's earliest disastrous relationship.

In a child as severely damaged as Henry was, the psychotherapist would probably also have delayed dealing with the full impact of the early trauma and might have concentrated initially on supporting Henry's ego. Eventually, however, the emotions and fears of early injuries would have been re-enacted in the transference relationship. In art therapy such material should be expressed insofar as possible in the art work rather than in the relationship.

Some elements of transference from earlier to later relationships are present whenever people are together. We must, however, be on the alert for moments when the relationship becomes so much more important than the art work that it impedes the creative process. Then we must suspect that transferred feelings have become dominant, particularly when there is much inexplicable affect and compulsive repetition.

Martin: The workings of transference and counter-transference were made devastatingly clear to me in one of my earliest experiences as an art therapist. I was working at the time at Wiltwyck School, a residential treatment home for disturbed boys. Among my pupils was a very talented ten-year-old whose main difficulty stemmed from a fixation on his disturbed mother. Martin provoked her to cruel punishments which ended in reconciliations, and this pattern of sado-masochistic excitement was re-enacted unendingly between mother and son.

Martin was one of my most gifted painters. Even though he was often almost insufferable, I greatly admired him and enjoyed working with him. I found it easy to understand him because I too had been an isolated, gifted child burdened with a strong mother-fixation.

One day Martin painted unusually accurate and malicious caricatures of the school's executive director and of the president of the board. Then, in anger, he smeared the picture over with black paint, spoiling it past redemption. Furious and heartbroken, I pushed Martin roughly against the wall and shook him violently by the shoulders. A crazy grin spread over his face, his hand went to his genitals, and he said, "That makes my dick itch." I realized that Martin and I were re-enacting the whole familiar drama between him and his mother. I also knew that this could only have happened because my counter-transference had played into his transference.

I had identified with Martin. By painting the caricatures Martin had expressed for me my own hostility against the school's directors, and on a deeper level he had expressed my childhood rebellion against parental authority. As long as his caricatures were good, he had gratified my aggressive desires in a way that was acceptable to me. I had indulged in more vicarious gratification than is permitted to the therapist and so I was doubly hurt when Martin reverted to raw destructiveness. I was not only attacked in my role as Martin's teacher who had helped him to make the picture, but I was much more deeply hurt because identification with Martin made me experience his regression as my own. Since breakdown of sublimation was to me the most serious menace to my integrity as an artist, I experienced Martin's attack on his painting as an attack on me, and I reacted with panic, regression, and counterattack.

Martin's telling me so bluntly about his sexual excitement was probably at once an act of seduction toward me as a representative of aggressive, seductive womankind, and an appeal to me as his therapist whom he knew to be not really seductive and on the whole rational. By making me realize what was happening between us he made certain that it would not happen again.

To set the reader's mind at rest, no disaster followed this incident. Martin and I had both learned a lesson and our relationship was from then on under much better control. Indeed, I count Martin's case among my most successful ones in a long career.

This story shows the difference between empathy and identification.[2] It is permissible, even essential, to draw upon one's own childhood in order to better understand the child. However, an identification that is not consciously experienced may impede our understanding and open the door to irrational behavior. When emotional scenes repeat themselves always in the same way, we must suspect a dovetailing of transference and counter-transference such as occurred in the encounter between Martin and myself. One must then find ways of breaking the vicious circle.

In evaluating the harm that may be done through experiences such as these, we must remember that the disturbed child's life is a more or less unbroken succession of disasters brought on by the dovetailing of his own and his environment's pathology. One more event of this kind is to him nothing extraordinary. Experiences free from such dovetailing are the exception and therefore

2. See Christine Olden, "On Adult Empathy with Children."

memorable. Occasional slips are, therefore, seldom disastrous if only the relationship survives the incident. It is different when a relationship that has been strongly invested by the child is destroyed or permanently distorted by the adult's counter-transference. Such experience, reinforcing the child's worst expectations once too often, may do serious damage.

For instance, if I had been so frightened by the violence of my reaction to Martin that I had withdrawn my interest from him and his art, or if I had continued to re-enact the sado-masochistic incident in spite of the warning which he gave me, either reaction might have been harmful.[3]

Ordinarily our powers for both good and evil are moderate, and as long as we can admit a mistake children will forgive us more readily than will most adults.

PRACTICAL SUGGESTIONS

Having gained some theoretical understanding of art therapy, we must ask what are the practical requirements that should be met to make it an effective factor in the therapeutic milieu.

Before all, art therapy needs a room of its own, separate both from the general play area and from the crafts. The latter condition is seldom fulfilled. All too often, a hybrid of "arts and crafts" is supposed to take care of the children's creative needs.

Even from the purely practical point of view such a situation is detrimental to both fields. The crafts require order, cleanliness, methodical procedures. Art is notoriously messy and needs improvisation. When they must coexist at close quarters, antagonism inevitably develops.

Under such conditions art usually remains of secondary importance to all but a minority of very gifted children. Crafts, offering set rules of procedure and promising predictable end

3. For an example of such an event, see Rudolf Eckstein, Judith Wallerstein, and Arthur Mandelbaum, "Counter-Transference in a Residential Treatment Home."

results, are more immediately attractive, and the situation does not give most children the opportunity to acquire a taste for the more elusive pleasures of art.

The greatest enemies of both art and crafts, however, are predigested kit-crafts, commercial plaster molds, precut patterns, and similar devices which circumvent both creativity and craftsmanship. In a room where such commercial aids are used and the resulting objects are displayed, creative work has very little chance.

The art therapy room should have running water, a large sink, and ample storage space for materials, for work in progress, for finished work.

Simple materials that lend themselves to a wide range of uses, such as charcoal, tempera paints, pastels, and ceramic clay, and a kiln for firing clay sculpture, constitute the basic necessities for our work. A program that serves adolescents will need a greater variety of media. Particularly valuable for such a group are space and equipment for making large sculptures.

To foster the production of art that embodies profound personal meaning, the art therapist conducts sessions in a nondirective way. He encourages each child to choose his own subject. Projects or assignments can be helpful at times, for instance to get children started, re-inspire them when they have become jaded, establish a more disciplined atmosphere when sessions have become too chaotic, or teach some specific techniques. But such approaches should be no more than occasional departures. The atmosphere should be one in which the child feels that the art therapist wants neither to impose his ideas nor to elicit any specific information, but that the therapist is there to help him in any way he can to achieve what *he* wants to do. All examples of art work given in this book were produced in sessions where neither subject matter nor technical procedures were prescribed.

Art sessions should be so scheduled that the children can invest in the activity intensely. For most children one- to one-and–a–half-hour sessions held at least twice a week seem adequate. However, when a child becomes very absorbed in his work every effort should be made to give him the opportunity to spend extra time at it. It is advisable to maintain both regularly scheduled art sessions and free periods (preferably at the end of the day) when children can work more informally. As a rule, a lively and intense working atmosphere is best established when children are seen in groups so that they can inspire one another. The size of groups that can be profitably handled depends on the children's disturbances, their age, and other factors. One art therapist may be able to take care of six to ten delinquents, but three or four borderline children may be all he can deal with at one time. Some children, of course, are so disturbed or so handicapped they can be helped only when they have an adult's exclusive attention.

Is art therapy desirable for all disturbed children? Are there situations when art may be detrimental or where it is bound to be ineffective? We have said before that the making of symbolic images is differentiated from the playful experimentation that precedes it roughly between the ages of three and five. It follows that children who have not matured beyond this early stage or have regressed to it can profit from the handling of art materials, but they do not need the assistance of a specialist. An understanding nursery school teacher can supervise such activities equally well. The art therapist, however, may be called upon to work with a child who seems about to make the transition from the more primitive stage to the creation of symbolic objects.

Art therapy may be contraindicated for brain-damaged children who are neurologically so impaired that they are overwhelmed by the profusion of stimuli and the freedom of art, and frustrated by demands that they cannot fulfill. For such children, art materials can be useful as a means of training perception, but teaching is, in the main, directive, and creative work becomes at best a distant goal.

However, the art therapist must not admit defeat too readily. Often it is possible to find ways of circumventing the brain-damaged child's handicaps so that he too can enjoy using art materials expressively. For instance, many children who are hopelessly confused when they attempt to draw or paint can create in clay or wood, where touch supplements visual perception. Others who are unable to concentrate when confronted with too many stimuli can nevertheless produce when the material offered is simple and distractions are kept to a minimum.

My own limited experience with such children has taught me that it is extremely difficult to conduct art therapy sessions for groups that include both the brain-injured and the emotionally disturbed who are not neurologically impaired. Their needs are so different that either one or the other type of child necessarily suffers.

Creative art may also be either temporarily or permanently out of reach for children whose functioning depends mainly on obsessive-compulsive defenses and who break down in situations that cannot be handled by these mechanisms.

Children who are easily flooded by material from the unconscious are at times menaced by an activity that stimulates fantasy.

It is hard to make any definite rules about the degree of obsessiveness or of disorganization that would make art therapy unsuccessful or harmful at a particular time. Luckily, children usually sense their own needs, and in both admitting them to art therapy and allowing them to withdraw, the therapist fares best when he takes his cues from them.

III

Art Therapy and the Problem of Quality in Art [1]

IN ART THERAPY and education we use the word "art" to denote a great variety of products. Perhaps all they have in common is that form has been given to matter with the intent of making a symbolic rather than a useful object. This does not mean that we are blind to the enormous qualitative differences between these products which, for want of a better word, we call art. [2]

The practicing art therapist or educator finds that he necessarily orders the great variety of products which he encounters into a number of loosely defined categories. He distinguishes work that is predominantly formless and chaotic; art that is conventional and stereotyped; pictographic communications that can be understood only if the painter explains their meaning; and complex, aesthetically valid creations that possess to a greater or lesser degree the qualities which we associate intuitively with art in the full sense of the word.

It is not always easy to discriminate between the various kinds of products. For instance, certain seemingly unrestrained chaotic pictures reveal themselves upon closer examination as

1. The introductory passage of this chapter is based on the first section of my two-part article "The Problem of Quality in Art."
2. The question arises: Would it be better to coin a new word, free from value judgments implied in the term "art," to designate the objects created in art sessions conducted with the principal aim of alleviating suffering or bringing about beneficial changes in personality? This problem has been discussed by Elinor Ulman, "Art Therapy: Problems of Definition," and M. L. J. Vaessen, "Art or Expression: A Discussion of the Creative Activities of Mental Patients." See also Ainslie Meares, *Shapes of Sanity.*

nothing more than banal stereotypes in the modern manner, tame in a way that we associate more readily with conventional pictures of flowers and fruit. On the other hand, a picture may seem stereotyped at first glance because subject matter and composition follow a familiar pattern, while actually the artist has filled this conventional form with fresh experience. Though no foolproof method of distinguishing between various kinds of art can be devised, and though judgments remain subject to error and controversy, we cannot doubt that such distinctions are valid. We feel intuitively that scribble, stereotype, pictograph, and artistic creation differ not merely in intensity but in kind, though all four may be manifestations of related processes.

In practice our responses show that we appreciate these differences. For example, we may feel that uncovering the secret meaning of a schizophrenic's pictograph constitutes a therapeutic victory. We know, on the other hand, that it would be nonsensical to apply the same kind of literal translation of symbols to an aesthetically conceived work of art. When a scribbler attributes very special meaning to some element in one of his scribbles, we would see this as an act of projection comparable to a response to Rorschach blots. The projected idea would interest us, but we would not mistake the scribble itself for a pictograph made with the intention of expressing meaning.

Underlying our actions and attitudes are certain general assumptions which we can accept as self-evident in the majority of cases. For instance, we can safely suppose that paintings or drawings consisting entirely of chaotic colors or lines are created at a time when impulses have ascendancy over controlling forces. Beyond this, no conclusion can be drawn. Unless we know more about the specific situation, we cannot guess whether the artist purposely abdicated his controls and permitted the impulsive elements of his being full reign, or whether he was overpowered by an upsurge of emotion. Assuming that he was overpowered, we must remember that a weak ego may be overwhelmed by a relatively slight increase of pressure, but that even a strong ego may be thrown off balance by an infuriating or devastating experience; and again, areas of strength and weakness differ. A person who in art easily resorts to angry gestures may have considerable self-control in other situations, while the opposite may be true for another.

We can also be reasonably certain that the balance is reversed in stereotyped, conventional work and that such painting serves mainly as a defense. Some conventional art seems to be less a defense than an expression of helplessness and emptiness such as I have described in the section on Art and Emptiness. Even in these cases the mood is submissive rather than impulsive. The painter of stereotypes confirms this by his attitude, for he is usually happiest about those pictures which deviate least from his chosen prototype, thus revealing least of his own personality. On the other hand, there are painters who make a conscious effort to be original and nevertheless end up copying someone else's manner. We suppose that in such a person an unconscious need for conformity is stronger than the conscious wish for self-expression, or that the person lacks sufficient feeling of identity.

As before, we cannot tell without further information why the stereotype was painted or what function it serves. A stereotype may have been painted because any departure from conventional norms arouses anxiety in the painter, or it may have been manufactured to please a public that prefers conventional art, or for a variety of other possible reasons.

It is hard to make generalizations about pictographs. They are intended to convey meaning, but in each instance a key must be found before that meaning becomes intelligible.

Finally there are products more complex than chaotic expression, more original than stereotypes, more immediately intelligible than pictographs, that possess to some degree the quality of art in the strict sense. Again we may ask whether we can discern properties common to all such products, and try to guess their function in the artist's psychic economy.

From the outset it seems debatable that specific processes distinguish true art from other forms or pictorial expression. Art, it can be argued, is always emotionally charged; it arises from and evokes feeling. An emotional outburst captured on canvas or paper may be deeply moving both to the artist and to the spectator. Where, then, is the difference betwen art and a passionate scribble? And where should we draw the line between stereotype and art, when it is virtually impossible to create art that is not influenced by tradition and convention? Finally, may not the same process that leads to the making of simple pictographs also contribute to artistic creation? For every work of art holds within itself a secret story, matter concealed even from the awareness of the creator, which influences the choice and arrangement of pictorial symbols.

The arguments are persuasive, yet we are convinced that art is an entity, however elusive, however open to controversy, that is distinct from all other forms of pictorial expression. Art is characterized by economy of means, inner consistency, and evocative power. Beyond such very general description, art defies definition. Prominent critics of the past and present have admired rubbish and condemned great art, and whole societies have been blind to the merits of certain schools of art. Even the critic with faith in his own judgment knows that he can never absolutely trust his evaluation of any single work of art. Nevertheless, we feel that there exists a core of objective truth and that it is, therefore, worthwhile to seek understanding by investigating the psychological processes that are active when art is made.

The problem is less complex in children's art. If we define as art any kind of formed expression, regardless of the level of talent, skill, or mental age, that has some degree of inner consistency, and, again within the limitations of the child's capacities, a certain evocative power, we can usually decide without too much hesitation whether or not the goal of art has been reached in a child's picture.

ARTISTIC FAILURE AND SUCCESS

Herman: Plate I was painted by a ten-year-old boy, Herman, shortly after his admission to Wiltwyck School. The picture shows considerable skill, but it is perturbing. Two contradictory messages seem to cancel each other out. The figures in the picture, a rabbit, two trees, two birds, three angels and one fairy-like female figure, and a sun are all tame, somewhat saccharine subjects more appropriate for a good little girl at Sunday school than for a ten-year-old boy. The background with its passionate orange brushstrokes tells a different story. Its vivid color and strong movement nearly obliterate the figures and also isolate each of them so that the whole picture gives a fragmented impression.

Herman's figures appear to represent the part of him that he is ready to show in public, while the background betrays his hidden anger and passion. The figures of his picture would have called for a pink or light blue background; the hellfire which invades Herman's effeminate paradise is inappropriate. The isolated, fragile figures floating in the fiery orange have a certain eloquence, but the picture is not altogether an artistic success. It is diagnostically interesting, but we find that the psychological truth comes through not in accordance with the child artist's intentions but in spite of them. It is an example of self-betrayal more than of self-expression.

Plate II, Herman's next picture, also tells of a conflict between two forces. This time the negative power does not intrude against his will; instead the struggle has become the overt subject of his painting. Herman's lady-angel, clutching her harp, is pursued by a red devil, and we can follow their endless chase all over heaven in the blue maze that fills the page. We need no diagnostic training to get the message. The economy of artistic means in conveying the story is remarkable, indeed the deepest meaning is conveyed entirely through the handling of the paint. Both the angel's dress and the maze were originally painted in red—the blue has been superimposed. In the dress the mixture of the two colors made a dramatic purple. Blue has won out in the maze, but the underlying red remains in part visible, so that we perceive how both powers have indeed covered the same ground; this makes the kinesthetic feeling of endless, directionless chase even more dramatic. We feel how angel and devil are truly and fatefully inseparable.

Naturally we cannot assume that all this was consciously planned. Rather we see how conscious intent and unconscious message converge to make the painter's intuitive handling of his subject more powerful and convincing, whereas in the first painting conscious and unconscious meaning diverged and enfeebled the picture's aesthetic quality and emotional impact.

Plate III, painted when Herman was eleven years old, still shows the cleavage between two forces, this time overtly depicted as male and female but not explicitly identified with good and evil as in the picture of the angel and the devil. It seems that Herman's values have shifted, for the mare is black, while stallion and colt are both a golden (good) color. Also the father's sex organs are conspicuously delineated while the mother's udder is not drawn, even though its presence is implied by the colt's suckling gesture. The palomino stallion and the black mare face each other across a division rendered by two vertical brushstrokes in green, but there is an attempt at reconciliation. The colt unites the pair, for it is suckling at the black mother but has the father's palomino coloring. The horses are beautifully drawn, but on closer inspection one notices that each horse lacks one leg.

We do not know whether to admire Herman's artistry in creating figures that correspond to our visual image of "horse" in spite of a missing leg, or to worry about Herman's fate, as we see the persistence of feelings of castration and inner division even while he is making a heroic effort at coming, to terms with his conflicts.

Artistically we can pronounce the picture a success, but with some reservations. The painting is evocative and well integrated. The bilateral composition, which gives equal weight and importance to the figures on both sides, conveys a feeling of division in a state of balance. The color repeats this. The strong contrast between gold and black is reconciled by the black shading of the golden palominos and the golden shading of the black mare.

However, the missing legs constitute an intrusion, albeit a well-hidden one, which diminishes the painting's evocative power. Herman's style has matured. The ideas are more realistic and the problem of sexuality is overtly stated. The disturbance is better concealed. (It takes close observation to notice the missing legs.)

Max: We must distinguish between confusion that *intrudes* upon a work of art and diminishes its inner consistency, and confusion as the *subject matter* which the work expresses. Figure 3, painted by Max, a nine-year-old boy whose father was Puerto Rican and whose mother was Negro, expresses his confusion about his race and color. It consists of two heads, one white with red features, the other brown with pink features, both at-

FIGURE 3. *Max:* Black and White (18″ x 24″)

tached to amorphous bodies. The theme is reiterated in a background of dizzily intermingling white and pink dots. Max is not as talented as Herman, but within the limits of his endowment the painting is successful. It is formed, evocative, and consistent, and expresses meaning with economy.

Having given an idea of what is meant by the quality of "art," we can turn to a more systematic observation of the forces that foster art and those that impede it.

DIFFERENT WAYS OF USING ART MATERIALS

Both the forces that converge when the creative process is successful and those that impede it are more transparent in children than they are in adults. The complex defensive system which in later life becomes inextricably interwoven with the total character structure is still rudimentary in the child. Particularly when we work with children at the borderline of psychosis we see them oscillate between different modes of functioning. To facilitate systematic thinking I have differentiated five ways in which art materials may be used.

1. Precursory activities: scribbling, smearing; exploration of physical properties of the material that does not lead to creation of symbolic configurations but is experienced as positive and egosyntonic.

2. Chaotic discharge: spilling, splashing, pounding; destructive behavior leading to loss of control.

3. Art in the service of defense: stereotyped repetition; copying, tracing, banal conventional production.

4. Pictographs: pictorial communications which replace or supplement words. (Such communications occur often in psychotherapy or in other intimate relationships. They usually remain unintelligible to the outsider. Pictographs are, as a rule, crudely executed and seldom attain the integration and evocative power of art.)

5. Formed expression, or art in the full sense of the word; the

production of symbolic configurations that successfully serve both self-expression and communication.

The following stories illustrate these different ways of using art materials. They were all collected from work with five- to eight-year-old children who were in-patients of the child psychiatry ward at the Albert Einstein College of Medicine. I will call them Tom, Michael, Robert, and Billy.

Precursory Activities

Tom (age 6): Tom enters the art room for the first time since admission to the hospital. He chooses to work with clay, pats a lump of it into a pancake, smoothes it with water, and is delighted by the wet, slippery sensation.

Seeing another child making a face from just such a pancake form, he takes a stick, draws a face on the clay, and attempts to add ears. He obliterates this face, tries again; finally in frustration he throws the clay against the wall. He then regains control of himself, washes his hands meticulously, and leaves the art room.

We see playful activity leading to attempted expression followed by discharge of affect and finally defensive behavior typical for this child. Tom functions like a child of three or four. This seems, at the moment, to be the best he can do; no attempt is made to push for more mature work. It can be expected that the other children's example will soon induce Tom to go beyond his present state.

Emotional Discharge

Michael (age 7), Robert (age 7): Michael and Robert are in the same art therapy group. The two boys also have the same psychotherapist, and sibling rivalry is bitter between them.

Michael, who is the stronger of the two, sets the tone. He pours a lot of paint on paper, folds it up, reopens it, and produces a series of Rorschach-like blots that ooze all over the paper.

He manages to cover a table and himself thoroughly with paint.

He vociferously demands that I admire his products, manages at the same time to cover Robert's work with paint, and wipes his hands on my smock. By now Robert has been drawn into Michael's orbit and the two boys proceed to paint swastikas on the wall. Michael also paints swastikas on my smock (despite my protest), while Robert adorns the smock with stars. The two boys dig up the half-broken clay head of a dog, put it into a coffee can, and pour paint over it, calling it a "fuck head." At this point they are told very emphatically that they have to stop or leave the room. Their behavior subsides to a more tolerable derisive banter, but no constructive work is done.

The session is clearly dominated by emotional discharge. The paint-pouring at the beginning is only a pretext for aggressive smearing. The anger vented against me is probably connected with the boys' anger at having to share many things, above all the psychotherapist. In their concerted attack on me they find the only common ground that is possible to them at the time.

The two boys' behavior and their use of paint is no doubt expressive, but it is formless and leads to loss of control.

Compulsive Defenses

There are times when creative work is impossible and chaotic behavior can be controlled only through a retreat into compulsive activities.

Robert (age 7): Robert enters the art session extremely disturbed. He can't settle down, climbs on furniture, throws clay, bothers the other children, and does everything imaginable to get hurt or punished. Since I know that Robert is not able to do expressive work when he is in this condition, but that he can function within strict limits, I suggest that he do something about school work. Eventually he settles down to make clay numbers. He works diligently and I praise his work.

The session begins with symptomatic behavior which can be controlled only by flight into a compulsive, defensive activity. In this emergency the art therapist supports Robert's defenses. His compulsive work is preferable to chaotic wildness even though it has little educational value.

At times attempts at expressive art work may have to be abandoned after a struggle. To restore control, a child must resort to stereotyped work.

Robert wants to model the head of a German shepherd dog. He produces a solid shape for head and neck. Trying to make the neck still stronger, he adds lumps of clay so that it loses its shape. At the same time he squeezes the neck so that it actually gets thinner. I attempt repeatedly to help Robert restore the original form, but inevitably it is again destroyed. Later Robert digs a deep hole representing the mouth and tries with dogged persistence to insert a narrow strip of clay for a tongue. The tongue breaks again and again. Finally Robert smashes the head with both fists and drums on it.

He calms down and takes a piece of paper, puts his foot (in new sneakers) on the paper and traces it. He then sets out to copy the intricate design of his rubber soles with meticulous care (Fig. 4).

In starting his dog head, Robert made an attempt at formed expression. We can surmise that, if he had completed it, the sculpture would have embodied Robert's psychosexual pathology with its chaotic confusion of body openings and body functions. The sexual excitement and the ambivalence and anxiety aroused in the making of the head interfered with the creative process, leading to contradictory actions which destroyed the form and ended with an outburst of temper. After this emotional discharge, Robert retreated into his preferred mode of defense—obsessive-compulsive drawing with delusional overtones (Robert has fantasies about a "magic power" residing in his sneakers).

Billy (age 6): Billy draws a triangular Christmas tree with ornaments. Scattered over the paper, drawn with a light pink crayon, are primitive schematic representations of children and toys. Each child consists of a head with rudimentary features, to which two lines are attached that serve to denote both legs and

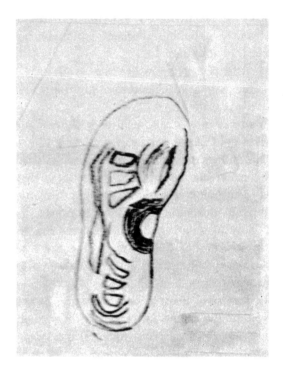

FIGURE 4. *Robert*: Sneaker (9″ x 12″)

body. At a right angle to these lines are two short lines denoting arms. The area that suggests the body is empty and undefined. There is no distinction between male and female.

Billy is dissatisfied and tears up the picture. He then begs me to cut out a "regular" Christmas tree for him, meaning the stereotyped pattern of the coloring books. He discards several of my offerings, insisting on absolute symmetrical perfection. He traces this pattern carefully, adds a row of neatly beribboned packages, and colors the tree with green crayon. He cannot be induced to add any people.

Billy's first attempt, though infantile, was expressive. It was a good image of home as it really was, a crowd of neglected children in a chaotic environment. Billy's schema for people is symptomatic of his deep feelings of insignificance, helplessness, and castration.

He cannot endure this projection of his incomplete self. He turns toward neat and impersonal stereotypes that will not confront him with unbearable truth.

Pictographs

The kind of therapy described in this book is not designed to particularly encourage the production of pictographs. These belong on principle to psychotherapy rather than art therapy. There are, however, moments when pictographic communication is essential in art therapy as well.

Emergency Measure: When several children had undergone psychological tests that include a maze, one of the group began drawing his idea of this kind of maze—in his words, a "trap." He drew a confusion of roads with a house somewhere in the middle, but none of the roads led to the house. The idea spread like wildfire. Soon all the children were drawing traps. They began adding all sorts of terrible dangers, such as monsters, ghosts, and wild animals, to their drawings. They drew traps for each other and traps for me, and they invited me to draw traps for them. The session became loaded with anxiety, and the work more and more formless.

Evidently the maze tests had touched upon the children's worst fears, and this could be easily understood. They were far from home, confined in an enormous building full of mysterious goings-on. At the hospital's entrance they encountered people in wheelchairs, on crutches, armless and legless people. Ambulances came and went. Beyond this, each child was lost in the maze of his own confusions.

I felt that I had to somehow free the maze-traps of their sinister implications. I set out to draw benign traps for the children, with roads where they encountered mild dangers that could be overcome so that they came safely home. For example, one of the roads led to a stream crossed by a broken bridge, but there was a path to a log which also spanned the stream and could be safely crossed (Fig. 5).

The children were delighted. Every child got his benign trap, and they in turn drew traps for me that would lead me safely home (Fig. 6). The art session ended peacefully. We had not produced art, for the drawings had been too quick and rudimentary. We had used graphic symbols to relieve immediate anxiety and restore confidence. I had performed a kind of psychological first aid, using the pictorial language in response to the children's pictographic communications.

Reconciliation: Robert had been very destructive during one art session. I was angry with him and had finally put him for a short time in seclusion. During the rest of the afternoon he wept inconsolably. After I had finished with the other children, I invited him for a short individual session in the art room on condition that he would control his weeping.

He stopped, entered the room without looking at me, and never said a word. Instead he drew a picture (Fig. 7) which eloquently expressed his state of mind. The tall stem of a daisy-like flower with a very dark center, like a black-eyed Susan, divides the page in the middle. The right part is dark and contains a faintly drawn stroke of lightning. On the light side we see a second, smaller daisy, also with a dark center, a large cloud-face with a sad mouth and tearful eyes, a smaller cloud with a similar expression, and a number of tear-shaped raindrops scattered over the page. Robert was not ready to talk about the drawing, but he left the art room composed, and later honored me with a smile and a friendly goodbye.

The drawing stands between pictograph and picture. It is more formed and expressive than most pictographs, but the message it contains is directed specifically to me and refers to the immediate situation.

Since Robert would not talk about the picture, we do not know what conscious ideas were tied to it; nor have we any help from his associations to suggest what unconscious material found expression. We cannot know whether the dark half of the picture

FIGURE 5. *Kramer*: Benign Trap (12″ x 18″)

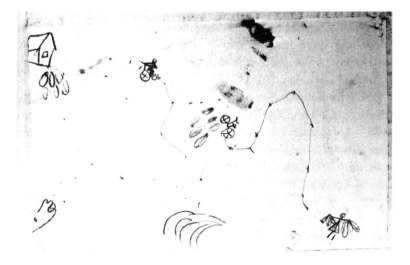

FIGURE 6. *Angel*: Benign Trap (12″ x 18″)

FIGURE 7. *Robert:* Reconciliation Picture (18″ x 24″)

and the stroke of lightning in it is an image of my anger or of
his, or, as seems likely to me, a condensation of both. We do not
know why there are two clouds and two flowers—are those the
two actors in the drama or does the repetition serve mainly for
emphasis?

Whatever unknown content the picture may include, it constitutes both an eloquent message and an excellent image of the
child's personality. Robert was divided. Both anger and tears
were always close. He also was a child who tried desperately to
hold onto relationships even though his pathology threatened to
disrupt them all the time. The drawing tells of black anger, tears,
division between darkness and light, and of hope.

At the time when Robert drew the pictograph-picture he
could not have put such complex ideas into words, but he was
able to communicate them in graphic language.

Formed Expression

Robert (age 7): Robert's expressive attempts did not always end in chaos or retreat. Sometimes he managed to sustain the creative act to the end.

Robert makes a sculpture of a dog (Fig. 8). He constructs four solid legs and models a head and neck. When making the body, he repeatedly squeezes it so hard that it breaks in half, just like the neck of his dog-head sculpture. With my help, the body is restored several times and ultimately stays together. Robert places the dog on a slab of clay and puts little pieces of clay beneath the dog's hind legs representing "caca" (his word for feces). He also gives the dog a huge collar, and later paints the dog white with black features and paints the caca black. Beneath the dog's front legs he paints a red spot—"blood"—and makes the collar green. The dog's small white face with large, sad eyes,

FIGURE 8. *Robert*: Dog with Blood and Caca (6″ high)

its forehead covered by black hair, looks remarkably like Robert at his most appealing. He gives me the dog as a present.

The figure expresses not only Robert's pathology (his pre-occupation with blood and feces), but his personality as a whole. It shows his need for and attempt at control (the collar) and a plea for acceptance in spite of, or including, his troubles. This is expressed both in the choice of a domestic animal as subject and in offering it, blood and caca included, as a gift.

Production is threatened when Robert keeps squeezing the dog's body in half. This time Robert is able to accept the art therapist's help in warding off the impulse. In contrast to the experience with the dog head, where sexual fantasies impeded creation, this time Robert's fantasies are incorporated in the artistic product.

Robert represents a borderline case between those children for whom art is beneficial and those for whom it is upsetting rather than helpful. His control depends largely on compulsive defenses, and art often leads to chaotic behavior. But on the rare occasions when he is able to create art, Robert is elated, and he remembers each such incident with pride. It is, therefore, worthwhile to keep on giving him the opportunity to create, even though one must be prepared for breakdowns. When art is too exciting, I encourage Robert to seek shelter in compulsive occupations.

Michael (age 7): Sometimes expressive form can be attained only after the danger of emotional outburst has been warded off through compulsive defensive activities. After a severe temper tantrum at school, Michael enters the art room soberly, declaring that he intends to paint a circus scene, a picture that should be good enough to sell so that he can help to support his family.

He sets up his table and materials with great care. Then he begins to draw a ladder leading to the flying trapeze. He places it close to the margin of the paper and spends the whole hour patiently painting in the rungs.

He returns to the picture in the following session and now

swiftly paints an acrobat about to catch the woman partner who is leaping through the air toward him.

Michael is a talented child who has learned to protect his creative work from his own impulsive behavior. He often uses systematic craftsmanlike procedures for their calming effect.

Michael (now 8 years old): Creative work can help a child master anxiety and make emotional preparations for change, but when anxiety becomes too intense the creative process may break down.

When Michael's discharge to a treatment home approached, he set out to model a deep-sea diver, complete with oxygen tank. He intended to add the figure of Angel, a boy who had been Michael's competitor in art and who had already been discharged to another institution. According to plan, the sculpture was to represent both Michael and Angel in divers' outfits, shaking hands. The work extended through several art sessions. In the beginning all went very well. The first figure (Michael) was nearly completed; only the oxygen mask had to be fitted to the diver's face. Michael had great technical difficulty making this small object and fitting it properly over nose and mouth.

He became frantic. I suggested that he eliminate the mask and make believe that the diver had already reached land, but he would not accept this solution. Suddenly Michael struck the sculpture with his fist, destroying it beyond repair. He broke into loud sobs, overturned the table, and had to be forcibly removed from the art room.

Deeply anxious about his impending departure and his survival in a new environment, Michael expresses his situation symbolically in the diver. He tries to build up a manly idea of himself and conjures up the image of another boy with whom he already identifies (because he also is a good artist), and who has survived transplantation. Thus Michael acts according to our fondest hopes. He creates a symbol which serves as an analogy to the impending danger, and he almost succeeds in mastering his fear.

Unfortunately, anger and anxiety erupt when the breathing apparatus, which most emphatically symbolizes survival, is constructed. Michael ends by destroying the image of his hopes and fears. (It is conceivable that anxiety was exacerbated because nose and oxygen mask may also have a sexual meaning, and the act of joining the two thus touched upon deeper fears and ambivalences.) Michael's despair is the more intense because he is unable to master his feelings through creative work, on which he can usually depend for comfort and reassurance.

Michael is not too weak to sustain creative work at all, like Robert or Billy who attain formed expression only on rare occasions, but this time the pressures are too great even for Michael's considerable creative powers.

Our examples show how the categories we have established can help us think more systematically about children's art, but they do not constitute a rigid system. We see on the contrary how even in the making of a single object different kinds of functioning may come into play: a child may progress from precursory playful experimentation to formed expression, may regress to chaotic behavior, retreat into compulsive defensive production, and move back again to formed creative work. At another time a child may be content to produce fragmentary pictographs that serve immediate needs.

Although the art therapist is on the whole committed to helping children to produce work that is both expressive and formed, he knows that he cannot always attain this goal. There are times when creative work is out of reach, and situations when other modes of functioning are more helpful to the child.

IV

Sublimation

THE CONCEPT OF SUBLIMATION

IN THE SECTION ON Artistic Failure and Success we approached the problem of quality in art by analyzing the finished product. We recognized evocative power, inner consistency, and economy of artistic means as hallmarks of good art. We saw that the harmony of art is attained through the integration and balance of tensions, never through simple elimination of dissonance. It mirrors a complex balance of inner forces. In psychoanalytic terms this harmony is identified with the process of sublimation.

To understand the concept we must consider man's basic dilemma. He can never unconditionally obey his instinctive drives or be guided by his primitive affects. In him the evolution of intelligence and the concomitant atrophy of instinctively regulated behavior have reached a point where the instinctive inhibitory mechanisms which safeguard much of the impulsive behavior even of the highest animals have ceased to operate effectively. Thus man's survival depends on the continuous appraisal of and adjustment to reality. The drives, nevertheless, remain his chief source of energy, and the gratification of instinctive needs his basic source of pleasure. Yet, since they are no longer held in check by instinctive mechanisms which determine when they can be gratified and when they must be denied fulfillment, the drives are, in their primeval form, a source of mortal danger to man.[1]

1. See Konrad Lorenz, *On Aggression.*

The dilemma is inescapable. According to Freudian theory it has brought about a fundamental cleavage in man's psychic organization. It has become divided into the original primitive system, which he has named the id, and the more recently evolved ego. The latter is an organizing force which develops anew in each individual and constitutes man's most indispensable organ of survival. To it are ascribed all the higher mental functions, such as the capacity to perceive and manipulate reality, to postpone gratification, and to maintain the inner unity of personality. Ultimately the ego serves the instincts, which, through the ego's efforts, obtain the gratification they could never achieve through the impulsive discharge which is all the id remains capable of at this late stage of evolution.[2]

As the individual matures, the superego develops, and social demands and inhibitions become internalized. The superego's power to compel or to inhibit can never attain either the reliability or the force of instinctive inhibiting mechanisms that govern the social behavior of other species, but it fulfills some of the same functions, making individual behavior more predictable and protecting the continuity of social organization.[3]

The ego could not fulfill its manifold and contradictory tasks of controlling impulses, avoiding dangers, warding off anxiety, and obtaining pleasure without the aid of simple repression as well as various more complex mechanisms. Among the latter, sublimation constitutes one of the most efficient means of dealing with dangers threatening from the drives and of making constructive use of their potentially destructive power.

It is a process wherein drive energy is deflected from its original goal and displaced onto achievement, which is highly valued by the ego, and is, in most instances, socially productive. The obsessive single-minded quality that characterizes the drives in their original form is modified through sublimation, so that

2. See Sigmund Freud, *Complete Psychological Works: Formulations on the Two Principles of Mental Functioning*, pp. 213–26; *The Unconscious*, pp. 159–215.
3. See Lorenz, *On Aggression*, chap. 5.

energies are freed for action beyond the narrow circle of infantile conflict and primitive needs. Because ego strength and autonomy increase in the process, we surmise that a shifting of energy from id to ego occurs and that aggressive and libidinal energy is neutralized.[4] An essential feature of sublimation is the great amount of genuine pleasure the substitute activity affords.

Neither the development of the ego as a whole nor the process of sublimation is as yet fully understood. It would certainly be an oversimplification to describe sublimation as mere ersatz gratification. Even though the capacity for it can develop only when the human environment fosters it, and even though the form it takes depends in part on the environment, the inclination toward sublimation is as much a part of the human heritage as is the need for ego development itself.[5]

The pleasures of direct gratification and those of sublimation differ in kind. Abandoning oneself to impulsive pleasures is intensely gratifying, but the danger of excess and of the letdown that follows it is ever present. When excitement reaches a certain threshold there is anxiety, for the loss of ego controls endangers both physical safety and the ties upon which emotional survival depends.

The pleasures of sublimation are more lasting and often they are more exquisite, but they cannot be as intense. Sublimation depends on partial renunciation, for an instinct that spends itself through full gratification is not available as a source of energy for any modified activity.

No instinct, on the other hand, can be successfully modified and socialized unless there has been sufficient direct fulfillment at the time of its first appearance and unless a certain measure of direct gratification remains available later on. In the absence of such gratification, instinctive need remains too overwhelming and obsessive. If the lack of gratification has external causes, the

4. See Heinz Hartmann, "Notes on the Theory of Sublimation"; Heinz Hartmann, Ernst Kris, and Rudolph Loewenstein, "Comments on the Formulation of Psychic Structure"; Ernst Kris, "Neutralization and Sublimation."
5. The following four paragraphs contain ideas previously presented in the introductory chapter of my book *Art Therapy in a Children's Community.*

instinct will find ersatz gratification, however bizarre. If the sanctions against instinctive gratification have been internalized, the effort of maintaining repression will exhaust the individual's energies.

In practice, few social achievements are brought about through sublimation alone. Compliance with social demands are also enforced by fear of loss of love or fear of castration, and these fears are apt to lead to neurotic defenses rather than to sublimation. But, since socialization is necessary if there is to be any growth at all, we cannot expect entirely to eliminate these harsher means of achieving it. All we can reasonably hope for is that, in the course of growing up, sublimation will outweigh other, more debilitating mechanisms of coming to terms with the conflict between instinctual and social needs.

Sublimation increases the ego's power, while neurotic defenses lead to the diminution of its available energies. Each person has areas where sublimation is easily attained and others where it is more difficult. The capacity for sublimation varies. Some children sublimate with a minimum of encouragement; others seem nearly incapable of sublimation even under the most favorable conditions.

DISPLACEMENT AND SUBLIMATION

Substitution which channels actions and emotions without changing their nature remains a safety valve throughout life. When we strike a table with our fist, we express anger, substituting table for person. The psychotherapist who works with aggressive children keeps a punching bag, a game of darts, or the like in his playroom, mainly to allow expression of hostility without danger to himself, the patient, or the furniture, but this alone is not yet sublimation.

In sublimation we expect a change of the *object* upon which the interest is centered, of the *goal*, and of the *kind of energy* through which the goal is achieved. The following story will illustrate this.

Danny: A group of deprived, mildly disturbed eight-year-old boys and girls were working with clay. One of the little boys rolled out a large clay sausage and held it against himself like a penis. Soon the whole group was making clay penises. As could be expected, the session ended in wild hilarity, obscenity, and fights; a good measure of sexually colored hostility landed on the therapist. Why had this happened?

Some of the manifestations of guilt, hostility, and dammed-up sexuality can be explained as reactions to the excessive horror with which exposure of the genitals is regarded in our culture. However, even in an environment that treated nudity more casually, there probably would have been trouble.

When the boys tried to substitute large, adult clay penises for their own small ones and the girls tried to replace the missing penis with a clay one, they were confronted with the full absurdity of their wishes. The activity brought their longing for the large penis to a high pitch, while the crumbling soft clay which kept falling off inexorably demonstrated the futility of their efforts. I, who had permitted—or rather had been unable to prevent—the incident, naturally became the object of the children's scorn and derision.

A few sessions later Danny, who had been one of the penis-makers, asked very shyly whether I thought it would be possible for him to make the Empire State Building out of clay. I assured him that this was a very good idea and he set out to model the building, working hard and earnestly. He achieved a structure about ten inches high that satisfied him. He painted it red and adorned it with a flag, placed above the door (like the flags on school buildings and post offices).

Danny was inordinately proud of his work. In the following days he frequently dropped in to visit his building. He developed enthusiasm for clay modeling, and produced in quick succession a dinosaur, a large battleship, a swimming pool with diving board, a fort complete with large guns, and so on.

No doubt the Empire State Building was a penis symbol, and the subsequent sculptures also symbolized aggressive masculinity.

What was it that made modeling a clay penis lead to disaster, and modeling penis symbols lead to constructive work, civilized behavior, pride in accomplishment, and a positive relationship to the art teacher? Neither the desire for a bigger and better penis nor the admixture of aggression has disappeared. However, it seems that the overt wish has been put aside and that it is at least temporarily suppressed while Danny works with clay. He has displaced his interest in the size of the penis to the general qualities of size, magnificence, and power in many different guises. His ambition awakens; he strives to become a good sculptor and builder. Thus Danny attains his wish in a way that is possible for a little boy, by creating objects that symbolize to him the idea of masculinity.

In this sequence, substitution of a penis symbol for the literal clay penis was only the first step. If Danny had done no more than displace his preoccupation, he would have become just as obsessively fixed upon the Empire State Building as he had been fixed to his penis. His new preoccupation would have been more socially acceptable, but that would have been all. It is Danny's growing capacity to vary and broaden the scope of his interests, and his pleasure in his accomplishments, that prove that there has been a fundamental change beyond simple displacement.

Danny's way of dealing with sexual pressures is typical for the stage of latency. Had a similar incident occurred in a group of adolescents, sublimation would scarcely have been possible through turning away from the human body toward more impersonal sexual symbols. The latency child can set his sexual preoccupations aside. The adolescent must prepare himself for adult love. I should have tried to interest a group of adolescents in realistic sculpture and drawing of the nude. Sublimation would have been achieved if the single-minded preoccupation with the sexual organs had broadened into appreciation of the elegance and beauty of the whole body.

SYMPTOM AND SUBLIMATION

The same areas of conflict tend to become focal points both of sublimation and pathology. At times symptom and sublimation are so amalgamated that it is difficult to separate one from the other. Displacements can lead to the development of faculties that ultimately make sublimation possible; sublimation can become neurotically distorted. How can we tell whether the process that transformed the urge for immediate gratification into socially productive strivings has been sublimation or a mere neurotic formation?

In spite of similarities and overlapping, I believe that it is possible to distinguish between sublimation and other psychic processes. Our next example will give us the opportunity to observe how displacement, symptomatic behavior, and sublimation intermingle in an area of emotional turbulence.[6]

Christopher: At birth Christopher had minimal vision which then gradually diminished. At the age of seven he was totally blind but retained light perception. He was an out-of-wedlock child, who had lived in the same foster home since infancy. Throughout his childhood there had been contact with his mother, but he never met his father. Because of learning difficulties and aggressive behavior he was admitted to the Guild School, a day school for disturbed blind children, when he was eleven years old. There his behavior soon became less aggressive. He began to learn, and he was able to profit from psychotherapy.

I began to work with Christopher shortly after his admission. In the first session he told me how he loved birds, and he sculptured a well-articulated pair of birds in clay. His concepts were clear and realistic. He could perceive form by touch and remember it, and he was able to shape the clay according to his

6. The following case material was developed at the Guild School of the Jewish Guild for the Blind. The school is the therapeutic arm of the Guild's psychiatric clinic. The Art Workshop conducted by the author is part of a varied program of group and individual activities designed to develop intellectual, social, and physical skills.

ideas. Whatever Christopher's troubles were, the faculties of perception, imagination, and constructive action were intact.

Though his interest in birds was present from the beginning, Christopher spent most of his first year making images of both living and mechanical symbols of power, such as cars, buses, airplanes, and ferocious animals. He always chose them for some particular capacity—the cheetah for his swiftness, the wolf for his ferocity, the bull for his horns.

About a year later, when Christopher was twelve years old, he developed a method of making birds out of pipe cleaners, paper, and masking tape. He soon became so skillful that he was able to work at home without help. He produced innumerable birds, insects, bats, and fantastic winged creatures of his own invention, always in pairs, male and female. As his inventiveness and technical skill grew, his passion gave purpose to his free time at home. His birds were much admired and made excellent gifts. Even though there was an obsessive element in his constant output, making birds gave pleasure to him and to others.

At the same time Christopher developed an obsessive preoccupation with the speed, endurance, and strength of birds. He asked endless questions. Was an eagle faster than a goose? Could a goose fly farther than a duck? If an eagle pursued a duck, would the duck escape? Could a hummingbird escape an eagle? And so on, ad infinitum.

The questioning was obsessive, irrational, and joyless. It had the character of compulsive questioning which some children develop when they are preoccupied with the riddle of birth and sex. Christopher's habit of making birds always in couples points to this area as one of the motivating forces of his behavior.

It seemed, however, as if Christopher were also displacing onto birds a more general need for information. He had at this time great difficulty in admitting to any ignorance that would have put him at a disadvantage as compared with sighted people, and had developed many ingenious ways of covering up his handicap. This made it impossible for him to learn to distinguish between those things that escaped his notice because of his blindness and those that even a sighted person could not possibly know without asking.

Torturing his teachers and schoolmates with incessant questions about birds seemed to give him considerable sadistic gratification. It looked as if the birds had come to stand not only for all that was good and desirable, but also for what was unattainable and frustrating.

While Christopher was in the throes of his bird-information mania, he produced a powerful clay sculpture of a two-horned rhinoceros. It was big enough for him to sit on, and pleased him enormously. He took it home in triumph and kept it in his back yard, where it was much admired by family and friends. Inasmuch as Christopher's compulsive questioning expressed anger and the desire to be well protected and strong, the double-horned, thick-skinned beast seemed to have been created out of a similar mood. However, in making it he was dealing with his difficulties in a constructive rather than in a neurotic way. The rhino was both culmination and end of a phase in Christopher's artistic production. From then on he no longer needed to make ferocious animals.

Meanwhile Christopher's questions were becoming more and more irritating, and answering them seemed only to perpetuate the symptom; therefore, we tried to force him to ask only sensible questions for which there were realistic answers. Thus the sadistic gratification he had gained through his compulsive questions was no longer available. It is likely that the frustration this caused him helped bring about a change for the better, for somehow during a period when teachers, psychotherapist, and art therapist were making this concerted effort Christopher became more rational. His interest turned from exclusive concern with the power and speed of birds to curiosity about the lives of the local wild birds whom he could hear singing in his back yard.

He conceived a clay sculpture of a large tree with all the small domestic birds he knew sitting on its branches. The tree was to be a present to his classroom teacher. It was a major undertaking and required wooden armature. It consisted of a roughly finished trunk from which branches, complete with large leaves, stretched in all directions. More than six bird-couples were placed in the branches and on the ground beneath the tree. While Christopher knew each bird's position and species, everything had been executed crudely and some of the birds had been mashed out of shape as he placed them, but Christopher was in such a hurry to complete the job that he could not be bothered to repair the damage. At this point Christopher's classroom teacher visited the ceramics shop and offered to help him to perfect the work if he and I would tell her what to do.

While they were working on the tree, I suggested that he could add some nests and perhaps some eggs. Somewhat reluctantly he set out to make one. Soon there was a nest for each couple, complete with baby birds or eggs. His fervor grew and as he vividly imagined the form and position of each nest and the members of each family, the crude, somewhat disjointed structure took on a new organization. There was one couple that had eggs only, another one had both eggs and baby birds; a male woodpecker was busy making a hole in the tree trunk to accommodate his family, while another father bird was about to pull a worm out of the earth beneath the tree. Thus Christopher created for himself a representation of family life in many different constellations. It was impressive to see the sculpture become beautiful, not because Christopher was striving for aesthetic perfection but because he was so totally absorbed in giving form to ideas that were alive to him.

Christopher named the sculpture the "Spring Tree" (Fig. 9). In creating it he passed from quick, prolific production toward the beginning of concern with quality.

The tree became possible after Christopher had relinquished some of his symptomatic behavior. This implied a certain recognition of the futility of his preoccupation with fabulous feats of strength and endurance. His new interest in real birds meant renouncing fantasies—at least up to a point. (Since Christopher's emotional development at the age of thirteen was still in many ways like that of a ten-year-old, a certain amount of grandiose fantasy was in keeping with his stage of development.) Renunciation of sadistic gratification may have made it possible for him to move from preoccupation with the aggressive components of sexuality toward the expression of love and of Oedipal fantasies.

It is not surprising that Christopher's magnificent gift of love was followed by a certain amount of negative behavior toward his teacher, whom he proceeded to tease and resist obstinately.

In the space of a few weeks Christopher re-experienced both symbolically by creating the tree and more directly in the relationship with the teacher some of the gratifications and frustrations that belong to the Oedipal phase. Ultimately, of course, he, like every child, had to renounce the desire for full possession of the love object, and this could not be achieved without a struggle.

It seemed that at every juncture Christopher's emotional state was expressed in two ways, through creative work and more directly in his behavior.

Christopher's new renunciation was again followed by creative expression. After the idyllic family scene of the Spring Tree, Christopher established his independence by making a life-sized sculpture of a blue heron that was explicitly made *for himself,* not as a gift for anyone. It stood as tall as he and its wings were spread wide (Fig. 10). The sculpture was to join the large rhinoceros at home. The difference between the crudely executed monster and the long-necked, graceful bird epitomizes the transition from defensive belligerence to a more mature and proud masculinity. It was a major undertaking and its completion took the better part of a year. The history of this creation will be described in detail in the next chapter.

Just because Christopher's blindness constitutes an unusual situation, the story demonstrates particularly well how a basically sound ego responds to injury and conflict. We have seen a variety of mechanisms, some constructive, others potentially harmful, and have observed that their dovetailing can produce new and unexpected constellations.

When eleven-year-old Christopher entered the Guild School, his love for birds was already fixed. Also, he already had a great

FIGURE 9. *Christopher*: Spring Tree (15" high)

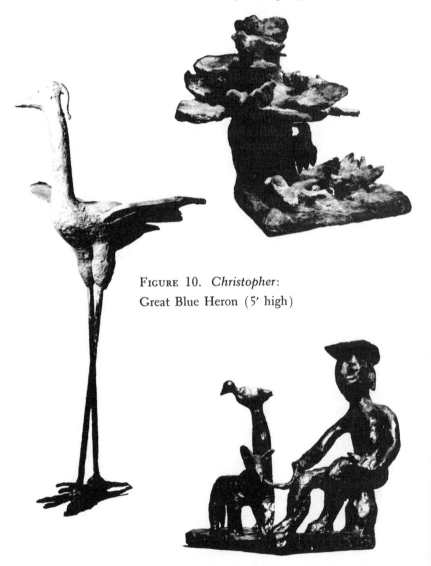

FIGURE 10. *Christopher*:
Great Blue Heron (5' high)

FIGURE 11. *Christopher*: Man with Dog and Bird (10" high)

reluctance to sculpture people, although the few attempts he could be induced to make proved that his body-image was intact and free from gross distortions. Since we know that children's art is above all self-representation, we conclude that Christopher identified with birds.

It seems reasonable to assume that these elusive creatures with powers that even the seeing cannot match stand for sight and all that this has come to mean to Christopher. We can also be certain that there is some unconscious equation of blindness with castration, potency with seeing. (We can also assume that the idea of sight had become in some way linked to those unfulfillable childhood wishes which Christopher shares with all children, but we do not know the exact nature of these relationships.)

If this reasoning is correct, then making birds is an attempt at denying the blindness and at restitution of sight and of all that it has come to symbolize. (It must be understood that Christopher did not deny being blind. Indeed, when he had completed a sculpture of which he was particularly proud, he was apt to exclaim how much he wished that he could see it.)

Because displacement helps us avoid facing a problem, it has its dangers, but it may also be a helpful detour. Since his fascination with birds enabled Christopher to mobilize energies for building up his mental and creative powers, and this in turn strengthened his feeling of self, it could in the end help him to fully accept himself. Christopher's last sculpture before his discharge to a day school for normal blind children points toward such an outcome. Using sculptor's wax, he created a seated man who holds his dog by the lead while a bird is perched on a tree (Fig. 11).

If all goes according to our fondest hopes, the unusual measures taken to overcome frustration and deprivation may in the end result in exceptional creative achievement. At present displacement, denial, sublimation, and obsessive-compulsive behavior converge and mutually influence each other, and we cannot foresee the ultimate outcome.

SUBLIMATION IN PROCESS [7]

The process of sublimation is for the most part unconscious. It is, therefore, seldom possible to trace a finished product to its emotional source. The story of Christopher's Spring Tree gave us a glimpse of the last stage of the transformation of feeling into form. In the other incidents which have been described it was possible to surmise the course of sublimation, but much remained elusive. I shall now present three instances where I could, more directly than is usually possible, observe the transformation of experience into picture.

Mary: Eight-year-old Mary was an energetic, highly intelligent child who suffered from a variety of neurotic disturbances. She was given to impulsive behavior, crying spells, and temper tantrums. Because of her talent and interest in art, painting sessions were arranged in Mary's home, mainly as a supportive measure. At the time Plate IV was painted she was struggling to gain some degree of self-control.

Mary began the art session by mixing colors without deciding on a subject. At first all went well; Mary was pleased as she found new and exciting colors and color combinations. But soon this total freedom became too much for her. Mixing more and more wildly, she reduced most of her paint to a brownish mess. Her mood became destructive. One could foresee that Mary would soon cover not just the paper but also the furniture and herself with paint. Unless something was done quickly, it would all end in tears and a tantrum.

Mary had covered about two thirds of her paper with splashes of different shades of brown interspersed with red and orange spots. I made her stop painting and look at her picture for a moment, saying, "To me this looks like the mountains of New Hampshire in the fall." I had visited Mary in the mountains and knew that her stay there had been happy. The wild splashes of

7. Ideas and case material presented in this section have been published in another version under the title "The Problem of Quality in Art."

color on her paper reminded me indeed of the blazing, turbulent colors of the New England autumn.

Mary's expression changed. Yes, she declared, she would paint the mountains. She bounded the rise and fall of her masses of color with a strong, deliberate brushstroke which defined the mountain range. Then she added bright spots of yellow and light gray-blue to bring out the fall colors. Finally she very calmly and carefully painted a blue sky and a yellow sun, taking pains to keep the blue paint from turning the sun green. When the painting was completed, Mary was radiant and proud.

How can we explain what happened? Working with color, especially in the absence of form, is exciting. Mixing and splashing paint, and the appearance of more and more brown color led to an upsurge of anal-aggressive impulses, which in Mary were ever ready to come to the surface. Her feeble controls were about to be swept away.

When I made Mary stop her splashing and reminded her of her beloved mountains, she was able to link her inner turmoil and the turmoil she had created on the paper to a memory that contained some of the same qualities but that was charged with positive feeling. As she transformed her wild and messy painting into the image of autumn mountains, chaotic aggressive energy was channeled into constructive action. Mary finished by adding sky and sun, graphic expressions of the calming, reassuring forces that had gained ascendance.

However, a teacher's request to stop destructive action and reflect is not always heeded; the invitation to see an image in a mess of paint is not necessarily accepted. We presume that Mary was ready to make the step, and that the teacher only supplied the extra push necessary to bring it about. That I could draw upon our common memory of the mountains may have made Mary feel very close to me, and this may have contributed to the successful outcome of the painting.

Throughout the session I performed both ego and superego functions. By inhibiting destructive action I supported her own still weak superego. When I helped the child find a satisfying alternative to destructive behavior, I became the ally of her ego.

To what extent did the event that occurred while the painting was made determine its final form? What would we see and feel if we did not know the story behind the painting? The brushstroke that outlines the mountains and separates them from the sky is the most dynamic element of composition. This line, we recall, marked the transition from random activity to creation.

There is a marked contrast between sky and sun, painted in a schematic, childlike manner, and the mountains which seem at first glance to be painted in a more sophisticated style. However, sun and sky are not altogether conventional. The shape of the sun is childlike, but its position, rising above a sudden dip in the mountain, is unconventional and dramatic.

The apparent sophistication in the handling of color in the mountains is in part deceptive, since in splashing paint Mary had obtained accidental effects. Later, however, some color was put in deliberately. In addition, although Mary had not planned all her effects, she was able to appreciate the visual possibilities of the accidents and utilize them.

There is, then, a clear connection between the picture and its history. The decisive creative act became the most important element of composition. The balance between destructive and constructive forces is manifest in the particular kind of balance between earth, sun, and sky. Although no one could guess the specific events that led to its creation, the painting expresses the quality of the experience.

Lillian: The next picture (Pl. V) was painted in direct response to a dramatic event. A group of children at camp were working in a little cabin on a hot, sultry summer day when a violent thunderstorm broke out. As the rain poured down, the whole group ran into the open to roll in the wet grass. Only nine-year-old Lillian, seeming rather frightened, stayed indoors. I invited her to paint a picture of the storm. Thereupon she chose a tan-colored paper, and on it painted a tree struck by lightning.

The picture is constructed entirely of rhythmic lines. The

dark-brown tree, burning with red and yellow flames, reaches out diagonally toward the middle of the paper. There it is cut off by the lightning which streaks across in the opposite diagonal direction. Its motion is repeated and emphasized by white scribbles. Only the green grass growing straight up and the black raindrops falling down counterbalance the dramatic movement of tree, flames, and lightning.

The painting depicts not the actual storm but a much more destructive event. We can surmise that the outburst in the sky found an echo in Lillian's own fantasies of violence and passion, and aroused fear of their uncontrollable power. The symbolic shape of the tree, the position of its branches, the red flames that are densest in the crotch where the tree's crown divides in half— all strongly suggest a bloody, violent sexual fantasy. The specific meaning of the fantasy in Lillian's life cannot, of course, be guessed. But here we are not primarily concerned with uncovering unconscious content; we are interested in the quality of Lillian's picture and how she was able to paint it.

Being frightened by the storm, Lillian might have done a number of things. She might, for instance, have decided to be a brave girl and go out into the rain with the others. To do this she would have had to override her fear, probably by denying that she was afraid; she would have repressed perception of her inner world. On the other hand, Lillian might have helped herself by shutting out the storm, perhaps by concentrating on a picture that had nothing at all to do with storms. In this case she would have turned away from part of her perception of outer reality. Finally, she might have succumbed passively to her anxiety.

When Lillian created her own storm on the paper, perception both of her inner life and of the outside world was heightened. Unconscious material could come close to the surface and find symbolic expression without endangering her necessary defenses. Lillian could allow herself to be moved by the drama and grandeur of the storm outside without being flooded from within by unmanageable excitement. Her response to stress was the most economical one. In painting she retained full command over her power to perceive, to imagine, and to act. She had transformed a potentially upsetting experience into creative adventure.

The teacher's suggestion to paint the storm may have demonstrated to Lillian that the adult in charge was not afraid of it, and this may have stimulated her to imitate the teacher. More important were the child's previous experiences which had taught her that turning to art under stress can be helpful.

Again we can ask how much of all this would come through in the picture. While no one could guess that the painting was made in direct response to a storm, it can be seen that it is carried by a swift, powerful, inner rhythm. We can feel that the painter responds strongly to moods in nature and observes well. No layman would connect the burning tree with the primal scene, but violent drama is visibly expressed in line and color. The picture cannot, of course, tell how anxious Lillian felt at the beginning, or how pleased she was with her finished work.

The young painter's capacity to integrate a subject that contains great tensions is impressive. In a painting that includes opposing forces—fire, lightning, and rain—one of them might easily overpower and obliterate the rest. Fire might consume tree, rain might drown fire, lightning might tear the paper. In Lillian's painting a balance is maintained wherein each force is given full play.

Gordon: The third example, Moby Dick (Pl. VI), was painted by Gordon, a twelve-year-old emotionally disturbed boy,[8] during an art therapy session when only he and his friend, John, were in the room. In the course of the session the two boys embarked on a bout of so-called "slipping" or "playing the dozens," a ritual of mutual insult where each boy accuses the other's mother and grandmother of every conceivable and inconceivable kind of sexual perversion and promiscuity.

This exchange of vituperation constitutes a conventional

8. I have presented Gordon's case history more fully in Part III of *Art Therapy in a Children's Community.*

social pattern among slum children whose mothers are in fact promiscuous. It can be embellished with all sorts of colorful inventions, but the crowning insult remains the disdainful declaration, "You don't even have no mother." Both partners to the abusive exchange get relief through projection. While the child could not possibly accuse his own mother of desertion and immorality, he can freely accuse another child's mother, and have the accusation thrown back at him. Such loaded banter may remain playful among friends, but more often it ends up in a fist-fight.

This time peace prevailed. While insults were passed back and forth almost mechanically, Gordon began a large painting of Moby Dick (its actual size is 1½ x 4 feet). The subject gave occasion for additional obscenity over the double meaning of the word Dick. One might expect that a painting created while such talk was in the air would be crudely obscene. Instead, there emerged a powerful, beautifully executed image of evil that comes close to embodying the symbolic meaning of Melville's masterpiece.

The white whale is floating on the surface of a light-blue sea, spouting a blue jet of water. The sky is indicated by loose blue brushstrokes. The whale's body is painted in subtle shades of gray with dark-gray accents. The light, silvery atmosphere of the painting contrasts sharply with the whale's evil expression. His mouth is open in a crooked sneer, baring a dark-red cavity surrounded by sharp, white teeth. There is a sly, evil look in his small, black eye. The whole body conveys a feeling of nakedness.

The sexual symbolism of the painting is obvious. We see a composite of male and female elements. The whole whale can be interpreted as one gigantic penis, conceived as a dangerous weapon with teeth. The whale's mouth, on the other hand, can be seen as a vagina dentata, devouring the male organ. The whale as a whole also recalls a woman's body, with the forked tail standing for her thighs and vulva.

The painting symbolizes a composite of dangerous, evil sexual fantasies, the kind that haunt the masturbation of a boy whose experiences do not correct but rather confirm his most confused, primitive sexual theories. Yet, in spite of all its contradictory symbolism, the painting remains a well-integrated picture of Moby Dick, the White Whale.

It was impressive to see the intensity with which Gordon painted the whale's body. Again and again he brushed over its surface, adding more and more subtle shading. Although his way of painting was reminiscent of masturbation, it did not become obsessive or purely repetitive. Gordon never lost command over paint and brush; he knew what he was doing and when to stop. He was proud of the completed painting, and his friend and slipping-partner was filled with admiration. The session ended in a spirit of contentment.

If we compare the talk that had accompanied the work with the symbolic meaning of the painting, we find that they both relate to the same painful situation; the boys' unfulfilled longing for mother, their rage over her unfaithfulness, shame over her behavior, and guilt and shame over their own degraded desires and fantasies.

On the surface all this seems to be expressed more directly in the boys' talk. "Your mother," it implies, "is promiscuous; furthermore you, her son, are ready to degrade her by attacking her sexually." When we listen closely to the merciless words, we find that the abuse is quite impersonal, uttered so mechanically that it becomes meaningless. Talk circles endlessly around the boys' most profound longing and grief, but it brings no insight or relief. The longing for mother is denied, drowned in the flood of mutual abuse.

When Gordon paints a gigantic image, half fish, half mammal, frightening, fascinating, and unfathomable, he creates it out of the same ambivalent feelings, the same fears and pressures that drive him and his schoolmates to relentless vituperation, threats, and fights, but he is no longer obsessed, forced to repeat stereotyped behavior with no will of his own. By transposing his conflicts from the narrow confines of his life into the wider world of imagination and adventure, he frees himself from meaningless repetition. Painting does not alter the nature of his trouble. He is too deeply injured to make an image of goodness. He can only make a monstrous composite of love and hate, male and female, but in making it he has ceased, at least for the duration of the creative act, to be the helpless victim of his conflicts.

Again, how much of what we have constructed by using several sources of information is actually visible in the painting? Most striking are the proportions (the length is more than twice the height), an unusual, extravagant length suitable for the whale, which indeed fills the paper completely. This conveys a feeling of hugeness and power that comes through even in the much reduced reproduction. The obsessive, overpowering emotions the white whale symbolizes are expressed in the spatial organization of the picture.

Next there is the tactile quality of the body. This whale is no decorative symbol; it is a three-dimensional living thing. More than any specifically symbolic shapes, this quality makes the whale sensual and sexually charged. Finally there is the evil expression, the half-open mouth which is the more menacing because of the tactile quality of the painting. The whale invites touch, but at the same time threatens to bite. While the picture does not reveal the exact circumstances of its inception, it does express obsession, ambivalence, aggression, and sexual excitement.

In each of the three examples there is evidence of strong emotions pushing toward direct discharge.

In each case discharge was inhibited, but none of the three children suppressed his dangerous feelings altogether. Instead, each child linked his emotional state to a pictorial idea with similar qualities: a mood in nature, a dramatic event, a figure from a story. Out of this linkage the child created an image that contained and symbolized his emotions. In each instance, it was possible to trace in detail the transformation of emotional content into pictorial form. We observed how the union of form and content brought about the qualities essential to art: inner consistency, economy of artistic means, evocative power. In this process, the constellation of inner forces was so altered that the child's ego gained control, at least temporarily, over energies that originally belonged to the impulses.

The emotions and conflicts we observed or could infer appear with little or no change in two of the finished paintings—in Lillian's burning tree and in Gordon's Moby Dick. Evidently the neutralization of aggressive and sexual energy we associate with sublimation does not extend to the emotional content of these pictures. Mary's mountains, on the other hand, do not express her initial mood. The painting, which began as an expression of anger, ended with the restitution of a loved object wrought from chaos and destruction. Mary's submerged positive feelings found form in the act of painting.

In all three cases, emotion reaches a high pitch, and the threshold of repression is lowered, but this lowering of defenses does not bring about a lowering of artistic performance. On the contrary, the intense personal feeling Gordon put into his white whale enhances the painting's evocative power. The symbolic impact of Lillian's tree makes her picture of a thunderstorm more alive; and Mary's dramatic change of mood comes across in the dramatic quality of her mountains.

In each instance private meaning and universal message intensify each other. This process widens horizons and opens avenues of growth beyond the confines of personal disturbance.

Substitution of an analogous subject for the original source of conflict facilitated sublimation, but it was only the beginning. Beyond the finding of the artistic theme, dramatic as it was, lay the struggle for execution. Here a division sets in. While the picture may contain any kind of emotion, no matter how disturbing or negative, the act of painting must be carried out in relative calm and serenity. Mary can paint her mountains only when she stops furiously hurling colors. We admire Lillian's discipline as she handles lightning, fire, and rain without excess. We are impressed when Gordon restrains himself from being carried away by the excitement of painting the whale's body. (Still earlier we have seen how Danny's sexual excitement gave way to serene craftsmanship as he passed from making clay sausages to constructing more complex penis symbols.)

The neutralization of aggressive and sexual energy characteristic of sublimation occurs in the area of *artistic execution*. No matter what emotion he expresses toward the act of painting and toward his medium, the painter must maintain a positive feeling equally removed from obsessive sexual excitement and from aggressive fury. This state is not easily maintained. It is constantly menaced by untamed drives on the one hand and, on the other, by the ego's tendency to apply radical, stifling mechanisms of defense.

Therefore, we find two main difficulties among artists, be they children or adults. There is the quest for subject matter, for access. to that area of the inner life where experience and affect meet, and analogies are found that can contain and express them both. Here the artist is in conflict with the ego's inclination to ward off indiscriminately anything that might disturb the existing equilibrium.

There is on the other hand the struggle for form. Here the subject matter has been found, but execution is fraught with anxiety and irritation because insufficiently neutralized energies push toward direct discharge.

As therapists we are more accustomed to failure than to success. We are used to seeing paintings of volcanos become a mess of red and black because explosive feelings were not depicted but acted out. We see carvings end up as slivers of wood because the act of cutting unchains aggression that cannot be confined to producing a given shape. Before our eyes, drawings turn into tangles of half-erased lines because ambivalence paralyzes the capacity for making decisions. We see symptomatic behavior more often than we see sublimation.

The performances of Mary, Lillian, and Gordon are exceptional. The process of production is unusually smooth. We see that form and content become one, but we observe no struggle for form. We do not really know why all went well when all might as easily have gone wrong. These are a few of the miracles which therapists hope for but experience only from time to time.

True art defies simple definition. Chaotic impulse, traditional form, pictographic symbolism—none of these is alien to art, yet none encompasses it. Art derives emotional impact from the same primitive energies that find direct expression in the impulsive manipulation of art materials. But the artist imposes form upon these raw emotions, and, when he does so, his work is linked to the mechanisms of defense which are active in stereotyped art. However, whereas the painter of stereotypes employs established techniques, symbols, and conventions to ward off and deny conflict, the very same means are used by the artist to contain and express it. Finally, there are in most works of art traces of personal meaning that link it to the simpler pictograph; but while pictographs mainly satisfy the need to state an idea that remains private, in the work of art any element that contains private meaning is so integrated that it contributes to the universal message.

Is there any essential difference between art and other forms of sublimation? The contemplation of all outstanding feats of sublimation can inspire feelings that are similar to those evoked by works of art. When we admire a bridge, a beautiful carpet, a precision instrument, a heroic deed, a mathematical equation, or any other valuable achievement, it is not only its usefulness that evokes admiration. All of us have experienced the difficulties of taming the instincts, of building ego structure, of becoming human. Therefore, we can experience something of the struggle and of the triumph of sublimation even when we do not personally benefit from its results and when we have no technical understanding of the specific difficulties that had to be surmounted.

Most products of sublimation, however, are in themselves emotionally neutral,[9] even though they can arouse aesthetic

9. The ideas in this paragraph have been presented in somewhat different form in the introductory chapter of *Art Therapy in a Children's Community.*

pleasure or even inspire awe. The results of a scientist's investigations, for example, will be an extension of the realm of objective truth, regardless of the primitive sexual curiosity which may have been at the root of his quest. The report of his researches will not reveal the process of his emotional and intellectual development. Primarily we benefit from the practical results of his labors, while only dimly sensing the magnitude of his struggle.

Art, on the other hand, retells the story of transformation; it offers primarily the pleasure of witnessing the process. Art's value to society consists in stimulating sublimation and influencing its direction. Kurt Eissler says in his *Leonardo da Vinci:* "One of the objective functions of all great artistic achievement, particularly in the visual arts, is not only to give pleasure of a certain kind, but to stimulate new ego differentiations in the personality of the beholder." [10]

Artist and audience travel together in two directions, from the primitive source of the creative impulse toward its final form, and again from the contemplation of form to the depth of complex, contradictory, and primitive emotions. In this adventure conscious, preconscious, and unconscious processes reinforce each other. It is thus probable that affect which is contained but not neutralized is essential to art, while other forms of sublimation would be disrupted by similar quantities of raw libidinal or aggressive drive energies.

10. Kurt Eissler, *Leonardo da Vinci: Psychoanalytic Notes on the Enigma.*

V

The Art Therapist's
Role in Sublimation

But it went with him the way it often does with children, they
make great plans and extensive preparations, even make a few attempts,
yet the whole thing is finally abandoned. . . . Wilhelm gave himself up
to his fantasies, experimented and prepared forever without completing
anything, built a thousand castles in the air and did not notice that he
had not laid the foundation even for a single one.
—Goethe, *Wilhelm Meister's Theatrical Mission*

IN ART, as in other areas of life, sublimation does not grow
untended in childhood. The urge to create forms and semblances
is strong, but unless the adult gives it direction and nourishment,
the art of children resembles a bean sprouting on a bed of cotton. It grows for a time, then folds over. The organizing force
that helps children's art transcend play and fantasy must come
from the adult world. Because this holds true in general, the
principles developed in this chapter apply also to work with
children who are not seriously troubled. The disturbed state of
the children whose stories are used as examples determines some
of the methods that had to be devised or explains the extent
of the help and attention that had to be given.

We have said before that the therapist is more accustomed
to failure than to success. Incomplete sublimation, symptomatic
behavior, the breakdown of sublimation are more frequent than
sublimation achieved. One of the prerequisites for becoming an
art therapist is tolerance for non-art, almost-art, and anti-art.

The art therapist must, on the other hand, be able to recognize sublimation in its inception and never abdicate his function of supporting it. How can this be done?

Let us return to our last three examples. What were my functions in each case? With Mary, Lillian, and Gordon I did not do very much. I performed the functions of a benign superego which limits but does not totally inhibit expression of impulses. By offering themes that could serve as containers for their affect, I performed ego functions for Mary and Lillian. And the presence of the person who had guided their artistic development constituted ego support for all three children even when I remained relatively passive.

The absence of a struggle for *form* makes these three stories unusual even for exceptionally gifted and highly practiced child artists.

THE ART THERAPIST'S FUNCTION AS AN EXTENSION OF THE EGO

Christopher: Christopher's story is somewhat different. Although he also came to art therapy with a previously developed interest in art and had unusual capacities for sublimation, I had, because of his blindness, to participate extensively in many of his creative ventures. At the same time I had to be extra careful not to impose my ideas. Just because the situation is out of the ordinary it illuminates the art therapist's function as an auxiliary ego particularly well, and therefore I will describe our work in detail.

Christopher's interest in wildlife was realistic, quite in keeping with his pre-adolescent state. Yet he could not, like another child, get his ideas by looking at pictures or going to the zoo. He could form ideas about the shape of domestic animals and the tame animals at the Children's Zoo by touch. When he wanted to make sculptures of wild animals I provided the missing information by making quick clay sketches for him, being careful to shape the models so that they were comprehensible to the touch. At the same time I told him to which familiar domestic animal the wild species I had made for him was related. Christopher then formed his concepts by piecing together information from these various sources.

In the beginning Christopher had wanted to appropriate these models and use them as his own. When I objected to such cheating, he got into the habit of first feeling the model and then destroying it simply by closing his powerful hand over the soft clay figure. Often he used this very clay as raw material for his sculpture.

Three processes succeeded one another. He first took in my ideas. Then he destroyed that which was mine, not his. Some frustration about his handicap and anger against the sighted was vented in the destructive gesture. Finally my contribution was both materially and mentally incorporated, and fantasy, experience, and information were fused in a sculptural whole.

Christopher needed assistance not only in finding out the shape of things; he also had to be helped with the building of his large clay sculptures. The blind are inclined to work on a large scale because details must be big enough to be distinguished by touch. Moreover, in a world in which much escapes them and where they are forced to form many concepts via scaled-down models, handling substantial, life-sized objects is in itself valuable.

Large ceramic sculpture entails complex technical maneuvers. It either has to be built hollow like a pot, or an armature must be devised that can be removed before firing or can burn away. Solid clay masses must be hollowed out before firing. Furthermore, large sculpture must be cut up into sections to fit the kiln, which in our case was eighteen inches in each dimension inside, large for a school kiln, but small for Christopher's needs.

Evidently Christopher could not have produced his Spring Tree (Fig. 9) or his Great Blue Heron (Fig. 10) had I waited until he had learned to execute all the necessary technical feats. Instead I helped him accomplish whatever he was able to conceive of at each instance, improvising as we went along. The detailed history of the making of the blue heron will illustrate how we worked.

Christopher had at first imagined a smaller bird, and consequently we had constructed an armature that would have been strong enough to hold up a moderate weight. As he began shaping the body and neck he kept adding more clay until the bird's volume had nearly doubled. He was entranced with the experience of feeling his bird grow under his hands, and as he added more clay the sculpture took on an increasingly decisive and graceful shape. This proved to me that making the bird bigger was not just an expression of a grandiose fantasy but a truly creative process. Therefore I did not discourage Christopher, even though the new structure was so heavy that the inside armature gave way and the bird would have collapsed had I not improvised an outside armature to hold it up.

Christopher managed to fashion the bird's wings by first making a cardboard pattern which he could easily hold up to the bird's body to get the right size and shape. Then he made two separate flat wings of clay, using this pattern.

During the months that passed while Christopher worked at his bird he outgrew some of his early ideas. At first the heron was rigid, neck and head pointing forward in a straight line. One day Christopher declared that the bird was too stiff. The neck ought to curve and he should be looking sideways, the way a live bird does. Thereupon he took the neck between his hands, wrenched it into the new position and tilted the head a little to one side. Indeed the bird looked much more alive now, but Christopher's radical action had wreaked havoc with the armature and the clay. Again I had to come to the rescue and make the new position stable. Thus the work went on with constant improvisation until, after a year had passed, the clay sections were fired, base and armature were built to hold up the finished structure, and the bird was successfully reassembled. When we had come that far I asked Christopher whether he had believed that the bird would *ever* get done. He said no, he had not *really* believed that the day would come.

(Sessions were held once a week only, and of course Christopher made other things besides the heron.)

We see that I went to considerable trouble to make it possible for a child to succeed with an ambitious—maybe an overly ambitious—project. This does not mean that I advocate assuring success to any wild idea a child may conceive of. I helped Christopher because I felt that his plan was founded on a well-imagined idea, not on vague fantasy. As he worked, his ideas changed, but not in the grandiose, protean way of shifting fantasy. On the contrary they became more definite and differentiated.

When he twisted his heron's neck into a new position he came close to destroying the bird altogether. Maltreating the clay so brutally contradicts the love and respect for the medium which the artist ought to maintain, but since Christopher's vision of his bird had changed he would either have had to change its shape or begin all over again. Risking the destruction of the sculpture was an act of moral courage. The violence of the act and the phallic quality of the bird's neck invited regression, but in the end the blue heron looked gentler, more like a bird and less like a crude phallic symbol than before.

Inasmuch as I helped prevent disaster I played Providence for Christopher, but my rescue actions also made demands on him. So long as I helped him, he felt morally obliged to persevere in a task that greatly taxed his powers of integration and his endurance.

Christopher's story illustrates the many functions an art therapist may have to perform. I had to empathize with another person's creative imagination to the point of guessing at his ideas, to actively lay hands on his work without imposing my style, to feed back to the child his own intentions clarified but not altered. I needed the courage to permit expression of affect, to risk regression, and to limit both when necessary. I also had to sense the nature of the child's projects and treat them accordingly. Was Christopher giving way to fantasies or was he pursuing a creative idea?

The difference between these two modes of psychic functioning becomes clear when we compare Christopher's Blue Heron to

Kenneth's Giant (see "Projection and Confrontation," p. 29). Six-year-old Kenneth's giant was a grandiose fantasy which consoled him for his rootless, ghostlike existence in a hospital ward. It was pure escape; Kenneth had formed no mental representation of it. Consequently he could not paint this giant, which was to have reached from floor to ceiling and to have been adorned in all the colors. It would have been futile for me to try to help him paint something he had not imagined and could not imagine, for, to become art, fantasy has to be transformed into imagination. To achieve this, Kenneth would have had to lay aside his escapist dreams and begin to take hold of his actual life. We recall that his next step was making a dog and doghouse in clay.

There was a period when Christopher's wild fantasies about the power of birds in flight had interfered in a similar manner with his capacity to imagine and sculpture them. By the time the heron was made, these fantasies had lost their hold on him. Although they persisted, they no longer interfered with his art. Our next story, also about a blind child, shows the transition from fantasy to imagination in process.

Tonio: Tonio, a mildly retarded, congenitally blind child, was, when I first knew him at the age of eleven, passive, uncommunicative, and fixed in his habits. Even though he seemed to have formed a fairly well-integrated body-image and had considerable manual dexterity, he could not be induced to model with clay because he abhorred the feel of it.

This is not unusual. For the blind, who are especially sensitive to the way their fingers feel, dried-up clay is often distasteful. Tonio's attitude expressed his highly discriminating sense of touch and a sensuous personality averse to incurring discomfort for the sake of a distant goal.

Tonio had an obsessive fixation on electrical wire and small machinery that was linked to his relationship with his father, who was an electrician. While this obsession impeded other learning, Tonio had attained considerable skill in handling electrical equipment.

His first imaginative work was made possible by utilizing his love for manipulating wire. He learned to make stick-men from pipe cleaners. The figures were simple and stereotyped, and they could not stand up because Tonio could not learn to attach the pipe-cleaner legs rigidly to the body. He invariably gave his men walking-sticks, also made of pipe cleaners, but would not explain to us why this had to be so. Were the men blind, or lame, or did they use the stick for adornment or in self-defense? Tonio would not tell.

Finally there was a change. Tonio considered making teeth for his pipe-cleaner man. I offered him small mosaic tiles and they felt very like teeth to him. Then we considered the necessity of constructing a head that would be big enough to accommodate them. I offered a skein of wool, which he wound around the wire until he had made a large ball to which the mosaic tile could be glued. This gave Tonio the idea of adding ears and nostrils by attaching rings of pipe cleaners. He omitted eyes and, since this is an extremely sensitive area for the blind, I did not bring the matter up. Now Tonio decided that this man should have arms as long as his own. By attaching pipe cleaners to one another he managed to measure out two long wire arms, each of which ended with *eight* pipe cleaners by way of fingers. Tonio was enchanted by this profusion of fingers. In his elation he decided to give the men not just one, but *two*, pipe-cleaner penises. The man's legs, on the other hand, he cut off short, so that they were hardly longer than the penises. Tonio became exuberant. He promised to make a woman with *two* vaginas for his man, and from there he went into a grandiose fantasy of making people with hundreds and thousands of penises and fingers.

I responded by unconditionally accepting Tonio's distorted representation of the body. The eyeless head with big ears and teeth, exaggeratedly long arms and fingers, large penis, and diminutive legs represents the congenitally blind person's body feelings. Because of his handicap, he is thrown back upon his body sensations, such as the feel of the teeth in his mouth or feelings in his genitals. He reaches out to the world largely with his arms and fingers, and must inhibit the impulse to run.

The two penises and eight fingers I accepted conditionally as a fantasy distinct from reality, stressing the artist's right to his invention. The wild talk about hundreds and thousands of penises and fingers I treated as a fantasy that one can talk about but that could not very well be realized even in art.

After this incident, Tonio no longer made his pipe-cleaner men with walking-sticks. He declared that he would make a life-sized man as big as himself. However, the man would have to be made without clay, from wires and other dry materials subject to Tonio's approval.

To my amazement he began this man by constructing the *upper arm*. He made a "bone" by twisting several strands of long pipe cleaners together, and then systematically wound newspaper around this core, until the whole attained the thickness of his own arm. From there he went to the lower arm, made in the same manner, and attached eight pipe-cleaner fingers to it. The procedure took several art sessions. For a while Tonio was inseparable from this arm and even took it home over the weekend.

Why was the upper arm so important? Tonio had a habit of gently patting people's upper arms when he wanted to speak with them or otherwise make contact. Later he also explained to his classroom teacher that the way people's arms felt reminded him of the way his penis felt when he played with it. Thus it seemed that Tonio's venture took off from the point where self-gratification and contact with others merged. Next he made a second arm, then the torso, legs, a penis complete with testicles, and finally the head.

The construction of the man took over a year (sessions were held once a week during the school year). In the course of making it, Tonio was introduced to an array of different materials, such as chicken wire, corrugated cardboard, foam rubber, plastic sponge, and masking tape. He tested each new material, first by touching it gingerly, and if he did not like the feel of it I had to remove it immediately from his reach. With time he became increasingly more accepting of new things, and aware of the technical problems involved in constructing his man. However, the use of many kinds of wires remained essential to keeping up his interest. We used pipe cleaners, electric wire, chicken wire, binding wire, and different sizes of aluminum armature wire. During every session, time was spent in obsessive manipulation of wire, and he had to be permitted to take some small piece back to the classroom.

The most interesting manifestation of his obsession with wire occurred in the construction of the man's head. It was made of tightly rolled corrugated cardboard. To it were attached small mosaic tiles for teeth. Lips were made of sponge, cheeks of foam rubber, the fleshy part of the nose also of sponge, and the nostrils of rings of heavy armature wire. Again eyes were omitted. When it came to hair, Tonio was at a loss for what material to use. I offered him fur, wool, rope—nothing seemed to be right. Finally he decided to make the hair of thick armature wire. He cut sixteen pieces of equal length and stuck them into the cardboard skull. Thus the wire-obsession was tangibly growing out of his man's brain! (Fig. 12.)

The whole man was ultimately covered with a layer of foam rubber representing muscle (Fig. 13). Thus it was satisfactory to the touch. The other blind children were pleased with the man and readily understood the meaning of all body parts, since they were constructed entirely from the point of view of the blind.

Certain aspects of my role in Tonio's creative work were similar to those I have described in relation to Christopher. For both children I functioned as an extension of the ego, helping them in everything that they could not do alone. By making it possible for their ideas to materialize readily, I helped them to develop, correct, and alter them as necessary. In doing this I had to be willing to have my offerings rejected, as when I offered Tonio various materials for hair and he did not like any of them and decided instead on aluminum hair, which would never have occurred to me.

Tonio's story shows how displacement that has taken on

I. *Herman:* Fairies
(18″ × 24″)

II. *Herman:* Angel with Harp
Pursued by a Devil (18″ × 24″)

III. *Herman:* Family of Horses (18″ × 24″)

IV. *Mary:* The Mountains of New Hampshire (18″ × 24″)

V. *Lillian:* Tree Struck by Lightning (18″ × 24″)

VI. *Gordon:* Moby Dick (18″ × 48″)

VII. *Andrew:* Design with Indian's Head
  (12″ × 18″)

VIII. *Andrew:* Portrait of a Friend
  (18″ × 24″)

IX. *Frank:* Indian Chief (24″ × 36″)

X. *Frank:* Mexican (24″ × 36″)

XI. *Mrs. Smith:* Angry Cottage Parent (12″ × 18″)

XII. *Willie:*
Suspicious Devil (18″ × 24″)

XIII. *Leon:* Horse
Against Master (18″ × 24″)

XIV. *Carl:* Lucifer
and Angel (24″ × 36″)

XV. *Carl:* Speedboat (18″ × 24″)

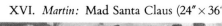

XVI. *Martin:* Mad Santa Claus (24″ × 36″

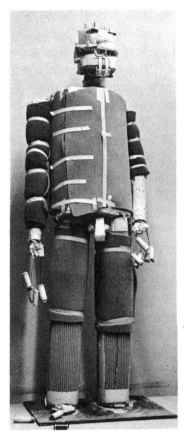

FIGURE 13. *Tonio*: Man (5'6" high)

FIGURE 12. *Tonio*: Man, detail (the two aluminum rings represent the nostrils)

pathological dimensions can ultimately lead to sublimation. Fixation on wire and machinery, initially a substitute for his conflict-laden relationship to the father, led back to relationships and to a new understanding of the world.[1] This process began with obsession only slightly adapted to a new venture, the pipe-cleaner man. The turning point hinged on assertion of Tonio's very personal concepts, even though they contradicted the ideas of the seeing, followed by expression of a sexual fantasy (the two pipe-cleaner penises), which lead in turn to spoken fantasies that had the abandon of primary-process thinking (he spoke about one hundred and one thousand penises). The expression of these fantasies and my conditional acceptance of them did not lead to fantastic art. It rather seemed as if the lessening of inhibitions increased the ego's strength, both because the exhausting task of maintaining repression was lightened and because formerly repressed sexual energies were liberated and some of these energies became available to the ego. In the transition from id to ego, the boundless, protean quality of primary-process thinking was modified so that it became more substantial without losing its vitality or becoming too rigidly fixed.

Thus Tonio succeeded in creating a sculpture that contained but transcended his earlier fixations. His man's upper arms were symbols both of masturbation and of a primitive way of making contact. The wire-fixation found expression in the man's crowning glory, his thick, aluminum-wire hair. Yet all of this was contained in a larger whole in which Tonio had achieved self-representation. We can therefore consider Tonio's work on his man a sign of a beginning capacity for sublimation. Sublimation did not eliminate Tonio's obsessions, however. It only broke their almost exclusive hold on his functioning, permitting additional modes of behavior to develop.

Naturally Tonio's growth did not depend on art therapy alone. The change was possible partly because the developmental spurt of pre-adolescence made new energies available.

1. For an early description of symptom formation leading to sublimation, see Anna Freud, *The Ego and the Mechanisms of Defense.*

These were well utilized at school. Tonio's skillful classroom teacher succeeded in bringing him out of his passivity. Sex education in which the children's fantasies, misconceptions, and uncertainties were discussed helped make the expression of sexual fantasies possible in art.

The classroom teacher's understanding and admiration of our undertaking helped sustain Tonio's interest in making his man. Meanwhile his fascination with electricity was channeled in his work with the shop teacher, who helped him construct a model elevator run by a small motor. Thus different approaches supplemented and reinforced each other.

I have used two examples of work with blind children mainly because unusual circumstances allow us to perceive universal processes in a new light. With a sighted child the same kind of support would not show up as dramatically, but the principles remain the same.

THE TALENTED CHILD AND THE GROUP

Everyone who has worked with groups of children knows that nothing inspires children more than the example of other children working well. The presence of even one child who readily responds to art can get a whole group going the way no teacher can, and luckily talent is so widely distributed that it is rarely missing in any collection of children. On the other hand, the talented child cannot function as a catalyst for the others unless the teacher sets the stage and supports the process.

The following two incidents illustrate the influence of a talented child on his two less gifted companions, and the art therapist's role in making this relationship helpful to all three of them.

Clyde, Allan, and Stanley: Clyde, who has already been introduced to the reader as the creator of a gorilla (p. 34), was the healthiest and most talented of a group of three eight-year-old boys in a children's psychiatric ward. The other two boys depended on Clyde in many ways and greatly admired his proficiency in art.

Allan declared one day that he would make a statue of his friend Clyde. However, he was afraid he could not stick it out. He warned me that I would have to help him all the time, because, as I knew, when he got frustrated he usually smashed up his work. This sculpture was specially important, so would I watch out for him? I explained to Allan that it would be impossible for me to watch him all the time because I also had to help the other children. I suggested that whenever he was in trouble he should call me and then remain seated with crossed arms till I came.

Allan agreed to this and kept the pact. The figure was successfully completed and painted. It was in every respect a departure from Allan's usual work. It looked like Clyde, calm and massive. Most of Allan's people looked like puppets, and he himself moved in a puppetlike, jerky way. Also, most of Allan's work ended up black. Clyde's portrait was colored realistically, with a red shirt and blue jeans (Fig. 14).

Allan's love for Clyde and his identification with him gave him the impetus to attempt the work, to seek controls, and abide by them. Before all, he managed to really *perceive* his friend, a great feat for this child at the borderline of schizophrenia.

Ordinarily Allan was immediately and helplessly influenced by Clyde's state of mind. When the other boy broke down he was desperate; when his friend was in control of himself Allan felt more secure. When he sculptured Clyde's portrait Allan replaced this primitive way of partaking of Clyde's strength with a symbolic act that made greater demands on his own capacities for perception, expression, and control. Therefore we can speak of the beginnings of sublimation.

To help Allan achieve his work, I had to make him share in the responsibility of controlling his temper. Had I assured him of my unconditional help he would certainly have failed, for he would not have mobilized his own controls. Also, I would have become an omnipotent being who could be readily blamed for all failure.

FIGURE 14. *Allan*: Portrait of Clyde (8″ high)

The rigidly mechanistic maneuver I suggested to Allan was the only kind of defense that seemed to be available to him at that time. It not only protected him against losing patience while he had to wait for my help, but also warded off the hostile element in his ambivalent feelings toward Clyde, which threatened this undertaking as it threatened all of Allan's ventures into relationship. Allan's behavior to Clyde was sado-machochistic. He served and obeyed him but also pestered him relentlessly.

Stanley was more disorganized than Allan, more dependent and overtly homosexual. Making a portrait of Clyde would have been quite beyond him, for he could not have separated himself sufficiently from the other boy to perceive him as an independent entity. He borrowed strength from Clyde by imitating his work or sometimes by working with him.

On one occasion Stanley begged Clyde to paint a picture of a horse with him, for Clyde could draw horses very well. Clyde was willing and began by drawing the outline of a horse, using yellow paint. Stanley filled in the horse with black, but he respected the yellow outlines. He contributed a wavy line denoting the ground, but he drew it so that the horse's feet did not touch it.

Both boys were distressed by this, but they accepted my suggestion that the horse could be jumping, and went on with the picture. Next Clyde drew a yellow sun, and Stanley impulsively painted it black. Clyde was disconcerted by this attack, but Stanley declared that the sun was in eclipse; the moon was covering it up. (Stanley possessed a store of scientific information which he habitually used for all kinds of rationalization.) Both children were satisfied, and the picture-making could continue.

Stanley then painted the sky dark purple but took care not to obliterate the horse, and Clyde colored the ground bright yellow, keeping within the confines of the blue, wavy line drawn by Stanley.

The two boys were proud of their accomplishment. I had to print a title, "Horse in Eclipse, made by Clyde and Stanley"; then they gave the painting (Fig. 15) to the head nurse as a present.

In the making of the picture, control and organization came from Clyde. He also contributed whatever gay or pleasant elements the picture contains, but he seems to have been on the defensive—yellow is a bright color, but not a very powerful one. Stanley's contribution was somber and aggressive, and narrowly skirted outright destructiveness. Both boys exercised what for them was extraordinary control—Clyde by tolerating Stanley's attacks and accepting his rationalizations, Stanley by controlling his usually irrepressible destructiveness enough to permit completion of the picture.

The picture itself is expressive. The black horse, still radiating some of his initial yellow, seems menaced from all sides by the purple and threatened from above by the large, black heavenly body. Even the ground beneath its feet, though a cheerful color, is unsteady, and besides, he is not standing on it. This well expresses both boys' precarious emotional balance and their insecure future. The picture is more coherent than anything Stanley

FIGURE 15. *Clyde and Stanley*: Horse in Eclipse (18" x 24")

could have produced alone. It was more expressive than most of Clyde's recent work, but Clyde was capable of being expressive without help from another child. Thus Stanley gained more than Clyde.

Except for offering the rationalization that the horse was jumping, I did not participate in the making of the picture. I only kept an eye on the boys, praised them for their work and their control, and showed them that I was prepared to come to the rescue if necessary.

Both incidents that have been described were helpful to all three children. The two weaker ones attained, although with borrowed strength, a degree of integration and sublimation that was ordinarily out of their reach. Such an experience hardly brings about immediate internalization of this strength, or any other direct improvement. It gives the child a taste of what it is like to function better, and this may stimulate growth.

For Clyde, who was often pulled back by his more disturbed

companions and who experienced his power for evil when his bad moods caused them to regress, it was reassuring to find that the best of him also could be powerful, and that it could bring pleasure to all of them.

Both incidents demonstrate how art has a way of counteracting those group processes that impede individuation. Making Clyde's portrait led Allan to perceive the leader instead of merging with him. Stanley experienced that he need not simply defer to the leader's will, but that another person's strength could help him organize his own ideas. Clyde experienced an expansion of his personality, but he could not use the other boys merely as tools and extensions of himself. He had to accept that his ideas, when he worked with Stanley, or his concept of himself when Allan portrayed him, were modified by the other child.

Even though all went well in the two incidents described here, there was danger that more primitive group-phenomena would win out in the long run, that the followers would become too dependent on Clyde and the art of all of them would turn sterile and repetitious.

Clyde had to be protected from being saddled with too much responsibility or from attaining too much power. Incidents such as the painting of the "Horse in Eclipse," for instance, should not be encouraged to become a habit, even though the specific event was helpful to both boys. The other two boys had to be supported in any constructive attempts to stand up against Clyde.

Among children who have more ego strength than Allan and Stanley, who needed very direct support, artistic production flourishes best when each child-artist is at once alone, communicating with himself, and yet in tune with the others who are engaged in the same kind of quest. Each child gains confidence by a communication that emanates from the *work* and its silent message more than from anything the children say to each other or the art therapist says to them. The common goal is good art, and this cannot be achieved by group action but only through supreme individual effort.

At times, the art therapist has to work against group pressures that push the individual into excessive submission and conformity, but there is no doubt that most children work better in groups and that they inspire each other more often than they hold each other back.

The stories of Christopher and Tonio demonstrate the great difficulties that arise when a child has to develop the forms that are to be the elements of his art in isolation, depending for feedback and stimulation entirely on an adult. These obstacles were overcome by empathy, trial, and error. Both Christopher and Tonio produced work that looked like them, not like me, but there is no telling what each child would have achieved if he had found an echo of his own ways of thinking and feeling in the art of other blind children who were on the same developmental level. This rarely occurred because the school was too small.

There is between children an immediate mutual comprehension founded on the community of psychic structure that even the most understanding and highly trained adult cannot match.

The gifted child, who has more access to his inner world, more courage and inventiveness, inspires his companions because his example proves that it is possible for one of them to achieve so much. On a deeper level the process of sublimation can be vicariously experienced because of the similarity of psychic structure and life situation of artist and audience.[2]

Paradoxically it is the. gifted child who often needs the art therapist's attention and support more urgently than the others. Talent constitutes a strength which leads him to approach potentially dangerous realms. As his art reaches greater depth, there is more pleasure and more despair. Art becomes loaded, and passionate outbreaks are frequent.

Even though such behavior sometimes taxes the endurance

2. In *Art Therapy in a Children's Community,* I have described at length the role of the gifted child as a catalyst, the rise and fall of fashions and fads, and their relationship to personality and to group processes.

of the group, the spectacle of the ups and downs of an intense struggle that ultimately succeeds can be a cathartic experience. At such times the group may become the chorus to the chief actor of the drama, taking sides, feeling joy and despair with him. At other times it may be the group that helps the art therapist control behavior and feelings that have gone out of bounds.

Walter: Walter, an excellent artist and a tortured human being, rarely finished a painting without reaching an impasse when he was desperate, ready to tear it up, or even driven to destroy all his previous work. At such moments the group usually acted in unison, helping me prevent a holocaust. Walter's portfolio was whisked away to another building, or locked up. The endangered painting was protected bodily. If his friend Jerry, who was also a good painter, was there, he sometimes helped him with his work and succeeded better than I could in calming him.

Eventually Walter's outbursts became a self-stimulating habit. Once, when he had threatened to tear up all of his work and I had locked up his portfolio in a closet, he nearly broke down the door kicking, wildly shouting for the key. At this point Jerry, supported by the whole group, very soberly demanded that I give Walter the key. I complied, feeling that they probably knew better than I what was best. Walter grabbed the portfolio but only tore up some unimportant sketches, by way of a symbolic gesture. Then he went back to work. Evidently the group had sensed Walter's genuine despair when they previously had helped me protect him from himself. They had also known the moment when it was possible and necessary to confront him with a choice, trusting to his ultimate good sense.

The extra attention paid to a child at moments of intensive struggle can usually be accepted by the others if the art therapist has proven to the group that she is ready to give as much to each one of them when he is in a similar crisis.

SUPPORT AND DEPENDENCY

Will such support as has been described throughout the preceding passages lead to excessive dependency? The danger is real, but refusing to give support is no solution. Problems of dependency are part of every disturbed child's difficulties. Neglected children whose dependency needs have been starved behave differently from children whose need for support has been exploited by overprotecting adults. Yet other children may be arrested on a level of symbiotic dependency that does not permit development of true relationships, or they may have frozen into withdrawn self-sufficiency.

Neglected children who have had to fend for themselves often present a defiantly independent front. "I trust only three people—me, myself, and I." Everybody, particularly every adult, is a fool and a liar. Such children often will not venture to try anything they are not certain to be able to do alone. They would rather produce the same thing over and over again than risk failure or ask for help. Words don't convince them that adults can and will help. It may be necessary to make oneself useful to the child even before he is ready to ask for assistance. One may have to rescue pictures by mopping up spilled paint or taping torn pieces together before the child can admit that he cares about his work. If such a child lets the art therapist in on the planning or execution of a picture, this may be a major victory.

However, it can and does happen that extreme dependency ensues, and that the child becomes unwilling even to do those things by himself that he was able to do before he trusted the adult. How much to give in to such irrational demands or when to call a halt depends on the specific situation. One has to avoid being exploited, but also avoid giving the child the feeling that he has been seduced into trusting someone only to be let down again.

It can also happen that a neglected child, upon becoming

dependent on the adult, mobilizes his earlier delinquent patterns and tries to cajole, manipulate, and dominate him.

Martin: Martin, of whom I have spoken in connection with transference and counter-transference (pp. 41–43), went so far as to offer to pay me money for drawing his pictures for him and berated me for "not wanting to earn a living." At other times he threatened to complain to the Director that I was not doing my job because I was not helping him, and to have me fired. But it was just this child who eventually developed a clear understanding of the art of teaching. He became an excellent assistant art teacher who could accept other children at their own level, encourage them and help them just enough but not too much. Thus Martin mastered the difficulty of having to relinquish his underhanded attempts at stealing my skills and maneuvering me into working for him. By learning to understand my ways of thinking, he attained what he had wished for— superior skill in art and a (modest) share in my power and position.

The overprotected child's healthy needs for dependency remain unfulfilled for different reasons than those of the neglected one. Never being allowed to venture forth on his own, he misses the experience of feeling reassured when the adult comes to the rescue in case an adventure proves to be more than he can handle by himself. Therefore it is often necessary to execute acts of independence with him or for him and to give reassurance at the same time. When I offered all kinds of new materials to Tonio for his approval (p. 100), I emphatically discarded whatever he disliked, dramatizing for him his need to actively reject things. At the same time I demonstrated that, while I encouraged him to dare to touch unknown matter which might prove distasteful, I was also ready to rescue him by removing such stuff quickly so that there would be no danger of his accidentally coming in contact with it again.

Whenever action is blocked by helpless submission or paralyzed by suppressed rebellion, support might take a similar dual form.

Whether the point of departure is defiant independence, dependency that covers underlying rebelliousness, frozen withdrawal, or merging with a stronger person, the road usually leads over periods of dependency to genuine independence, based both on self-confidence and confidence in the adult (for of course a child's independence is never absolute, but relative to his age and capacities).

Against inertia and the compulsion to repeat, one must mobilize the developmental thrust for change. Often there are moments of illumination when a child can see the pattern of his growth, realize how much depended on his learning to accept himself and on finding his own solutions, appraise what he has achieved, and envision what lies ahead.

It is therefore essential to keep some record of the child's development, such as portfolios, photographs, or slides, within easy reach. When Martin came to a point where he could relinquish his manipulative ways, he looked through his portfolio and threw out all pictures that were not entirely his own. At the same time he reminisced about the various tricks he had used to get me or others to work for him.

When Christopher visited an exhibition of blind children's sculptures, which included examples of his own work from the age of eleven to fourteen, he complained at first that the early pieces were not good enough and asked, "Why did you put them in the show?" When I asked him what would have happened if I had not liked his first attempts, he admitted that he would have stopped working with clay, because at that time he could not take any criticism at all. After fingering the sharp horns of a bull he had made when he was twelve years old, he went to feel the work of his schoolmate John, whose sculptures abounded with horns, teeth, and claws. He commented how much John's work resembled the things he used to make when he was younger. Like John, he used to like only ferocious animals that could defend themselves, but now strength alone no longer impressed him.

Sometimes when a child has reached a stage where his production is independent and fertile, he misses the attention he commanded when he was more troubled. He needs to be reassured that he has not done himself out of the adult's interest by being so good. My best painters at Wiltwyck, who would no longer think of asking me to draw for them, sometimes begged me to paint an area of blue sky for them while they went to lunch, or delegated other equally menial tasks to me, mainly to reassure themselves of my continued interest and willingness to give service. At such times it is important to comply at least by a token gesture.

APPROACHES AND DETOURS—FOR THE ART THERAPIST

Sometimes the art therapist must find detours around specific difficulties that impede creative work. By disentangling some areas of functioning from pathological impediments he often can create a sanctuary within which sublimation is possible, giving the child a taste of it even while daily life is disrupted by pathology.

To use an example that belongs within the range of normal functioning: there are children who can draw very well but regress when they touch paint. This usually occurs in a person who depends for control mainly on the intellect, repressing affect, which is felt as a threat. There are, on the other hand, those who can handle color beautifully but are helpless when attempting to impart form and organization. Usually these children have easy access to their emotions but find it hard to organize their lives. Ideally the capacity to handle color and form should balance. Even when this state is reached, one can often sense the weight of the two trends in the kind of harmony that is established.

Naturally one will try first to help a child who can only draw to get on better terms with color, or to help a colorist acquire a greater sense of organization. Sometimes it helps to confront a child with his difficulties, to mobilize his efforts at understanding them or overcoming them; but when a child exhausts himself wrestling with the same problem to the point of desperation, it may be better to call a halt.

For example, if a child invariably messes up his picture as soon as he tries to paint, yet unhappily persists because he has been told an artist should use color, it may be best to encourage him to be a graphic artist for a while, offer him black ink and sable brushes, charcoal, graphite, or some other rich graphic medium to help him attain the very best within the area in which he feels at home. Or a colorist who is quite unable to draw may be encouraged to build up his pictures entirely with paint, forgetting about drawing for the time being.

Angel: At a time when Angel, an excellent draftsman, was trying very hard to become more like other children, he repeatedly attempted to use tempera paint, but he could not find any relationship to color and was visibly unhappy and confused by the task he had set himself. At the same time his purely linear work had become so rigid that growth was impeded. I gave him charcoal and charcoal paper and showed him how he could modulate lines and planes to create depth, volume, and values. This he was able to comprehend, and his work lost its rigidity and came as close to the richness of color as was possible for him at this time.

Mervin: Mervin, an eleven-year-old boy, invariably spoiled his pictures when he used color because he could not control the flow of paint. Large masses of thick paint would always swallow up his people or objects. It was not a matter of skill, for he had great dexterity; it rather seemed an expression of some indefinable menace that threatened all his constructive efforts. Mervin loved color and was not ready to settle for drawing or for using crayons. I taught him how to use a dry brush, and this he could accept. He became adept at getting interesting effects by cross-hatching and, because he had found a way of controlling the paint, he ventured into subject matter that he had previously avoided. Eventually he learned to paint with a loaded brush when he wanted strong, solid color.

Andrew: When ten-year-old Andrew first came to Wiltwyck he only painted "designs." Not the common, empty, evasive kind, which have been described in the section on "Art and the Problem of Emptiness," but very full abstractions that combined unusual shapes and interesting colors in unexpected ways. Andrew seemed totally absorbed in his work and never asked for help. I left him alone and limited myself to showing my admiration for his paintings. Finally he explained to me that he confined himself to designs only because he could not draw. I suggested that we look for shapes in his designs that could be made into objects. This he could accept. Plate VII shows an Indian's face and headdress which he saw in one of his designs; he then added the features to make the idea clearer. Soon after this he was ready to tackle the problem of drawing people.

Andrew's representational work retained the decorative, colorful quality of his earlier designs, color dominating form throughout. At the age of twelve, shortly before his discharge, Andrew painted a portrait of a friend (Pl. VIII). In this sober attempt at clearly perceiving an individual, form for the first time dominated color. Only the friend's shirt collar, showing from beneath his gray sweater, was painted with Andrew's old abandon to color. Actually the friend wore a checked flannel shirt, but Andrew made it into a free design.[3]

To set at rest the mind of the reader who may regret Andrew's decline as a colorist as seen in his portrait, we note that such a development may be necessary when the child makes a supreme effort to organize himself. Andrew was facing his discharge from Wiltwyck, a very serious step. Also, the colorful shirt indicates that all is not lost and that the now submerged vitality may flourish again.

When the difficulty centers around confusion of the body-image, it is best to offer clay or wax, so that the body can be constructed by joining the various parts. The hurdle of projecting the image onto a flat surface is postponed until the funda-

---

3. For a documentation of the persistence of characteristic elements of form and color in the art of pre-school children up to the first school years, see R. H. Alschuler and L. W. Hattwick, *Painting and Personality.*

mental confusion has been clarified in sculpture. Here again talent plays a part. Some individuals are more gifted for sculpture than for drawing or painting and then this gift becomes an organizing force that commands the energies necessary for overcoming difficulties. We would of course like to know more about the nature of such talent, but this problem is beyond the subject matter of this book and the knowledge of the author.

More often than not, children prescribe for themselves, and the art therapist does best to follow the child's lead. When, on the other hand, some force seems to drive an individual to wrestle endlessly with the same difficulty, then the art therapist must search for a way to disentangle him.

Sam: Thirteen-year-old Sam had once more or less accidentally painted a beautiful sunset sky in many reds, oranges, and pinks. Subsequently he tried many times to repeat this triumph, but always reached the same impasse. He would begin by applying reds, yellows, and white to his paper, creating satisfactory color combinations. Then he added blue, mixed it with yellow, and was confronted with a grass-green area that did not fit his sky at all. When he tried to cover this up with other colors he got a muddy brown and then he tore up the picture.

I tried to reason with him, explaining how blue and yellow could not possibly give him a color that he could use in his sky, but although he had sufficient intelligence to have been able to understand the logic of it, the green intruded no matter what I said. Finally I took to simply forbidding him to put any blue at all on his palette. This worked. Sam succeeded in painting a sunset and then turned to other subjects.

As the child approaches adolescence, new obstacles to creative work arise. At this age both spurious originality and outright imitation make their first appearance. "Socialization" often means adopting a defensive mimicry which hides from view the real self with all its contradictions. To help an adolescent often entails his becoming consciously aware of such contradictions in his work.

A highly gifted adolescent girl was torn between intense rebellious, negativistic feelings and a capacity for constructive action which included a genuine talent for being motherly and protective to others. In her figure drawings she was troubled by the inclination to distort arms and hands so that they looked either ineffective and lifeless or more like claws than hands. She covered up by adopting an illustrative style, which could fool her companions but could not possibly satisfy her own high artistic standards, and she knew that she was evading the issue.

Her work took on new vitality when she began delineating figures by painting the surrounding area in black ink so that the figures appeared in the negative as white spaces. Their outlines were so well perceived that they gave all the clues necessary for "seeing" the figure. The tension created between the black and the empty white space moved the spectator to complete the picture by imagining the rest, and, since the outlines contained no contradictions, the spectator's effort led to something that could be felt as a pleasurable revelation.

Thus the negative brush-and-ink paintings fused into an integrated whole the intense negativism, the undamaged perceptions, and the equally intense desire to shield others from destruction. Her work demonstrated to the young woman the intactness of her perceptions and the extent of her integrative and creative powers. Naturally this did not resolve the conflicts that made the detour necessary. It only gave her an experience of undisturbed functioning which did not entail repression of important elements of her personality.

A misunderstanding of the meaning of reality in art sometimes feeds the adolescent's inclination to pursue goals that have no truth for him. When the therapeutic team feels that the adolescent should become more reality-oriented it is often suggested that the art therapist offer real things to paint or draw.

Still life is often presented in this spirit, the notion being that the objects the young people are invited to paint are unquestionably real, because they can be touched. This can be helpful at times. Painting a pot can lead to a revelation of the pot's substance, weight, hollowness, thingness. This can help to counteract flights into fantasy or to call the painter back to the real world. However, we must remember that only those things that are emotionally invested have reality in art.

For example, an ambulatory schizophrenic adolescent boy was perturbed by the weird, chaotic drawings he produced when left to himself. He wanted to draw more realistically, but he could not perceive a conventional still life at all. When a still life consisting of tools and pieces of metal was set up, he produced an astonishingly clear and expressive charcoal drawing. His father owned a machine shop. Subsequently he made many drawings in the shop and the backyard and eventually also included trees and other living things in his work. Art sessions were devoted to helping him to experience the texture, weight, and logical forms of these objects which were real to him.

A young woman could paint only skies with any kind of feeling and conviction. Her other work was competent but perfunctory and joyless. Only by pursuing this theme and subsequently adding other themes that became invested with meaning could she experience the pleasures of artistic creation.

Even though only genuine experience can lead to sublimation, there are situations when such experiences must not be forced upon people, when art must function in the service of defense rather than as self-expression, when the most sterile still life or most conventional landscape is a desirable achievement. But of this we will speak in the next chapter.

A great deal that has been said in this chapter applies to child rearing, education, and psychotherapy as well as to art therapy. There are, however, certain aspects of the work I have described that belong particularly to *art* as therapy.

It is not an accident that most of my examples told in circumstantial detail how a child produced a single work or what methods were used in helping him to overcome specific technical difficulties. Unlike scientific thinking, which proceeds from the observation of the specific to the recognition of general principles, the road of art leads from the nonspecific to the unique. At the inception of a work there are many possibilities. As it takes shape, this initial freedom narrows to compelling necessity until each move is inevitable in the sense in which a bean can grow only a beanstalk or a cat deliver only kittens. The reader who wants to understand what is at stake must accompany the child and the art therapist along this road, observing how the therapist speaks to the child in the language of the medium, respecting the specific problems that arise in the making of a piece of work, empathizing with the child's style, bearing with him until the work is completed.

When a child encounters difficulties it is not always easy to determine what ails him. When he insists on just such a brush, or becomes desperate because he cannot get a certain shade of color, or when he cannot decide what to make next, or feels he must destroy his work and begin all over again, is this behavior a symptom of general disturbance, or is he seeking the one and only way whereby his work can be completed?

To determine what is at stake, or what kinds of help should be given, the supreme test is the child's response. When help given within the realm of art bears fruit, then the difficulty indeed arose in this area, and seemingly trite measures such as mixing a special color, making a sculpture stand, or giving technical advice make the child feel that he is deeply understood.

When the creative act has reached a certain stage of complexity, and this can happen even with a six- or eight-year-old, the art therapist may have to bring his whole creative imagination and artistic experience to bear upon the problem of helping a child, disentangling him from snarls, or leading him out of a dead end.

For all these reasons it is essential that the art therapist should be a practicing artist, or at least should have practiced art long and intensively and with joy, so that he will have the technical ability, the empathy, and the commitment to art necessary to assist others. For even though there are many aspects of his work where these special skills do not come into play, the art therapist's unique contribution depends on his understanding of the language of art materials and of form.

VI

Art in the
Service of Defense [1]

IN THE PRECEDING chapter we discussed situations where children needed help in achieving sublimation. The process was under way but would have remained abortive or proceeded more slowly and painfully without assistance. In this chapter we will investigate instances where art has become subservient to defenses and has thereby lost most of its expressive function.

Defenses are not necessarily detrimental to art. In the passage on different ways of using art materials (pp. 54 ff.) we have seen that children, even in the making of a single work, often establish controls through compulsive defenses, and from this vantage point recapture the spirit of creative freedom.

Sublimation and mechanisms of defense may coexist, they may interlock, or they may be at war. Most artists, young and old, are inclined to establish some irrational rituals, some compulsive procedures which, however burdensome they may seem on the surface, actually facilitate sublimation. Mechanisms of defense become a menace to art only when they either make creative work impossible or distort it to the point where art no longer expresses experience.

It is not always easy to determine how this comes about. When does form, instead of giving order to expression, destroy its vitality? When will disguise no longer make truth more universal but pervert it?

1. Some of the ideas and case material presented in this chapter have been published in another version under the title "Stereotypes."

121

If we take stock of the products that look as if they were made under the pressure of defensive mechanisms, we find that they fall roughly into three categories: bland stereotypes that are dull, repetitious, and conventional; work that is rigid and stereotyped but presents unusual or bizarre configurations; work that is filled with false sentiment, such as saccharine sweetness, hollow heroism, or false piety. The third type of work makes its first appearance in adolescence or at the earliest in pre-adolescence. Younger children do not seem to be able to produce false sentiment in art. When defense gains ascendancy in their work, the usual result is merely impoverished, repetitive production.

Of course children are fully capable of lies and subterfuge; they are just as inclined to admire all kinds of rubbish as are adults, and they often like to copy such things. But they seem unable to create original work of this kind. Perhaps it is because their defenses remain on the whole sporadic. Even though preferences for specific mechanisms of defense develop early, ad hoc emergency measures predominate. Only as adolescence approaches and defenses are consolidated and integrated with the total character structure does it become possible to sustain pretense in a form of expression in which dissimulation is extremely difficult. For the production of convincing pseudo-art demands skill and sophistication and presupposes that art has become incorporated in the individual's system of defense.

Art has its own morality. In other situations we are inclined to condemn the outright lie and excuse unconscious falsehood, but in art the latter is more damaging.[2] The artist who lies only to others can sometimes preserve his artistic integrity through such subtle devices as satire or irony. For example, Velasquez in his court portraits used his exquisite craftsmanship to celebrate (through composition, setting, and costume) the power and magnificence of his subjects. At the same time his devastating likenesses show his full perception of their cruelty, cupidity, and perversity. Yet the very accuracy of the portraits so flattered and

2. For a lucid exploration of the nature of truth and falsehood, see Hannah Arendt, "Truth and Politics," *The New Yorker*, February 25, 1967.

pleased his patrons that his work was accepted and honored. When art serves to uphold defenses against the emergence of inner truth the process is unconscious, and art inevitably becomes tainted no matter how great are the artist's conscious efforts to be honest in his work. For example, the lovingly executed detail of Andrew Wyeth's figure paintings testifies to his honest desire to express his love and respect for his subjects. But when he portrays human beings this highly competent craftsman is totally unable to convey a sense of bone structure, volume, and weight. Thus the work betrays the profound isolation that makes it impossible for him to make his figures live.

While the best of taste and the best intentions may be powerless to bring about good art when unconscious forces work against it, art—particularly naïve art—can blossom even while the individual's taste remains atrocious. A child or an untutored adult may produce beautiful, honest work and greatly enjoy the experience, yet continue to admire the ugliest, most conventional kind of trash. Such adults are usually people for whom art is a late and new experience. Although their defenses may include denials and reaction formations, art is not incorporated into this system. Indeed, these naïve people, whose own art is free of false sentiment, often do not perceive the falsity of more sophisticated work. Such innocents may be able to take a garish picture-postcard, a saccharine flower piece, or a sentimental religious picture, "copy" it and produce something good. They have projected their own true feelings into the third-rate trash they set out to copy. The same thing often happens with children. Naturally this does not mean that I advocate distributing trash among children and amateurs!

ART EDUCATION AND DEFENSE

Simple neglect and lack of inspiration from adults usually lead to impoverished and stunted art among the children in their care. Teachers who would admire art, yet are disturbed by the element of improvisation that belongs to it, tend to induce more elaborate and specific stereotyped production. The children manufacture what they have discovered to be pleasing to the teacher. We learn about their personalities only when we try to bring about change. For instance, when skillful teaching soon leads to better work, we know that a student's creative capacity was not really damaged but only inhibited or misdirected.

The astonishing results of inspired teaching in classrooms, golden-age clubs, and adult-education or rehabilitation programs prove the indestructible power and resilience of people's creative capacity. They also demonstrate how indispensable is the teacher as a catalyst, for such faculties do not blossom when indifferent personnel dispense art materials.

However, one always finds a number of students who do not respond favorably even to the most inspired teaching. Inadequate guidance cannot alone explain their failure. One must seek the causes elsewhere.

Helen: When a child has the tendency to ward off truth by maintaining an artificial front, teaching that reinforces such inclinations may help the habit of misusing art to become deeply entrenched.

Helen, a seventeen-year-old girl, had been brought up in a home for dependent children. She had always been attracted to art. Unfortunately, art teaching at the home had been in the hands of conventional arts-and-crafts teachers who depended on commercial patterns and gave no guidance toward creative work. At public school, Helen's facility for making posters and decorations was exploited by the teachers and admired by her schoolmates who came to depend on her help.

When I first met Helen she could, with an uncanny facility, produce for occasions such as Christmas, Easter, birthdays, and so on, art of an exceptionally ugly, saccharine vulgarity (Fig. 16). She would not draw from nature, tolerated no criticism, and accepted no help. Her craving for unconditional praise was insatiable.

In sculpture, Helen's style was less set, and she was more

willing to experiment. Soon her sculptures became distorted and grotesque. For example, she began a cute clay kitten, then changed the kitten into a frog. Later she angrily squashed the frog and from the distorted, froglike lump fashioned a humanoid monster of ambiguous sex lying on its stomach, feet up, spine bent in an arch, much like a baby that is rocking on his belly (Fig. 17). She was pleased with this work and spent much time perfecting it. She also produced a number of grotesque heads; all these sculptures were infantile, weak, and at the same time monstrous.

Helen's grotesque sculptures help us understand why her "pretty" pictures were so stereotyped and ugly. Feeling so weak and monstrous, she could not possibly produce anything truly pretty on her own. If she wanted to make such things, she had to copy them. The special flavor of vulgarity she imparted to her pretty pictures betrayed the monstrous fantasies beneath the conventional surface.

After a period of making monster sculptures, Helen sculptured a reclining nude. It was obviously a self-portrait, somewhat idealized, but nevertheless an honest attempt to sculpture a human being, not an anatomically impossible fashion dummy. During the same period, she drew a self-portrait which also combined idealization with serious observation.

In the course of the year, it became evident that Helen's talent had not been completely perverted by commercialism. In retrospect it seemed as if her art could have been a positive force, that it could have helped her to deal more honestly with her feelings, and that this chance had been lost because her inclination to hide her true feelings behind a mask of compliance was supported by teachers and cottage parents. The result was anti-art on the aesthetic level and more firmly entrenched hypocrisy on the moral level. However, her facile performance bolstered her self-esteem and conceivably might have led toward a career in commercial art.

Although we can be sure that a chance for a certain amount of benefit from art was lost, we have no way of measuring the

FIGURE 16. *Helen*: Santa Claus (18″ x 24″)

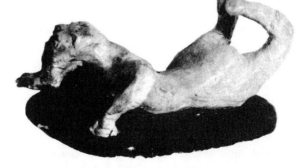

FIGURE 17. *Helen*: Pink Monster (10″ long)

extent of the loss. It would be presumptuous to maintain that better art instruction would have "saved" Helen. Conceivably, she might have grown up into much the same kind of person even with the best of art teaching.

What about Helen's teachers? Was their preference for stereotyped art a sign that they were warding off fantasies similar to those that emerged in Helen's grotesque sculptures? It is more likely that the teachers were merely people who were at ease in a conventional setting and felt justified in inviting the troubled children in their care to share this bland emotional climate with them. Encouraging this kind of pseudo-art may also have been an unconscious defensive maneuver on the part of the child-care workers. Had truly expressive art emerged, the adults in charge would have been confronted with the full impact of the children's mutilated and distorted personalities. This might have made it too difficult to like those children and to endure living with them.

It seems likely that the gulf between Helen's distorted inner life and the insipid emotional and cultural nourishment that was offered to her contributed to the particularly revolting flavor of her stereotyped production.

REPETITION AND STEREOTYPE

We must be careful to distinguish the sterile kind of repetition we call stereotype from repetition that remains alive and productive. For example, a five- or six-year-old child who is in the process of discovering various schemata that unmistakably denote for him men, women, children, or animals is thereby enormously increasing his power of expression. Just because he has succeeded in abstracting from the confusing variety of things certain definite forms which he can easily repeat and control, he is able to understand and depict the complexity of his world better than before. His schematic art is, therefore, full of vitality. There will be plenty of variety in organization, color, and subject matter, even though the basic patterns of representation remain the same.

Ralph: We also must not underestimate the stabilizing and reassuring function of repetition, and we should be careful not to push children into premature change. Seven-year-old Ralph's series of exactly identical "portraits" of his schoolmates (Fig. 18) was, for example, such a constructive repetition. Ralph was struggling to overcome his fear of other children, to relinquish his artificially belligerent front, and to establish positive relationships. As a step toward coming to terms with living in a group of children, the portraits were an enormous achievement, and the very fact that he had hit upon a formula that he could surely repeat every time was comforting.

If, on the other hand, there had been not as much conflict between his desire for friendship and his feelings of fear and hate, Ralph's style would probably have been less rigid and impoverished and he would have had less need for exact repetition.

We must likewise distinguish between stereotypes and varia-

FIGURE 18. *Ralph:* Portrait of Eddie (16" x 24")

tions on a theme. There are artists whose range is narrow and yet we never feel that they are imitating themselves. Vermeer van Delft's world is as narrow as a room, the things and people in it, and the light that falls on it all, yet each of his paintings is absolutely fresh and alive. The world of Pieter Bruegel is much wider, but it too is bounded by his culture and his personality. Neither of these two artists is ever mannered or repetitious.

A child who suffers from persistent inner difficulties is apt to paint many similar pictures expressing his state of mind. After Eric's mother had died, for a whole year he painted little else than monster faces. Each of them was imbued with a fresh sense of horror, and this lasted until he had overcome his excessive guilt.

Christopher, whose work we have described in the section on Symptom and Sublimation, made a great many sculptures of birds. This subject matter was related to his blindness, which was a permanent source of frustration and grief. Yet his sculptures were not stereotyped. Each new version was fresh and alive.

In these two cases the difficulty was so overwhelming that for a long time the child was unable to master it, but each creation constituted a new attempt at coming to terms with conflict or finding a way to endure it. The battle was inconclusive, but it was not in a state of deadlock.

Even in the face of persisting conflicts, a child's style of work needs to change as he grows older. New forms may be modifications of previous schemata, or they may be radical innovations. Whatever the change, if there is to be art, some framework is always needed to give unity and order to the artist's ideas. In normal growth, the process of finding form, modifying or breaking it, and finding new form, never ceases. Fallow periods occur when style has lost its meaning and no new style has yet been found to replace it. When all goes well, the anxiety and confusion generated at times of transition become a driving force for seeking new ways of expression. When things go wrong, the capacity for artistic expression may be inhibited, atrophied, or perverted.

What causes disturbances in the rhythm of growth? What makes an individual or a culture repeat the same worn-out patterns over and over again like a broken record? What can we do to bring about change, or when should we refrain from interfering and accept the status quo in spite of its sterility?

EXAMPLES OF STEREOTYPED ART

Conventional, stereotyped production does not always mean lost opportunity for creative expression. It can also be the first step toward any kind of organization in a chaotic person, or it may be a defense against the threat of chaos and confusion.

Ann (protective mimicry): Nine-year-old Ann was an adopted child suffering from mild brain damage and severe emotional disturbance. During several months' residence in a psychiatric ward, she diligently drew Christmas trees, Easter baskets, flowers, and little girls. She tried hard to learn to draw new things. With the art therapist's help, she acquired a number of new schemata such as a bird, a star, a house, and the like (Fig. 19).

Ann practiced drawing these objects rather as if they were arbitrary symbols, like letters that must be learned by rote; evidently this was the only way she could learn to make them. Her inability to learn more intelligently was probably caused by slightly impaired perception combined with suppressed rage that threatened to disrupt all her constructive activities.

Ann was painfully aware of her handicaps. She knew that her adoptive parents would accept her only if she somehow managed to control her rages and present them with the semblance of a nice little girl. Her efforts in art were devoted mainly to manufacturing a plausible imitation of a normal nine-year-old girl's production. Ann's work was rigid, meager, fragmented, and devoid of artistic quality. Nevertheless it served an important purpose, and at this time it would not have been advisable to interfere.

Later Ann was placed in a residential treatment home where

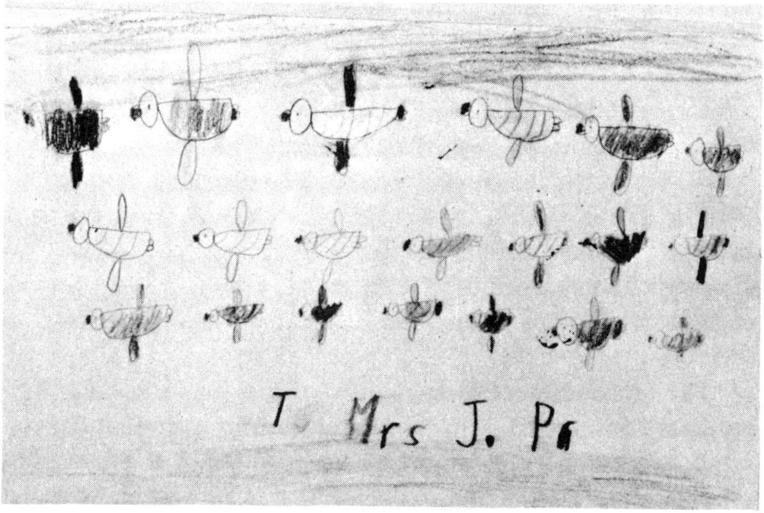

FIGURE 19. *Ann:* Birds (18" x 24")

she could maintain limited contact with her parents. It was conceivable that there she would be able eventually to work through her rages and fears, and experience a reorganization of her personality. If this were to happen, Ann's art might also become more spontaneous.

Henry (lifeless symbols for living things): Henry had lived in a psychiatric ward for two years following his psychotic mother's thinly veiled attempt to murder him when he was four and a half years old. He was capable of relationship, and his intelligence was above average. He also compulsively re-enacted destruction and rescue by incessant monkeylike destruction of toys and other objects alternating with skillful repair jobs, and by continuous fights and reconciliations with children and adults.

In art, Henry alternately spilled paint and cleaned up, destroyed other children's work and repaired it. He never drew solid figures but only stick-men, and he was compelled to destroy any of his own art work in which a living being was represented. He could, however, refrain from destroying abstract symbols that served for self-representation. He drew his initials and he drew the Star of David, which represented both his person and his belonging to the Jewish people. Sometimes he represented his initials in action, like living things: in one picture, they were flying a kite from the roof of the Empire State Building.

In his better moments, Henry manufactured innumerable Stars of David, initials, or combinations of both and gave them away as presents. Although the activity was compulsive and stereotyped, it helped him behave in a less chaotic fashion, cement relationships, and establish some tenuous feeling of identity.

The substitution of lifeless symbols for living things may have reinforced his alienation from himself, but in general his stereotyped production was beneficial. Indeed, the few fragmentary self-representations in human form that were not immediately obliterated emerged at times when a period of stereotyped drawing had built up temporary barriers against his impulse to destroy. Figure 20 was drawn after Henry had produced an enormous number of large stars and given them to all the nurses;

FIGURE 20. *Henry*: Stars of David (18″ x 24″)

it shows a rudimentary person finally allowed to survive beneath a tower of stars.

The Cobra (identification with the aggressor): Sometimes stereotyped art appears when a situational deadlock reinforces inner conflicts. The story of the Cobra is a good example.

A new counselor came to Wiltwyck School, a residential treatment home, to take charge of a group of eight- and nine-year-old boys. He was a tall, handsome man with shining eyes and a magnetic personality. Unfortunately, he was also narcissistic, brutal, and unpredictable. The boys were both fascinated and terrified by this man who was more like a gang leader than a child-care worker. They nicknamed him "The Cobra."

During his reign, the group's art work became almost exclusively centered on painting cobras. The fad was initiated by a particulary frightened, dependent little boy who begged me to draw him a cobra and then devoted hours to painting a yellow and black zigzag pattern all over it. The picture was a huge success. Soon many boys painted replicas of the black and yellow snake. They wanted to have them displayed right behind their table in the dining room, and they ate completely surrounded by cobras.

Although the children were so attached to the cobras, their pictures remained singularly meager. Nobody altered any detail of the first prototype, nobody painted a background or added new objects. Cobra-painting persisted unchanged until the cobra-counselor was dismissed, whereupon it quickly died down.

The children's stereotyped painting was a reaction to being terrified by a person who was also attractive to them and from whom there was no escape. Evidently the cobra paintings were signs of anxious preoccupation with their counselor. Their pleasure in making them tells us that painting cobras somehow diminished anxiety.

If we consider that children's paintings usually contain some form of self-representation, we can say that the boys turned themselves into cobras. As Perseus used his polished shield to petrify the Medusa with the reflection of her own terrible countenance, the little boys used their cobra paintings as protection against the cobra in their midst, declaring over and over again, "I am not afraid of The Cobra, I am myself a cobra."

We see that love and admiration led to identification, but since fear and hate also prevailed, identification was focused only on the dangerous aspects of the object of love. If the counselor had not resembled the boys' dashing but brutal fathers or other admired figures of their delinquent environment, they would still have hated and feared him, but they might not have been quite so helplessly fascinated by him, and conceivably they might have expressed their feelings differently.

Why did the paintings remain so sterile? That they expressed fear and hate would not necessarily make them fail artistically. A child who wants to be a dangerous snake could very well paint a magnificent picture of a cobra.

I suggest that the emotional and physical deadlock contributed to the sterility of the children's art. Emotionally the boys were torn between hate and love, envy and fear. Physically they were helpless against the counselor's strength and authority. In their paralysis, their artistic expression was reduced to the stereotyped repetition of a primitive mechanism of defense, "identification with the aggressor."

Naturally, this balance of forces depended not only on the counselor's strength but also on the children's weakness. Had there been an unusually talented child among them, he might have given a more moving expression to his feelings and might have influenced the other boys' style. Had the group been stronger and more united, they might have resisted the counselor's fascination and rebelled. Indeed, this happened when Cobra was transferred to a group of older, stronger boys who staged a mass runaway which led to the counselor's dismissal.

Angel (oscillation): Helen's case has taught us that talent does not guarantee creativity in art. For years her work was almost entirely stereotyped. Angel, another gifted child, oscillated between two modes of production.[3]

3. I have described this case at length in "Art Therapy and the Severely Disturbed Gifted Child."

Angel began to draw when he was in a hospital at the age of five. He suffered from delusional fantasies of being Superman, whom he impersonated in a homemade cape. Angel's earliest drawings all represented either Superman or similar omnipotent heroes of television and comic strips. His drawing was precocious and bold (Fig. 21) but endlessly repetitious.

Even so, art proved beneficial. As Angel's drawings became the vehicle for his fantasies, he ceased impersonating Superman directly and was able to accept the status of a small child in everyday life on the ward.

Angel's artistic gift soon attained a certain measure of autonomy. Sometimes he used his talent in the service of learning and of friendship. Figure 22, a picture drawn when he was six years old, represents his beloved occupational therapist.

Throughout three years in a children's psychiatric ward and two subsequent years' residence at a home for normal dependent children, Angel's art retained the same dual character. It was in part given over to obsessive renderings of Superman and similar figures; in part it was a means of observation, understanding, and self-expression. Figure 23, a portrait of the art therapist drawn when Angel was seven and a half, shows an astounding capacity to observe and depict the countenance of a person who had come to be important in his life. Figure 24, Hercules Fighting a Centaur, drawn when he was nine years old, is a more original elaboration of Angel's preoccupation with deeds of valor inspired by reading Greek mythology and by visits to museums. Figure 25, drawn during a trip to the zoo at the age of ten, shows how well he could observe and depict anything he encountered in the real world.

Angel's habit of turning toward fantasy in distress was a severely pathological response to neglect and desertion. He withdrew from reality before he was four years old and substituted the synthetic heroes of television for living people. Since relationship between a small child and those improbable shadows necessarily remains delusional, Angel's development was impaired in many ways. After his admission to the hospital, some of the dam-

FIGURE 21. *Angel*: Superman (12″ x 18″)

FIGURE 22. *Angel*: The
Occupational Therapist (18″ x 24″)

FIGURE 23. *Angel*: Portrait
of the Art Therapist (12″ x 18″)

FIGURE 24. *Angel*: Hercules Fighting a Centaur (18″ x 24″)

FIGURE 25. *Angel*: Gemsbok (14″ x 16″)

age was repaired through living in a benign milieu and through psychotherapy. In many respects Angel developed normally, and his intelligence and talent helped him to make good use of the cultural and educational opportunities offered to him, but his dangerous inclination to replace living objects with synthetic ones that were more completely under his control persisted. He could not invest new relationships beyond a certain point, and his identifications remained tenuous. Consequently Angel's ego ideals remained bound up with his early childhood fantasies.

Even at ten years of age this bright, artistic boy who was not at all belligerent dreamed of being a superhuman brute fighting monsters. At the same time he entertained ideas of becoming a famous artist, but under stress he reverted to his early Superman fantasies. We see that art plays a complicated and contradictory role in Angel's life.

In the beginning art provided a container for his delusional fantasies so that they no longer invaded all of his life. Even though this art was repetitious and stereotyped, it was helpful and indeed may have saved him from being engulfed by his delusions.

On the other hand, this stereotyped art also helped to preserve Angel's pathology, because the act of drawing enabled him to achieve a feeling of being one with his fantasied heroes. Pathological or not, this was useful in daily life. As Angel grew up, his drawing was a dependable source of gratification and an ever-ready means of escape, and this helped Angel to maintain himself at school and at a home for normal children. He learned to stave off temper tantrums and combat despair by drawing.

If stereotyped art was Angel's protection, creative art was one of his major assets. It was a means of assimilating new experience and knowledge. It helped him to fulfill his craving for fame in a legitimate manner. Wherever he went he was soon known and admired for his drawing. Art helped him to establish a sense of identity and the idea of becoming a Famous Artist provided a reasonable alternative to his infantile ego ideals.

Angel's stereotyped art, then, is a defense that protects him against further inroads of his pathology, but it also preserves his illness in its present state.

Angel's creative art pushes him toward change. It offers more mature kinds of gratification, but it also exposes him to new dangers and makes new demands on him. As Angel oscillates between regression and spurts of growth, his art oscillates between stereotyped and creative production.

Frank (stagnation and change): Even though his art never quite became stereotyped, Frank's story is included because it is a good example of a child's battle against repetition and stagnation.[4] At the age of ten, Frank was admitted to Wiltwyck School after his mother had deserted her husband and two little sons.

Frank loved art. In the beginning he painted many large pictures of heroic figures such as mounted policemen, kings, and Indian chiefs, of which Plate IX is a good example.

Frank's drawing was decisive and somewhat rigid. His figures and faces were still bound to childlike schematic concepts. His colors were vivid and solid, and strong contrasts, particularly complementary reds and greens, predominated.

When Frank was about ten and a half years old, he became dissatisfied with his pictures. He found his style of painting "babyish," his figures too stiff, his faces unrealistic and too much alike, his colors too even. He wished to paint in a more grown-up way, to give his people realistic faces, to use "wiggly" lines, to "shade" his colors.

Frank's self-criticism was justified. He was indeed beginning to repeat himself, and his work seemed to be in danger of freezing into stereotyped forms. He was at an age when the intellectual and emotional widening of horizons, which normally gains momentum in the second half of latency, is apt to influence the talented child's style. As his understanding of the world becomes more rational and objective, the child's power of visual repre-

4. I have presented Frank's case history more fully in Part III of *Art Therapy in a Children's Community.*

sentation expands. He discovers means of creating space and depth, and learns to represent objects not just schematically but with individual differences.

Such new powers also bring new difficulties. Periods of stylistic transition are never easy, but the convulsions that tore Frank's art asunder were beyond the ordinary.

Frank could neither relinquish his old style, nor could he accept it. He desired to be more expressive, but he could not endure imperfection. Often he began his pictures in his old rigid style and then tried to change them. When he succeeded in creating more expressive features or more varied color effects, he found the colors too "messy" and was upset because his people's faces were not, as he put it, "regular" enough. For a long time most of Frank's attempts ended in heaps of torn paper.

Still he returned to the art room again and again to do battle with himself, the art material, and me.

Frank's great desire for change in his art and the panic that overtook him whenever he was about to make this change ran parallel to his general emotional state. When he was admitted to Wiltwyck he had held himself aloof from all close relationships. He trusted only in his father and had never forgiven his mother for her desertion. Father, however, soon disappeared and was not heard from for over a year. Mother, on the other hand, visited Frank regularly, even though he ignored her.

In time Frank relinquished his isolation. He began to recognize that his father was not altogether good nor his mother wholly evil, but that there was good and bad in both of them. Necessary as this re-evaluation was, it was very painful. We can see why Frank's painting had to change and why this change was so difficult.

Frank's early paintings had been protective masks that upheld his isolation. Even though some feminine qualities could be noted in most of his figures (see for instance the long hair and protruding chest of his Indian chief), his paintings were before all representations of strong male figures. They fulfilled the emotional needs of a small boy whose feelings were rigidly divided

into hostility toward almost everybody—especially his mother—
and love for his father, who was both ego ideal and protector.

These paintings did not express the feelings or serve the needs
of a boy who had to reappraise himself and the world and come
to terms with disappointments and mixed feelings. But so long
as those feelings were too overwhelming, pictures that lacked
symmetry or that gave even the slightest feeling of ambiguity
because colors had been blended and shaded were extremely
frightening. Such irrational perfectionism, characterized by a horror of all asymmetry, is rather common among children and
adults whose inner balance is precarious.

The Angry Indian (Fig. 26) illustrates this state of mind.
Frank drew it after a stormy session during which he had been
dissatisfied with everything he did. Finally he picked up a brush
and said: "I will show you that I cannot paint." He drew the

FIGURE 26. *Frank*: Angry Indian (24″ x 36″)

picture in a kind of frenzied war dance, which can be felt in the rhythm of the headgear. The little face in the middle is an excellent and moving self-portrait, but Frank could not see this. To him the picture was nothing but a despicable mess. Still, if Frank was to attain his "grown-up" style, some of his rigid defenses would have to give way.

He succeeded in making the transition after he had once more re-enacted the disintegration of stereotyped forms, but this time with a positive outcome. He drew a rocket ship and painted it a flat gray against a darker gray sky in his old schematic manner. Then he added red and orange to the rocket and to the sky. Splashing on more and more paint, he explained that the rocket was "melting" in the sun, and indeed the painting was rapidly turning into a muddy mess. Then Frank decided to rescue the rocket. He restored its outlines and succeeded in changing the mess into an interesting but coherent painting in gray and blue with orange and red highlights. In spite of its explosive subject matter the painting was neither chaotic nor childishly rigid. Frank felt that he had finally succeeded in painting a grown-up picture.

From then on, Frank's painting suddenly took on more freedom and maturity. The Mexican (Pl. X) shows the change of style fully achieved.

Much, however, remains unchanged. If we compare the Indian Chief (Pl. IX) with the Mexican, we see the same powerful, broad style of painting. Both pictures are of heroically conceived men. Both have some feminine features (long hair, strongly accentuated chests). But while the Indian's face only reiterates the aggressive power contained in the body and in the barbaric splendor of the headdress, the Mexican's head adds a new human feeling to the picture.

Frank's story demonstrates how even an initially vital style is bound to succumb to stereotyped stagnation when form no longer expresses content. We also see why the transition to a new style is so often a time of pain and turmoil. When inadequate old forms are broken, while new ones are still in the making, chaos threatens until forms can again successfully contain and express feeling.

DEFENSE AND DEADLOCK

I have described diverse examples of stereotyped art. In each case art serves as a defense against conflicts that are in a state of deadlock, and this is what makes the defense so static. Let us recapitulate these various instances.

In the simplest case, that of the *bland stereotype* which is induced by the teacher, two forces converge to produce a nearly insurmountable barrier: the teacher's distrust and fear of art, and the inner resistance against the emotional rigors of creative work which exists in every child (or adult).

As a rule there are only two kinds of children who will not produce conventional stereotypes in response to such teaching: the very gifted child whose creative drive is stronger than his own inertia and the teacher's resistance combined, and the disturbed child who is too driven or too detached to be influenced by the teacher's standards, or is incapable of complying with them.

In Helen's case the situation is already more complicated. Helen might have been talented enough to have transcended the mediocre teaching that was offered when she was a child, but her inner difficulties made her respond avidly to its worst features.

Helen needed desperately to please and to be successful. This made her into the clever "artist for all occasions," and the environment encouraged her in this role. For children living in institutions, holidays are notoriously difficult times when the loss of family and love is most acutely felt. To function as the decorator-artist can be a constructive solution if the child uses it to rise above the bitterness of the loss. If, on the other hand, feeling of loss is denied, it is more likely that pseudo-art will result.

Helen also warded off the emergence of the warped aspect of her personality. The discrepancy between Helen's ego ideal (a sophisticated, sweet young girl) and her real self created a deadlock in which the strength of her considerable talent was used to uphold an as-if art. Although she succeeded in living up to her ego ideal in her art, the effort exhausted her, without contributing to her growth.

Later, the emergence of the repressed material can be tolerated and even useful, because the conditions that led to the deadlock are no longer in full force. Helen's need for success and approval is satisfied when I accept her grotesque sculptures. At seventeen she is probably not quite as weak as she was as a child. Gains, however, are tenuous, and Helen's art retains much of its original commercial quality.

Ann uses art to create the semblance of a normal little girl in order to defend herself against the danger of desertion. Since in reality she is no such thing, her art is impoverished and stereotyped. But Ann has no choice. The parents' demands and Ann's inadequate endowment produce a deadlock. Although I usually do not encourage such work, under these circumstances I helped Ann to enlarge her repertory of stereotyped patterns.

Henry struggles with internal conflicts. There is on the one hand his healthy desire to create and to give himself to the people he loves. On the other hand there is his compulsion to destroy all representations of living things as soon as they are made. He compromises by manufacturing abstract symbols that do not carry the full weight of his ambivalent emotions. In this way he manages to fulfill his need to give and at the same time to ward off those impulses that would destroy his labor of love.

Because Henry's destructive impulses were so overpowering and because he suffered intensely whenever he was engulfed by them, I supported every and any method of control he devised for himself, including stereotyped mechanical repetition.

The story of the boys and the Cobra tells of inner conflict reinforced by external conditions. These children were still bound to the primitive mechanism of identification with the aggressor as their chief defense against anxiety. In the presence of the counselor who personified such an aggressor they could not grow beyond it. Since I had not the power to fire the counselor, all I could do was help the children endure Cobra's reign by helping them paint better cobras.

The deadlock in Angel's case is in a sense the opposite of that in Helen's. Helen tries to live up to a relatively conventional, normal ego ideal and fails because of an infantile and disturbed personality. Angel's healthy need for ego ideals is tied up with imaginary figures that were fixed upon before he was four years old. While Angel has matured considerably, his ego ideals have remained archaic, attached to fantasies of superhuman, brutal strength. Unable to live up to these ideals, he continues to try to merge with them in fantasy and through drawing. The part of his art that is devoted to these vain attempts remains stereotyped and obsessive.

I have described the methods used in working with Angel at great length elsewhere.[5] The treatment went through several phases. In the beginning, all of Angel's work was unconditionally accepted. Later, a distinction was made between original work and stereotyped repetition; Angel was praised for any departure from his stereotypes. Eventually Angel developed the tentative ego ideal of a "Famous Artist" which coexisted with his earlier Superman ideals. From then on, efforts centered on diminishing the importance of the Superman fantasies, by nourishing and strengthening all those tendencies in him that could provide acceptable alternatives to his escape into delusional fantasies.

Frank's art never settled into a stereotype. It threatened to become sterile during those periods when his old ideas and established defenses had become untenable and new emotions were too frightening and too contradictory to endure. The attempt to uphold an outdated system of defense reduced the artistic forms —once full of life—to shells, no longer capable of containing truth. To help Frank, I had to understand what his battle was

5. See "Art Therapy and the Severely Disturbed Gifted Child."

about, endure the upheaval, pick up the pieces, and help him change his style, taking my cues from him.

In each of these examples we find the productive process dominated by ambivalence, defenses fixed, and growth blocked. Nevertheless the stereotypes protect each child's precarious equilibrium, and it would be foolhardy to try to weaken defenses without considering the cost.

We know, on the other hand, that defense which wards off conflict thereby keeps ambivalence alive. With the passage of time the defense itself may become a pathogenic force. Defenses are vulnerable to "the return of the repressed." When this occurs the defense gradually takes on the character of the repressed material. Helen's cute productions, for instance, could easily have grown more vulgar and distorted until her repressed fantasies reappeared, made more horrible by their saccharine disguise. Another danger is that the "secondary gain" may become so gratifying that the defense cannot be relinquished; the admiration that Angel's Superman cartoons commanded may be a case in point. There is the danger that affect warded off by defense may erupt disastrously. Ann, for instance, might build up immense aggression while busily conforming to her parents' expectations. Beyond any such specific risks there is the universal danger that those areas that are dominated by mechanisms of defense will be sealed off from maturation.

Our examples show that there can be no single rule of conduct. In each instance one must ask: What function does the stereotype serve? If we discourage the stereotype, have we anything better to offer? Has the individual the strength to endure the expression of more conflict, and is it likely that he can reorganize his personality through such creative expression? Will we be able to support him during a period of heightened turmoil? In case of explosion, will we be there to pick up the pieces? How much time have we at our disposal? Will the individual be hurt if he relinquishes his façade? Can his family endure him without it?

Luckily, people do not give up their defenses lightly. Children in particular are not easily pushed in the wrong direction. They let us know by behavior if not in words when they are wrongly treated. It is best to take one's cues from them. A very obstinate resistance often has excellent reasons. Nothing is more important than to observe the child's moods. Anything that brings about serenity and capacity to give is probably beneficial, however senseless or boring it may seem to us.

If we keep two basic rules in mind we cannot go very far wrong. One of them is Freud's dictum, "The patient is always right"; the second is that, even at those times when we accept the status quo or permit regression, we must also give stimulation toward growth.

VARIOUS STEREOTYPED WAYS OF USING ART MATERIALS

Not all stereotypes are caused by reasons as complex as those described in the preceding examples. Retardation or brain damage can produce stereotyped behavior that is a defense against confusion and feelings of helplessness but is not necessarily linked to inner conflict.

A global condition of emptiness can express itself in "stereotyped chaos," a syndrome I described in the section "Art and the Problem of Emptiness."

Sometimes children's work becomes stereotyped or mannered as they attempt to recapture former successes, and this may be an expression of insecurity rather than of deep-seated conflict. In this case the manner will change in response to simple educational methods.

A forerunner of art in the service of defense is the stereotyped handling of art materials that can be observed in some psychotic children. When given several colors of paint these children will invariably cover the whole paper with one color only. They also seem perturbed by having different colors at their disposal. When they are presented with trays filled with several colors, they mix them together until all the compartments look the same. We do not know enough about these children to ana-lyze exactly what their behavior symbolizes; however, it gives the impression of a global defense not just against conflict, but against the very idea of separateness and difference.

Some stereotyped art serves wish-fulfillment more than it serves defense. The art of psychotic children often constitutes an attempt to influence the world by magical means or to create a new world. A psychotic little girl of eight spent all her art ses-sions making identical clay figures representing herself and in-numerable relatives and acquaintances. Throughout each session she worried about whether there would be time to make all the people she needed; this, of course, was never possible, because the supply of people was endless. Conspicuously absent were both father and mother. Attempts on my part to induce her to represent them met with categorical refusal. It seemed as if the main purpose of her compulsive manufacturing of people was to crowd out her parents.

A psychotic seven-year-old boy, who had been sexually used by his mother and had also witnessed her prostitution, made penis-sized clay sausages to which he sometimes gave faces and tiny arms and legs. These personified penises were caressed, tor-tured, offered to me to suck, and in the end destroyed.

In cases such as these, the character of art in the usual sense is lost, as the child conceives of his creations not as symbolic representations but as a concrete object in his delusional world. Against the evidence of reality the delusion is upheld by reiteration.

In such children changes come very slowly. When the gen-eral condition improves, it is sometimes possible to help the child make the transition from a magic conception of art to one in which art has symbolic meaning in the generally understood sense.

A more common, less pathological form of art in the service of wish-fulfillment is the saccharine or obscene erotic art of ado-lescents or of adults who have not grown beyond this level.

The girl who endlessly draws profiles of pretty women with

exaggeratedly long eyelashes and elaborate hairdos escapes into narcissistic fantasies where she becomes irresistible to men. The corresponding art of boys, usually more openly pornographic, contains a similar narcissistic inflation of the male image and degradation of the woman into an impersonal object of sexual gratification.

If we include these categories in our survey, we may say that stereotyped art is most frequently produced in the service of defense, though at times such art serves wish-fulfillment more than defense. In either case the repetitiousness is symptomatic of a state of deadlock.

TALENT IN THE SERVICE OF DEFENSE

While great art demands talent and maturity, genuine art in its simplest form is within the reach of even the immature and the not particularly gifted. To produce anything but the most stereotyped and meager art in the service of defense, on the other hand, requires a certain degree of maturity and some measure of talent.

In our next story we can observe how a talented child's work turns to imitation and false sentiment as he establishes ego ideals at the expense of his feeling of identity.

Larry: When Larry was ten years old his compulsion to provoke the wrath of other children made him into one of the most cruelly victimized little boys at Wiltwyck. He sought protection from adults, but he provoked them by stealing and by disrupting the group, so that they too were inclined to punish him.

He found sanctuary in the art room, where the general atmosphere was serene, but even there he could not completely refrain from teasing the others. He worked huddled over his paper, in mortal fear of attack, glancing behind him frequently to make sure that all was safe.

During this period of masochistic suffering, Larry produced two versions of an African witch doctor with a painted face and wearing a pair of horns. These pictures, which remained unfinished, looked like Larry both in features and expression. The first showed the mad grin that distorted Larry's face when he was about to provoke another child (Fig. 27). Figure 28 showed the brooding expression that was characteristic of Larry nursing his grievances. We see that Larry projected his self-image at this time onto a sinister, mysteriously powerful figure.

Meanwhile the counseling staff made intense efforts to teach Larry to fight back when attacked, and they succeeded to some extent. Before the first year at the school had passed, he was more respected by the group and no longer victimized all the time.

Larry's masochistic behavior changed to sadistic cruelty. He began to mete out what he had received, and now he persecuted smaller boys. Most of the paintings of this period are suffused with a sense of arrogant pride and restrained cruelty. The Indian Chief (Fig. 29) is a good example of the skill and evocative power Larry commanded when he depicted themes that embodied such feelings.

When Larry had been at the school for over a year, he became attached to his tall, manly social worker. For his sake he tried to control his stealing which until then had continued unabated. He also admired the school's principal, a white-haired, upright gentleman, and tried to improve his behavior and to make progress at school. Larry came from a religious home, and he mobilized his faith in the effort to live up to his new ego ideals.

A large painting of a white man in a business suit holding a Bible (Fig. 30), which resembled the social worker, testified to the intensity of Larry's striving to firmly implant this new ego ideal. The painting, however, was somewhat flat and lifeless, as if the figure of this civilized gentleman was not completely real to Larry.

During the following year of heroic struggle for control over his delinquency, Larry's art was almost wholly devoted to pictures of guaranteed positive content. There were pictures of

FIGURE 27. *Larry:* Grinning Witch Doctor (18″ x 24″)

FIGURE 28. *Larry:* Brooding Witch Doctor (18″ x 24″)

FIGURE 29. *Larry:* Indian Chief (24″ x 36″)

FIGURE 30. *Larry:* Man with Bible (24″ x 36″)

churches, a painting of an elderly, white-haired man resembling the principal, and many landscapes. One winter landscape showing two small cottages at night in a wide white field with two bare trees and a light-yellow moon high in a black sky (Fig. 31) achieved a feeling of chilly solitude which was quite moving. His magnum opus of this period was a huge painting of the American flag waving in the breeze, with all (then still forty-eight) stars meticulously depicted.

He could do very little on his own, but copied the work of the other good painters at the school, especially of those who, like himself, aspired to the better things in life. It is interesting that the only painting of this period with aggressive content was a dragon after a drawing by Leonardo da Vinci. Here aggression was redeemed by association with a famous artist. Meanwhile, Larry's delinquency was only partially under control. His bullying of weaker boys was less cruel, but still went on. The look on his face remained sulky and brooding.

When the time for his discharge approached, Larry devoted many of his art sessions to religious paintings. Most of them were conventional renderings of Christ or of angels. His last painting, Christ with the bleeding heart (Fig. 32), was more expressive. The Christ figure, depicted as a light-skinned Negro, resembled Larry. It seemed as if the pressures of imminent discharge had brought forth more profound feelings. The bloodiness of the heart suggested persisting sado-masochistic tendencies now expressed as religious symbolism.

It has often been observed that children who are in trouble frequently produce more moving art than children who are well behaved. Particularly during periods when the struggle for control is intense, art often becomes meager, overly pious, or saccharine, or the child loses interest.

Up to a point, the fullness or emptiness of the art of well-behaved children can be a gauge of the balance of forces that uphold behavior. A child whose good behavior is founded on ego strength and the capacity for sublimation usually produces vital

FIGURE 31. *Larry*: Winter Night (24" x 36")

FIGURE 32. *Larry*: Christ (24" x 36")

art. When conformity is, on the other hand, upheld at excessive sacrifice by means of repression and guilt feelings, art tends to become constricted and empty.

This rule of thumb, which must be taken with a grain of salt altogether, does not work in reverse. The art of undisciplined children is not necessarily more free. On the contrary, it is often just as constricted as that of the cowed, conforming child.

In Larry's case there was a dramatic shift from self-representation of heroes that were braver and more successful than Larry, but not intrinsically different from him, to representation of ego ideals that contrasted with his delinquent, ignorant, and cruel self, and were white. This shift was accompanied by diminished expressiveness and vitality in his art. This alone would not have been sufficient reason for concern; the tendencies that appeared in his paintings need not have been a true indication of his total development. One could imagine that Larry might have been inclined to use art in particular to dramatize his capacity for conformity, for here he was certain of success. While busily producing pious art, Larry might conceivably have been wrestling with his conflicts in cottage life, at school, in his sessions with the social worker, or elsewhere.

If this had been so, I should have regretted losing Larry as an artist, but would have been at ease about him. But his continued relapses into stealing, his underhanded ways, his facial expression, which was still like that of the sulking witch doctor (Fig. 28)—though the mad grin of Figure 29 had disappeared —all corroborated the evidence of his painting, namely, that Larry's new virtue was insufficiently supported by structural changes in his personality.

One of the reasons for his making little real progress may have been the unchanging hopelessness of his family life. Throughout Larry's childhood his father frequently deserted his wife and her many children, leaving them destitute; when at home he treated them brutally. Larry, being the oldest, had often been in open conflict with his father. There was no hope of his being able to live at home in the foreseeable future.

Larry's despairing longing for a better family life found expression in a painting which he repeatedly began and never finished. It represented a group of horses, each of a different color—black, brown, and spotted—among them a mare and colt, with a black stallion standing guard. Each time he worked on it with loving care, bringing it close to completion, but he always discarded it in the end.

And so Larry made do by conforming, ingratiating himself with persons in authority or consoling himself with dreams of becoming his mother's and siblings' savior. Such a position could lead to development of ego ideals, but it would not help him to form the identifications necessary for profound personality changes.

When Larry was finally placed in a foster home at the age of fourteen, where he enjoyed material advantages which his mother and siblings lacked, he felt extremely guilty. He tried to live up to the role of savior both legally, by buying presents out of his allowance, and illegally, by stealing for them. Stealing, once resumed, did not stop at the purely altruistic level, and Larry also stole for himself. Thus he tragically perpetuated his old pattern of provocation and punishment.

Could this repetition have been prevented? We cannot tell. Character remains elusive, and while we sometimes feel that we can trace back what happened and how it came about, we can scarcely fathom what might have been.

Since the art therapist had an inkling that Larry was not working through his inner conflicts sufficiently, ought she have tried to encourage him to paint more expressively in order to confront him with his problems, particularly since Larry's art had been highly expressive before? I did try, but failed every time. Evidently Larry was so threatened by his pathology, so divorced from himself, and so intent on upholding virtue that it would have been both cruel and futile to insist on pushing him into emotional adventures for which he was not ready. The cause of his defensive attitude in art lay elsewhere, and it seemed that art offered no approach to the source of his trouble.

We see that Larry's very talent helped him to use art in the service of defense. Even before his conversion to virtue he had used art to enhance his self-image. His kings, sword fighters, and Indian chiefs are all imbued with arrogant, narcissistic pride. When Larry assumed a false front, it was natural for him to use art to uphold it; for while his performance in other fields fell short of his aspirations, he was indeed competent in art. Also, the more Larry was cut off from his inner life the more was he reduced to exercising his artistic skills by imitating others.

Could Larry's gift have helped prevent his loss of identity? Often art helps a child to remain true to himself even under pressure. I believe that an underlying current in this direction continued throughout the years. Larry never became that scourge of the art class, a slick, facile painter. There were moments of truth in some of his outdoor sketches, in his choice of color, in the sensitivity of his brushstroke, in the mood conveyed by some of his landscapes, even in some of his religious paintings. But the linkage of Larry's self-esteem both with his ego ideals and with success in art made it almost inevitable that art had at the time to function in the service of defense.

The story demonstrates once more the potentialities and limitations of art. Diagnostically Larry's unfortunate character development showed more clearly in art than in his behavior or his talk. Inasmuch as creative work helped stabilize his inner life and bring his psychic processes into the realm of the ego, art was helpful to Larry and might have made him more amenable to treatment. Art alone, however, provided no leverage for bringing about change.

ADOLESCENT ART AND DEFENSE

Larry's case has taken us beyond childhood into adolescence. In him we see tendencies common at this time of life, magnified by his personal tragedy. The talent of many children who are not as seriously endangered as Larry suffers a similar fate when adolescence is reached.

Owing to the profound inner changes of this period, the sense of identity is often shaky. Before the ego is again consolidated and a stable identity reached, pseudo-identities are frequently assumed. Imitation and false sentiment flourish, not only in art such as Larry's that is given to virtue, but also in the openly aggressive or erotic art of adolescents who take on libertine or hostile attitudes that are equally unreal.

Another menace to art arises when the adolescent makes efforts to achieve adult responsibility. At this time the makeshift defensive measures of the child, who ultimately depends on the adult for control and protection, no longer suffice, and a more consolidated system is established. Often this new system does not allow enough leeway for creative processes. Rigidity, whether rooted in health or pathology, is inimical to art, which flourishes best when the personality is in a state of flux. Consequently, creative work becomes impossible for many young adults who were talented as children. Finally, many adolescents lose interest in art simply because their energies become centered upon other goals, and art loses out as the chosen field becomes more highly invested.

Is it then sensible or even desirable to continue offering art as therapy or as part of education to pre-adolescents and adolescents? I believe that it is worthwhile, although one should not expect art to be as universally liked as it is in childhood, and should realize that some adolescents will pervert art and produce pretentious fabrications while others will not take to it at all, no matter how it is presented.

Adolescence is not only a time when sustained insincerity becomes possible but also the period when a more conscious recognition of the difference between inner truth and pretense can be reached. The adolescent not only imitates others, but also searches his soul. Like adolescent life, adolescent art is characterized by swings between extremes. The same individual's production may alternate between the trite and the sincere, the undisciplined and the highly formed, the banal and the original. If we accept these oscillations and put our weight on the side of truth, we can do our share in helping the adolescent become an adult who can stand on his own and who can tolerate conflict and ambiguities without resorting to rigid defensive mechanisms.

VII

Art Therapy and Aggression

THROUGHOUT OUR INVESTIGATIONS we have encountered aggression in many guises: as disruptive violence that made work impossible; as threat that called forth defensive counter-measures; as destructive force which, without disrupting the creative process altogether, interfered with the unity of a work of art; as emotional content that was expressed and contained. Finally, according to our theory of sublimation, we must assume that part of the constructive energy which goes into the making of art derives from neutralized aggression. Aggression seems to be both one of the most disruptive forces we have to contend with, and an indispensable source of energy for constructive work. It seems therefore reasonable to devote an entire chapter to the problem of aggression in art therapy.

Regarding the nature of aggression, both the psychoanalytic investigation of man and the study of the natural history of aggression as conducted by ethnologists such as Lorenz[1] and Tinbergen[2] leave no doubt that it is a primary instinctive drive. Stresses such as frustration or danger call forth unusually intense aggressive behavior, but these stimuli must not be mistaken for causes. The drive is innate, not a mere response to external conditions.

There is also evidence, derived from psychoanalytic study of human relationships and from the investigation of bonds among

---

1. Konrad Lorenz, *On Aggression;* Lorenz, *Über tierisches und menschliches Verhalten: Gesammelte Abhandlungen.*
2. N. Tinbergen, *The Study of Instinct.*

158

other species, that positive relationships always contain aggression. Neither man nor beast seems to be capable of forming a bond without simultaneously directing aggressive affect toward the same individual.

In *On Aggression*, Lorenz explains why the evolution of individual bonds has been of necessity tied to intraspecific aggression. The prerequisite for the development of personal relationships, he reasons, is the capacity for individual recognition. This ability did not evolve in the peaceful flock, since there is no need to distinguish among the various members. It is only when cooperation develops among members of species who are as a rule inclined to be aggressive toward one another that the ability to distinguish between friend and foe becomes essential. Therefore only among such species was there sufficient evolutionary pressure for the development of a faculty for individual recognition.

Furthermore, cooperation develops most often between male and female in the care of the young. Since adequate space is particularly important for new life, the functions of procreation and aggressive behavior are apt to be linked, and animals are often particularly aggressive in defending territory while preparing a nesting place or tending their offspring. Species that develop cooperation must therefore also evolve mechanisms that effectively control aggressive behavior between individuals who have formed bonds. The greater the individual's readiness to valiantly defend those with whom he has formed a bond, the more reliable must be the inhibitions that prevent him from also attacking them.

And so it seems as if the ambivalence that characterizes passionate human relationships is foreshadowed in the mental organization of these other species. For among them the individuals' intercourse with their chosen companions is shot through with mechanisms that divert, bind, or transform aggression against the very beings whose company is ardently desired; the time of closest cooperation often coincides with periods when both sexual excitement and readiness for aggressive behavior are at their height.

Naturally, the existence of analogous situations among other species constitutes no proof of the psychoanalytic hypothesis that aggressive and libidinal drives in man are inevitably linked. It only places it in a wider perspective, making the reasons for it more comprehensible and therefore easier to accept.

I have permitted myself this digression because I feel that it is essential to approach the problem of aggression in the belief that we are dealing with a primeval force. Only on this basis can we hope to understand aggression, or to find ways of dealing effectively with its destructive aspects. Particularly when we encounter some of its pathological manifestations, it is important to remember that aggression is a vital force, in itself neither good nor evil. All vigorous and purposeful action draws part of its impetus from the same drive which, misdirected, causes untold suffering.

DAMMED-UP AGGRESSION

The layman who considers the role of art therapy in the management of aggressive children usually thinks at first of art as a harmless outlet for the expression of pent-up anger. Such direct discharge can be beneficial when the individual's basic integration is not menaced by it.

For example, a child who has been forced into extreme cleanliness too early in life may be able to enjoy constructive work with clay or paint only after a veritable orgy of simple messing with the stuff. Or a very angry child may not be able to settle down to work unless he first gives vent to his anger directly. The hallmark of such healthy explosions is the sense of relief when they are over: the atmosphere is cleared and work can proceed better than before. We conclude that the outburst freed the individual from excessive pressure but left essential ego structure intact. If, on the other hand, the explosion is followed by lasting disorganization or extreme distress, we must conclude that important defenses have been swept away, leaving the child more vulnerable than before.

When it frees the individual from crippling inhibitions, temporary regression to crudely aggressive art may be an emotional victory. When ten-year-old Alice, on the day of her mother's expected visit, painted herself as a primitive manikin entirely scarlet with rage and surrounded by swirling streaks of paint on a paper edged in black (Fig. 33), she bore the picture in triumph to her social worker. It was the first time that she had been able to give vent to her rage at the psychotic mother who had left her in foster care, neglected her, yet pursued her with demands for filial affection.

Fifteen-year-old Philip, a very staid and stable boy whose art was usually contemplative and serene, felt great relief when he painted a crude caricature of his alcoholic father who had abandoned him and his dying mother when he was three years old.

When Mrs. Smith, after a day's vacation, found the cottage where she worked as a house parent in an unbelievable mess, she relieved her feelings by painting Plate XI. The red background,

FIGURE 33. *Alice:* Angry Girl (18″ x 24″)

she explained later, signified her towering rage, the primitive little figure in the middle her feeling of utter helplessness. By the time she had finished the picture, she had calmed down sufficiently to resume her duties and restore order in the cottage. The painting was more infantile than Mrs. Smith's usual work. Rage, it seems, had made her regress. It was, on the other hand, stronger than most of her more adult paintings, so that we can see in it also the seeds of sublimation.

Since the two children as well as the cottage parent had sufficient strength to reintegrate after their temporary regression, they experienced relief, and their emotional equilibrium had not been upset.

AGGRESSION AND CONTROL

When adequate channels for the discharge of impulses have failed to develop properly, it is entirely different. Painful tensions are felt not only under unusual pressures; even the ordinary flow of drive energy is experienced as catastrophic and is discharged chaotically, or the ego tries to defend itself against the onslaught by unusual emergency measures that constrict or distort the child's life.

The self-representations of such children often portray this situation vividly. Like most children, seven-year-old David liked having the art therapist trace the outline of his body while he lay stretched out on a piece of brown wrapping paper, but whenever he tried to fill in the outline he soon reduced it to a seething black mess in which all body parts were lost. In his very best moments, David was able to draw a person with head, body, arms, and legs, but then it was always a robot, constructed of squares and straight lines and complete with push-buttons for making it work.

This of course does not mean that it is never advisable to offer art materials to children like David, or that aggressive manipulation of these media can never be helpful. It only means that we must not forget how easily children of this kind feel threatened by experiences that in any way tend to upset their equilibrium.

Robert's story (p. 56) provides a good example of various modes of dealing with aggressive and libidinal impulses in a child just a little healthier than David but still suffering from grossly defective ego development. We saw how Robert usually oscillated between chaotically disruptive behavior and rigid ritual. Only on rare occasions could he produce work that was both organized and expressive. These moments, however, were so precious to him that he was ready to endure a great deal of turmoil in order to reach this state of well-integrated functioning.

Such oscillation need not be the only possible response to art even for a severely disturbed child. I have observed three atypical children, for whom relatively untroubled artistic production became possible at a time when daily life was still hedged in with avoidances and rituals. None of these children had developed normal speech at the appropriate age. Instead, each of them had communicated by elliptical, symbolic expressions such as reciting rhymes or stories, singing, playing instruments, or by gestures and ritual acts. During the severely troubled phase of their development, art materials could only be used for very primitive manipulations, such as spilling, smearing, or covering sheets of paper entirely with one color.

• However, when they improved sufficiently to begin talking and had reached the Oedipal phase where art usually blossoms, the form and imagery of their art became almost normal. Two of the children even created unusually beautiful and expressive work. It seemed as if much of the capacity for growth poured into artistic creation, at a time when normal functioning in life was still beyond reach.

It is conceivable that the earlier pathological avoidance of normal speech for which they had substituted various forms of idiosyncratic communication via analogies had prepared the way for subsequent healthy artistic production. For art implies the capacity to perceive analogies and invest them with personal meaning.

Shirley: Six-year-old Shirley, a day-care patient at Jacobi Hospital who had only recently begun to speak intelligibly, kept herself completely isolated from the other children. She looked through them as she looked through everybody and was entirely passive when they attacked her. She first gave indications that she wanted contact when she voluntarily shared her art therapy sessions with two other girls. Although she neither spoke to them nor looked at them directly, she used the subject matter of each of their pictures, producing her own versions. Thus she expressed her realization that she was also a little girl, and her readiness to communicate and compete. Those symbolic attempts preceded direct contact and probably prepared the way for it, for Shirley soon began to play with children and to defend herself when attacked.

Rose: Rose, an atypical child, had been in psychotherapy for three years. When she was six and a half, art therapy sessions were added with the idea of helping her develop new modes of expression and of mastery. In her gradual individuation, imaginative play had served a double purpose: it had enabled her to approach ideas that were particularly disturbing by symbolic elaborations which came close to the original meaning; however, these elaborations also isolated the frightening material, wrapping it in a smokescreen of play, or in stories and poems that were repeated endlessly.

When Rose learned to make things out of clay, purposeful action began to take precedence over play and fantasy. The process of making things slowed down her fantasies and forced her to consider what objects looked like and how they could be constructed. Clay sculptures do not lend themselves to being used as toys. They rather invite further creative action. Thus Rose's ideas became more defined, following one another in a logical progression rather than turning in repetitive circles. She learned that all making entails vigorous action which includes destructive gestures: to make windows in a clay house the solid walls must be pierced and cut. The result, however, is not a wound, but a necessary architectural feature which makes it a better house.

Rose's subject matter centered around those family situations and conflicts that ordinarily occupy much of the art of children of her age. Being an only child who lived alone with her mother, she symbolically fulfilled her wish for family unity and for siblings by creating a large family of clay figures.

Both penis envy and fantasies of castration were symbolically expressed in making trees, bushes, and fountains and cutting them down to the right size. However, none of this play became destructive, or lost its pleasurable quality. The sense of mastery that came to her through such creations extended beyond art therapy sessions. Rose became more independent at home and more willing to make things for herself, even if this meant risking failure.

We see that, even for children who are unusually threatened by their aggressions and who make extraordinary efforts to control them, art need not be limited to defensive production. Sublimation can be reached and can in turn help the child to transcend some of the crippling constrictions he has imposed upon himself.

Margaret (aggressive control): The problem of aggression and control in the young child who is impulsive but not psychotic is exemplified admirably in Margaret's picture of a caged lion. She was a lively, emotionally deprived seven-year-old, insatiable in her demands for attention and for material goods, and much given to bullying her little foster brother, Ralph. Her favorite threat, "I'll break your penis," left no doubt of her strong and open envy, but her general behavior indicated that more primitive oral aggression mingled with her overt phallic preoccupation.

One day Margaret was at a loss for subject matter. I reeled off a great many possible themes, among them a number of animals. When I pronounced the word "lion," Margaret immediately lit upon it. She produced a large, humanoid creature, which did not look particularly fierce except for a smiling but very big black mouth. Then, using the widest paintbrush, she painted strong red bars across the whole paper (Fig. 34). When I regretted that the bars had nearly obliterated her lion, she explained that this was very necessary because "the lion is dangerous and might hurt people."

We note, however, that the lion, which officially signifies

Figure 34. *Margaret:* Caged Lion (18" x 24")

aggression, does not look very fierce. The red-hot bars, on the other hand, don't inspire confidence. We feel that they could melt any minute, join forces with the lion, and destroy us all.

I have chosen this example to present our problem in its simplest form: archaic aggression embodied in the devouring lion, crude external controls represented by the bars. Naturally the simplicity is only relative, all psychic processes being extremely complex and contradictory. We cannot just say that the lion stands for Margaret's aggression, the bars for control. The lion might also stand for the controlling adult seen as aggressor; the bars, for Margaret's need to ward off external controls. Or the lion might be another child (maybe Ralph) whom she wants to put behind bars. All we can be certain of is that Margaret felt both aggression and aggressive control when she painted the picture, and that both positions were internalized and sufficiently invested to produce a powerful image.

Ultimately the subject matter seems to be aggressive control per se—lion, whatever he stands for, being nearly obliterated by it. Margaret's picture draws its vitality from the state of flux which gave rise to it. Lion is obliterated by cage, but the picture began with him. When control reigns supreme, expression is apt to be lost.

Among the borderline psychotic children at Jacobi Hospital who have figured frequently in this book, a trip to the zoo brought forth an array of *empty* cages constructed of clay and sticks from all but Clyde (who was healthier than the others). These children were so fascinated by the cages that the animals did not figure at all. Even though their preoccupation might in part have reflected their actual caged condition at the hospital, it also represented their state of mind. Since their pathology left them little choice between chaotic abandon and paralysis, control meant for them that they became all cage.

Our attempts at interpreting the meaning of Margaret's caged lion made us aware of the protean quality of aggression. There is no way of knowing which one of the two, lion or cage, represents Margaret—whether lion represents Margaret's enemies or her own aggression which is perceived as a hostile force. Any number of interpretations are possible, and all of them probably contain some truth.

Complexities of this kind are characteristic of aggression. It is never easy to distinguish between the genuine enemy and the target of aggression which takes on the guise of enemy in the aggressor's eyes. It remains extremely difficult to distinguish between aggression that has welled up from inside and aggression that is stimulated from outside.

The situation for which intraspecific aggression was originally programmed does not require making these distinctions. The prototype of such aggression is (to stay within Margaret's imagery) lion fighting lion, not lion pursuing lamb. In such a fight aggression is mutually stimulating and there is little point in distinguishing between the one who made the first move and the one who responded to it. It is equally immaterial to question whether such a lion's aggressive mood led to his search for an adversary, or whether the sight of the enemy made him feel aggressive.

Such distinctions, however, are extremely important in the

life of a child. Margaret must learn to distinguish between genuine hostility and benign controlling action that feels to her like an attack because it makes her angry. She must differentiate between angry responses which her aggressive behavior provokes and anger vented against her for reasons that originated in the aggressor. She must learn that mishaps and pain frequently are caused by impersonal forces which are not at all motivated by personal hostility. She must learn to modify her responses in accordance with these distinctions.

In the never-ending struggle for mastery of these conflicts, we encounter Margaret at a time when she has attempted to come to terms with aggression by putting the dangerous force into a cage, which in turn constitutes an act of aggression against it. Later she may attempt to tame the lion. If she is at this time still aggressive, her ways of taming him may remain cruel and castrating.

Michael (identification with the aggressor): Rather than putting them behind bars, some children are inclined to join forces with the ferocious beings they have imagined. Eight-year-old Michael (who has figured already in the passages on pp. 55 f. and 64 ff.) was the terror of the children's ward of Jacobi Hospital. Aggression permeated his life. At the time he made the father dragon and baby dragon (Fig. 35), art constituted an island of relatively controlled and organized functioning in a sea of trouble. Making the sculpture extended over several art sessions. The father dragon was constructed first. He is heavily armed with spikes, blowing fire, and adorned with a golden crown.

The baby dragon is already able to blow fire, but he lacks the adult dragon's spikes. According to Michael, these would grow as he got older. In our reproduction the baby dragon is placed for better visibility upright on the base of a clay baby carriage which Michael built for him. To it belonged an orange hood which has been removed in our picture.

Even though the sculpture looks ferocious, a great deal of Michael's play with his two dragons was tender. Talking in a soft, cooing voice, he would place baby dragon between father's

FIGURE 35. *Michael*: Father Dragon and Baby Dragon (16″ high)

front paws, or put him to bed in the carriage, carefully protecting him with the hood. Whenever play was aggressive, father and son presented a united, fire-spitting front against their enemies. We see that Michael plays two roles—that of the well-defended dragon king and that of the still defenseless baby. It seems as if he tried to attain strength by identification with the aggressive male while preserving his babyhood by placing himself in father dragon's power. By playing the defenseless baby whose spikes have not yet grown, he probably also defends himself against the dragon-father's hostility. We surmise that the sculpture has grown out of a mixture of love and hate, envy and admiration, desire for independence and need for protection. There is no indication that the idea of control of hostility itself, or of good and evil, played any part in the making of the group.

We can say that Michael's pair of dragons embodies his identification with the aggressor. In psychoanalytic terms, this is a mechanism whereby a child defends himself against both his fear of attack and the helpless anger which such attacks arouse in him by identifying with the aggressive qualities of those persons who cause him such feelings. The most common objects of such identifications are the frustrating and controlling aspects of the parents and parent-substitutes. The process is in the main unconscious, and the identifications the child establishes constitute an amalgamation of actual experiences and the feelings and fantasies to which they give rise. What we see in images such as Michael's dragon is not the actual father, but the dragon aspect of him as it is perceived by the immature and exceedingly aggressive little son.

A child like Margaret who masters her own aggressions by aggressively controlling herself, and masters her fear of attack by controlling others, fights a battle on two fronts. She has not much energy or leeway for expressive art.

A child like Michael who attempts to master the same kind of difficulty by identifying with the power that is both admired and feared, turning all aggression against the outside, avoids inner division and preserves his narcissism. He is, at least for the time being, better able to express himself forcefully in art. Even when only the aggressive component of an authority figure has been internalized, identification has a stabilizing effect. Although father is a dragon, Michael conceives not only of his ferocity but also of his protective strength. As he forms mental representations of these qualities, his inner life is enriched.

We see that in the process of maturation both the establishment of aggressive inner controls and identification with the aggressor can be temporarily helpful. Frequently the two mechanisms complement each other. Neither position, however, is tenable for long.

Margaret's aggressively controlling personality caused her much internal suffering and brought her into unending conflict with others. It took years of struggle until Michael established reliable inner controls. At the time of the two dragons, to be alive meant being aggressive. The only time I saw him entirely well behaved and peaceful was during an art session he spent making a sculpture of his own grave, with his mother kneeling in prayer beside his tombstone.

In Michael's case there was reason to suspect some deficiency in his psychic organization which made it difficult for him to withstand the ordinary pressures of the impulses. Although there had been stresses in his life that could have led to disturbance, there was nothing known to us that could account for his severe and intractable pathology.

Michael's story explains how it can come about that highly belligerent children become deeply and even more or less peacefully engrossed in creating pictures or sculptures.

Since the aggressive child sees enemies everywhere and indeed makes himself enemies, he also is in constant need of protection. He is preoccupied with ideas about powerful, well-defended figures, and to create their images is reassuring. For this kind of work the child is therefore ready to muster whatever controls he can. Since art is not tied to any set morality, the creative process is not disturbed by the children's delinquent, often cruel imagery.

Beyond giving child and adult a moment's respite, what good can we expect of this? The process of identification is in itself beneficial. Giving form even to asocial ideas also gives substance to the aggressive child's inner life. It reduces the impact of fluctuating moods and helps to bring formerly elusive fantasies into the realms of the ego. As the child learns to love art, the activity can become a sanctuary wherein feelings and perceptions otherwise drowned in constant hostilities can be experienced for the first time. Even the most belligerent child is capable of tenderness and can enjoy some experiences that are not connected with strife. (Michael, for example, could express tenderness between father and son in his dragons.)

Thus art can prepare the way for change, but it rarely brings it about unaided. When inner difficulties are not too severe, its civilizing influence may suffice to free a child from undue preoccupation with violence and self-defense. When we observe a profound transformation in the art of more deeply troubled children, we usually find that there have been, beyond the artistic experience, other events that helped change their outlook.

THE EGO IDEAL AND IDENTIFICATION WITH THE AGGRESSOR

Frank: Frank's case (pp. 139–43) is a good example of the interdependence of art and life. His early art was devoted to painting ferocious, well-defended heroes such as his Indian Chief (Pl. IX). We observed a change in his Mexican (Pl. X), which expressed a more mature concept of masculine power and dignity. The transformation was brought about by his mother's changed behavior, a more benign environment, and psychotherapy. It was accompanied by an intense struggle for new forms in art. We surmise that this struggle deepened the impact of the experiences that transformed Frank's life. We see how the force which is initially vested in self-defense becomes inner strength that makes the conspicuous display of aggressive power unnecessary. The last painting is both self-representation and ego ideal. The Mexican is older, stronger, and more serene than Frank, but not essentially different from him. Liberated from the eternal vigilance that circumscribes the aggressive child's life, Frank could, with luck, grow up to become the benign, powerful man he depicted.

If all goes well, the image of aggressive authority, which was the child's initial object of identification, is with time transformed into a power that stands for virtue rather than mere force. The child begins to develop more benign ego ideals.

Walter (delinquent ego ideal): There is, however, another possibility. Having identified with the aggressor, the child may extol delinquency rather than virtue. Even though such an ideal does not contradict his previous identification, it nevertheless makes new demands on him: Michael did not have to work on himself to live up to being a dragon or a dragon's son. For the sake of a delinquent ego ideal, a child may force himself to become stronger, braver, or more cruel and ruthless. He may develop skills in handling switchblades, guns, or skeleton keys. He may build up his body, or destroy it by the use of drugs. Thus, even though its values are negative, the ideal exerts moral pressure. The constellation contains the seed of tragedy.

Walter who was discussed in the passage on Pg. 110 painted two monumental figures, each measuring 48″ x 36″ shortly before his discharge from Wiltwyck School. He was then thirteen-and-a-half years old. The pictures were the last of a series of images of ego-ideals that had oscillated between openly delinquent ones; exponents of lawful violence such as boxers or soldiers; and hunters, Indians, and other figures representing an adventurous but not necessarily destructive way of life. The boxer, Fig. 36B, a light skinned Black man, is depicted in profile, silhouetted against a sky painted in subtle shades of blue and white. His gesture and facial expression tell of self-confident belligerence. His hands, however, are safely muffled in boxing gloves and he is confined by beautifully painted ropes. The painting was created in honor of Floyd Patterson,

FIGURE 36A. *Walter:* Young Man with Switchblade (36″ x 48″)

a former Wiltwyck boy who had risen to fame as a light weight champion, and continued to show much interest in Wiltwyck School and its mission.

FIGURE 36B. *Walter:* Boxer (36″ x 48″)

The young man with the switchblade (Fig. 36A) is shown in full face. He stands against a city street at night; his face, that of a light-skinned Negro, looks luminous against a dark building which is lit from the inside; the yellow windows contrasting with the dark walls compete for our attention, creating a feeling of restlessness. The top of the young man's head remains below the skyline so that the street envelops him completely. Both the features and the figure as a whole show a combination of weakness and strength characteristic of the art of many delinquents. The young man's forehead and nose convey an impression of strength, but the mouth and chin are weak. The lower body seems flat and insubstantial compared with the heavy bulk of chest and arms. The hand holding the switchblade is turned toward the youth's own body and the knife is painted with meticulous care. The whole is a moving image of the young delinquent, dominating the scene in narcissistic pride, yet shut in by the city; weak in spite of his overgrown muscles, but dangerous to himself and to others.

Walter was a boy of considerable personal charm with a capacity for warmth. He was a talented and prolific artist and a good student. His major weaknesses were an uncontrollable temper and suspiciousness verging on the paranoid. His saving grace was his willingness to try to reconstruct, after his frequent outbursts of temper, the actual events that had lead to it. On such occasions he was willing to make amends for the damage he had wrought. Although these insights prevented hostilities from mounting indefinitely, Walter could not learn from experience. Similar incidents invariably recurred. However, the institution provided a number of additional safeguards. For example, Walter learned to anticipate his outbursts and to remove himself in time from the person with whom he was in acute conflict. He ran to seek shelter in the orbit of some adult with whom he was at the time on friendly terms. Once he had cooled off he would return in a more amenable frame of mind. Such maneuvers worked well at a residential treatment home where a large staff was on duty. They would have been inadequate on the outside.

Walter was justly afraid of the irrational forces that menaced his precarious balance. Violence both attracted and frightened him. Walter's father was at the time serving a long prison sentence. Walter's paintings of prisoners[3] showed his identification with the father as well as his ambivalence toward him.

3. Described in *Art Therapy in a Children's Community*.

Of the limited number of possible ego ideals Walter could conceive of, only the delinquent one was realistically attainable. It is not easy to become an adventurer in our days, and he lacked the strength and self-discipline for becoming a sportsman. When, after his discharge from Wiltwyck, Walter was picked up on a minor larceny charge, he tried his best to pass as an adult so as to be sentenced to prison. Attaining the status of full-fledged delinquent had come to mean an assertion of manhood.

To fit into the mold, Walter had to repress the softer side of his personality and relinquish his more civilized aspirations. His painting expresses both the power that he gained by identification with his ideal, and his tragedy. In its muted colors, in the tensions between light and dark, and in the expression of the boy's face, we sense a capacity for introspection and for inner suffering that we have not seen in paintings that express belligerence only.

Walter's personality, though twisted, is more mature and more complex that that of the child who only turns his aggression against the outside world, and his chance for recovery is greater. Having internalized some of his conflicts, he conceivably could change his outlook.

Willie (the vicious circle): Willie's three pictures (Figs. 37, 38; Pl. XII) demonstrate the vicious circle that encompasses the life of such children. They were made in the course of a year—the first two in close sequence, the last one several months later.

His first picture (Fig. 37), made when Willie was ten and a half years old, shows a rabbit riding a canoe while a vulture hovers overhead. The rabbit's sadly downturned mouth. shows its hopelessness and helplessness. The vulture's expression is thoroughly evil and his claws are menacingly extended toward the rabbit. Thus both sides of the coin, helpless fear and vicious aggression, are represented. In his second picture (Fig. 38), Willie has turned himself into a magnificent, fire-spitting dragon, ready to defy the whole world, and has thereby alleviated his anxiety.

The last picture (Pl. XII), an avowed self-representation

FIGURE 37. *Willie*: Rabbit Pursued by a Vulture (18″ x 24″)

FIGURE 38. *Willie*: Dragon (18″ x 24″)

(Willie had declared, "I am a devil"), is a devastatingly cruel but recognizable self-portrait. The picture is painted entirely in red and brown, giving a feeling of all-pervading danger and excitement. The devil's red face is disfigured by yellow scars. Fear and suspicion have come back. The devil's small eyes are turned sideways, as if to intercept an oblique attack. If the attack materialized, the devil might again become the rabbit persecuted by the vulture, and if he rallied, there might be once more a full-force counterattack, and so on ad infinitum.

What makes it impossible for a child to move beyond this stage? The cause seems to be in the main a surfeit of aggression, either in the child or in the environment. Michael, being unusually aggressive, projected his hostility onto the world around him, interpreting even those actions that were motivated by genuine concern for his welfare as attacks, and eliciting hostility even from those who could have been his friends. Thus his personality early acquired a paranoid cast. Willie, having been brought up by cruelly punishing adults, had good reason to fear and hate authority. Since he had lived in an atmosphere of gang warfare, experience had taught him to be constantly ready to meet an attack. Whatever constitutional factors might have contributed to Willie's paranoid personality, there is no doubt that the environment greatly favored such a development.

ASPECTS OF AGGRESSION

Herman (male and female): In the section on Artistic Failure and Success we have already encountered art which expressed internalized conflict in Herman's work (p. 51; Pl. I–III). Herman had come to equate good with womanhood, evil with masculinity. This forced upon him a choice between emasculation and damnation.

We surmise that Herman had internalized parental controls that were either actually charged with castrating aggression, or appeared to him in this light, or both. (Herman's mother was indeed a castrating woman, who used religion to dominate the son.)

Herman's art derived its vitality from his continuing struggle against surrender to the irrationally cruel controlling forces which he had internalized. The act of painting itself constituted an assertion of masculine struggle against the inclination to passive compliance. It gave Herman occasion to openly state his conflicts and to sort out the various positions he was able to assume. It strengthened what was healthy in him without forcing upon him a false front of masculine belligerence. However, if we contemplate his last picture of a family of three-legged horses, we are inclined to doubt that two years of milieu therapy have sufficed to undo years of injury.

In this context I must mention that painting was not considered unmanly at Wiltwyck School. Although the art room constituted a sanctuary from violence, and although some of the boys who loved art had homosexual inclinations, Wiltwyck's important artists were not as a rule effeminate. In general I believe that the identification of art with feminity is more often than not induced by adults who have come to look upon it as belonging, along with interior decoration, to the domain of women. Teachers who favor a tame, emasculated style of art help to confirm this view. Most of the boys at Wiltwyck soon found out that it takes more courage to paint a picture than to start a fight, and while they accused each other frequently and mercilessly of homosexuality, they seldom used a child's love of art as evidence of his feminine personality.

Leon (conflict as a major theme of art): Herman's conflicts were centered upon one circumscribed theme. The severe constrictions that narrowed his life could be felt in the muted quality of his work. The power of Leon's art was unbroken. His main theme was conflict, expressed in many different guises.

Leon was the fifth of nine children. The family was matriarchic. Though the father had visited often enough to keep his wife with child, he had been absent frequently and contributed next to nothing to his children's support. The mother had been an alcoholic before Leon's birth. When he was eight years old, she had to submit to a major operation and was confronted with a choice between abstinence or early death. She reformed, became sober and God-fearing, and from then on tried her best to salvage her family from ruin. However, by this time Leon and his siblings had already been thoroughly traumatized. (Among the hardships they suffered was temporary placement for several months in a shelter when Leon was in his second year.)

At the time of the mother's conversion, the family found itself caught in the vicious circle of psychic injury breeding disturbance which closed the door to chances for rehabilitation. Drunk or sober, the mother could not find adequate housing for a fatherless family of nine children, several of whom already had a court record. From time to time most of the children were confined in institutions. The mother's parental duties became centered upon visiting them at these different places, dealing with numerous social agencies, and battling to extract financial aid from the welfare department.

Leon was admitted to Wiltwyck at the age of ten. He scored an IQ of 124. Psychiatric examination found his fantasy life unusually rich but not psychotic, his sense of identity weak. His symptoms included, besides the usual delinquency and learning difficulties, enuresis and a history of soiling that had occurred throughout his childhood when he was angry or overexcited. Leon also suffered from a minor deformity of the hip which caused a slight limp.

There were no incidents of soiling at Wiltwyck but he remained enuretic. There were few delinquent acts. He adjusted well to routines. Even though he was slightly handicapped, he could hold his own in fights and soon rose to leadership. His reign was on the whole benign. He upheld justice according to his lights and defended the weak against the bullies, but he was inclined to be aggressively self-righteous. He did extremely well in all the arts. The remedial-reading teacher was impressed by his lively curiosity and eagerness to learn, and reported progress. Leon also seemed to maintain good relationships with his family.

He returned from home visits in a positive frame of mind and made presents for his mother and siblings in arts and crafts.

In spite of all these initial signs of progress, things were not really going well with him in the long run. During his four years of residency Leon's IQ score went down from 124 to 104. Psychiatric examination at the age of fourteen found him preoccupied with fantasies, his relationships shallow and unstable, his ego weak. He felt himself the victim of a cruel and capricious fate, unable to control his own destiny. After discharge to his mother, Leon did not become delinquent, but he failed at school. He did not continue to practice any of the arts in which he had excelled at Wiltwyck. At sixteen he scored an IQ of 91. He had stayed out of trouble, but was in no way fulfilling his potential.

Leon's art showed the internal turmoil beneath his controlled behavior. The pencil sketch of a battle at sea (Fig. 39) was drawn when he was ten years old. One of innumerable similar pictures, it shows Leon's vivid and circumstantial imagination. The fluidity of his line, his ability to depict people in action,

Figure 39. *Leon:* Sea Battle (18″ x 24″)

and the freedom and verve of the whole testify to his intelligence and creative power. There is nothing bizarre or excessively cruel. The drawing corresponds to the psychologist's evaluation, showing fantasy that remains just within the range of normality.

Among Leon's numerous paintings, there was only one where aggression was directed outward and the enemy was reduced to a simple target of hostility. This was a large painting consisting of two vertically arranged rows of boys' profiles facing each other across an empty space. The profiles on the left were brown, with black hair and eyes, and they were intact. Those of the opposing row had pink skins and yellow hair. Their eyes had been blackened and their cheeks crosshatched with scars.

In the space between, Leon had sketched in charcoal subjects that to him represented positive values: several horse heads, a number of stars, and a cross. He never managed to paint these symbols, and finally discarded the picture.

We see that Leon could permit himself the expression of open hostility when it was directed against the white race. (The picture broke down not when he disfigured the white faces but when he found himself unable to paint the "good" objects.) However, this painting remained an isolated event. Although the same constellation could be discerned in a number of pictures which showed conflicts between white and brown horses, strife was never expressed as crudely or with as much cruelty.

Figure 40 shows a kind of kicking dance between a brown horse and a white one which can be interpreted either as a battle or as love play. (Leon's own comments on it were ambiguous: the horses had kicked each other and were going to kick again, but then again no one would get hurt.) The brown horse seems to be in a position to kick the white horse, while the latter looks as if he had just landed a blow on the brown one. However, the motion of both is so reciprocal and flowing that positions seem at the point of being reversed, and the whole has the elegance of a ballet rather than the ferocity of a real fight.

In Plate XIII, representing a golden palomino rising against

FIGURE 40. *Leon*: Brown Horse and White Horse (18" x 24")

its cowboy-master, there is no indication of racial conflict. The picture is one of Leon's most powerful and most disturbing creations. We see a small cowboy dressed in black and brown raising his arms to ward off the blows of a huge yellow-ocher horse with flowing orange mane and tail. The background, painted in wild brushstrokes of red, brown, and dark blue, underlines the horse's motion. The whole sky seems about to descend together with the horse upon the rider. The ground below is brown. The space between the legs of both horse and man is painted solid red. This color seems a foreign element that is not justified by any demand of form or composition. The picture is not improved by it; on the contrary, the group would stand out better if the sky were seen between the legs of man and horse. Also, the horse's great body would convey an even stronger feeling of being in motion if it were held up by two slim legs rather than being fused massively to the ground. Thus the red seems inconsistent with the rest. We are reminded of a similar inconsistency in Herman's picture of a family of horses

(Pl. III). There each of the horses had only three legs to stand on; the fourth was missing. We felt that his pathology had intruded upon an otherwise well-conceived painting.

Diagnostically, the red is interesting (as were the missing legs in Herman's painting). It points to the origin of excitement in the area of the genital and excremental organs (we recall that Leon's symptoms included soiling and enuresis). The equal treatment given to horse and rider seems to symbolize their community. Would this mean that the rider was unable to master the horse because he was himself infected with the same sexual excitement? (We recall that Leon felt that he was at the mercy of a cruel and capricious fate and incapable of controlling his destiny.)

In both art and psychology it is idle to attempt to ascribe any single meaning to a symbol, for overdetermination is the rule. It would be too narrow if we declared that horse stands for impulses, rider for control; or horse is destiny, rider Leon; or that, on still another plane, the horse may represent the Negro race revolting against its oppressors. It suffices that the picture conveys to us an impression of revolt; of wild natural forces overriding man; of primitive sexual excitement that drives both man and beast—that the imagery is powerful. We cannot doubt that Leon gives expression to very strong feelings.

Leon's behavior was on the whole controlled. As we have said before, he was not given to temper tantrums or to violence. If his painting is an indication of the power of the affects which he felt welling up within himself, how did he manage to attain dependable controls?

We imagine that both his fantasies and his art acted as safety valves. We can also assume that he helped himself by taking on the role of protector of the weak, avenger of injustice, and defender of the Negro race. In these actions, aggression was diverted to socially valuable goals.

However there were no indications that processes were at work that would have neutralized aggression and thereby reduced the pressure of disruptive impulses. Why should it have been so difficult for a child who was bright and creative, who knew right from wrong and could control himself, to neutralize his aggressiveness sufficiently so that he could fulfill his potentials?

One of the reasons may have been that controls were established too late and too suddenly. Leon's mother only made consistent efforts to establish discipline after she had reformed, and at that time Leon was eight years old. Even though he identified with his mother and had adopted her moral values, he only began controlling his delinquent acts and his soiling after placement at Wiltwyck School, when he was ten.

Another difficulty was the actual situation which gave him ample reason for resentment and bitterness. In spite of the mother's efforts the family remained poverty-stricken, unable to rise above its slum existence. Thus, whatever aggressive feelings Leon had accumulated in his early years were compounded by new frustrations. All this seems to have kept him fixed upon his aggressive fantasies.

When Leon was discharged to his mother at age fourteen, returning to the same environment that had contributed to his initial disturbance, he did not revert to delinquency but he also made no further progress. He neither pursued any of the interests he had developed at Wiltwyck, nor did he find new ones. Rather he seems to have kept a tight lid on his feelings, becoming passive and withdrawn. We must remember, however, that we are leaving Leon at a time of transition. Life does not end at sixteen. If Leon failed to make good in public school, it may have been that the system offered little to inspire him. This does not mean that Leon's intelligence and talent need stay permanently submerged in apathy. It remains entirely possible that he will in time find his way into a productive life.

Leon's story shows why art is so often attractive to delinquent children, or to those who are in the process of overcoming delinquency. Children who are laboring under an excess of unneutralized aggression are handicapped in fields where it is necessary to suppress aggressive fantasies or deeds. Art can absorb and contain more raw affect than most other equally complex and civilized endeavors. In art a child such as Leon, still deeply engrossed in his conflicts, can make the transition from fantasy to imagination, exercise his faculty for creating images that contain and express his feelings, and learn what it is like to function successfully. This can reduce the inclination to withdraw and may even help to stave off a break with reality. But no matter how beneficial artistic expression can be, ultimately there also must be other changes that can alter the child's outlook. Otherwise art is reduced to repetition and may finally lose its attraction.

Harry (capsulated aggression): Harry was another child who used both fantasy and art as protection against inner dangers.[4] Like Leon, he was intelligent and talented, but while Leon's improvisations and his flowing style reflected his emotional abandon, Harry's work was soberly planned and carefully executed. While Leon's fantasies remained within the boundaries of normality, Harry's ideas were weird and cruel. Figure 41, painted when Harry was eleven years old, is a good example of both the technique and the spirit of his work. It represents a giant squid which has entered the hull of a sunken ship. There will be a fight between the monster and the diver who has come down looking for treasure. The diver's doom seems sealed. The painting conveys a feeling of suspended menace and monstrousness.

We note that the squid's body as well as each of its eight tentacles is carefully outlined in black, as is the ship's architecture and the diver's body. Harry invariably delineated all of his objects in this manner and then filled the areas with color. This gave his art a decorative character suggestive of stained-glass windows.

The subject matter was inspired by a movie featuring a giant squid and a sunken vessel. We see that Harry has grasped the situation well and represents it clearly. The combination of weird content that implies horrible and violent deeds but stops short of depicting them, and precise, methodical representation was typical of most of Harry's work. It showed even more clearly in his major opus, a series of pictures of instruments of execution.

---

4. Harry's work has been described in the chapter on "Kings, Prisoners and Monsters" in *Art Therapy in a Children's Community.*

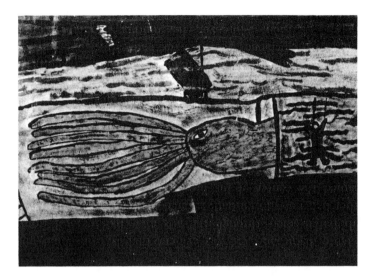

Figure 41. *Harry*: Giant Squid (18″ x 24″)

Each of them clearly showed the mechanism for executing the victim, as well as traces of blood, an open grave, or other signs of recent killings. However, none of the paintings depicted the act.

Harry's paintings of supernatural beings, such as walking skeletons, ghosts, or monsters, were never just conventional stereotypes. His cool, methodical inventiveness in the field of horror was beyond the ordinary. His affinity for the monstrous was apparent also in his paintings of benign imaginary figures. Under his hands, even the Santa Clauses, angels, or fairies produced for festive occasions took on an indefinably sinister cast.

This does not mean, however, that Harry himself was altogether sinister. He was a charming child with a good sense of humor, able to enjoy the many activities the school offered. He was not actually cruel and was, on the whole, well liked by his peers. His behavior during art sessions was exemplary. He worked hard and rarely got into fights. He took pride in his creations and liked to give his pictures away as presents.

It was singular that even at the ages of twelve and thirteen he never considered the content of his work when making a gift of it. He was inclined to give his most gruesome pictures to the nurse, seemingly unaware that these offerings might grate upon the sensibilities of this kindly, middle-aged lady. (The nurse bravely rose to the occasion and not only gracefully accepted his gifts but even hung them on the clinic's walls.) While such unconcern is not unusual in younger children, I was puzzled to find it in a boy of Harry's age and intelligence. Why did Harry, who otherwise covered up his aggressions with painfully polite, even servile behavior, feel no need to assume a false front in art?

Harry had been admitted to Wiltwyck at the age of eleven because of parental neglect and disruptive behavior at school. He had been without supervision after his mother's commitment to a mental hospital when he was nine years old. His mother, a paranoid schizophrenic, had suffered mental breakdowns after the birth of each of her two children, and had been hallucinating for some time before her final hospitalization.

When he was tested at the age of ten and a half, it was found that Harry was suffering from schizophrenic symptoms which included benign auditory hallucinations, anxiety, and paranoid ideas. Overly polite, placating behavior, which occasionally gave way to severe temper tantrums, concealed extreme repressed hostility. However, his intelligence was above average and there were signs of considerable ego strength. In view of these assets Harry was admitted to the school, where he made a good adjustment.

During two years of residence, although the basic illness remained unaltered, he developed more reliable and socially useful defenses. He became obsessional and capable of sustained interest in academic learning. He was able to ward off anxiety and control anger by concentrating on his obsessions or by flights into fantasy, and by combining these two defenses in his art.

Even though his fantasies were woven around the very ideas that threatened him, their power was diminished by the control he exerted as he built them into elaborate stories. Those controls were further strengthened when he transformed his fantasies into pictures. Thus Harry's art did not serve communication and self-expression in the usual sense; rather, it constituted a means of capsulating ideas and impulses that threatened to invade his life. For children who can distinguish adequately between reality and fantasy, art can be a way of giving their imaginative life more substance. For Harry, on the˙ other hand, beset by ideas that threatened to take on reality, it was reassuring to prove their imaginary character by painting pictures about them.

Although his production contained imagery that verged on the psychotic, the consistency and artistic logic he imposed upon his work kept it free from the fragmentation that characterizes florid schizophrenic art. The rigid boundaries that separated each object from the other also kept them whole. The black line itself created harmony that could contain division.

The cold cruelty of his imagery and his lack of guilt about it were signs of profound illness. Within this illness, painting constituted a relatively healthy activity. Harry's expectation of praise from adults for his gruesome pictures was therefore entirely justified. He was indeed doing the best he could to control his pathology.

Toward the end of his residence at Wiltwyck, between thirteen and fourteen years of age, Harry developed new defenses in art. He lost interest in painting pictures and turned to writing stories and drawing cartoons which he assembled into little books. In these stories he rendered harmless some of his worst fears by making them ridiculous. Figure 42, a cartoon of a "protection coat" that can only be assembled by a robot, expresses in a weirdly humorous form his excessive fear of attack and need for total protection. Figure 43, an "all-purpose animal," not only combines in a single body the two archenemies, cat and dog, but incorporates what seem to be a turtle's shell and part of a bird. The cartoon expresses Harry's schizophrenic divisions and splits transformed into a grotesquely comic contraption. The notebook from which these two examples were taken abounds in similar inventions.

We see that Harry's pathology remained the same, but that his ways of controlling it became more sophisticated, less cruel,

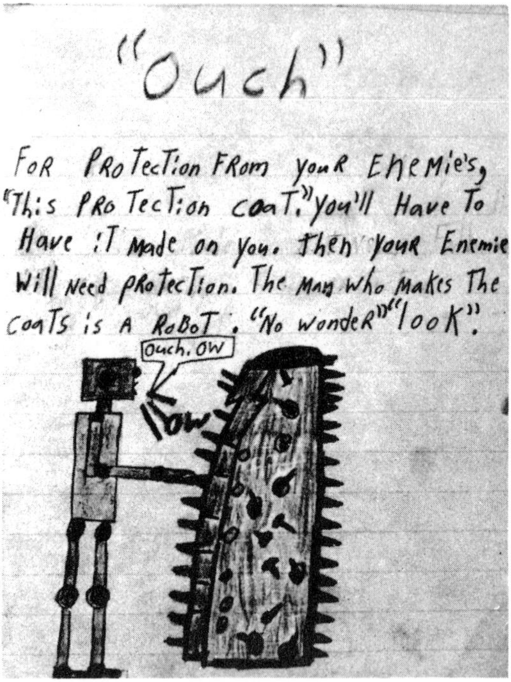

Figure 42. *Harry:* Protection Coat (7" x 8½")

and, conceivably, more effective. His earlier paintings had fulfilled a beneficial function in an entirely amoral manner. His highly organized, beautifully executed paintings had rendered his psychotic ideas harmless simply by capsulating them. In his cartoons he went a step further. He combatted anxiety by finding ridiculous analogies for exceedingly frightening states of mind, reduced his sadistic fantasies to absurdity by inventing improbable and funny contraptions for carrying them out. Thus he attempted to break the power of his psychotic ideas through grotesque humor. Sublimation was no longer limited to exerting his skill in giving his ideas form, but the content of his fantasies was also modified.

We have little information about Harry's artistic development

FIGURE 43. *Harry*: All-Purpose Animal (7" x 8½")

after his discharge from Wiltwyck School. He seems to have continued to be interested in writing but we do not know whether he also continued painting or cartooning as he grew up. His ways of dealing with his psychotic problems in life, however, corresponded to the solutions he had found in art.

Although his pathology persisted, he maintained a precarious hold on reality. With continued help from the agency, his defenses carried him through high school and vocational training, and he finally joined the air force. Thus he managed to fit his pathology into a niche where obedience to regulations, compulsive attention to detail, and obsessive preoccupation with destruction and defense were acceptable, indeed desirable, and where external rules and regulations helped to keep his pathology within safe bounds.

Carl (good and evil): Although both Leon's and Harry's art is centered upon conflict, neither of the two boys conceived of it in moral terms. Harry's art, as we observed, is entirely amoral. Leon's shows conflict internalized to the extent that both contending forces are fully imagined. In his picture of the horse rising against its master, we sense the ego's helplessness as it is overcome by impulsive forces, but even here it seems that Leon feels no personal responsibility for the conflicts he depicts.

In Carl's work [5] there was, from the beginning, evidence of moral conflict. The forces of good and evil were frequently personified in his pictures. When he was twelve and thirteen, their exponents were taken mostly from adventure stories. There were cowboys and Indians, masked assassins and their victims, and similar figures. As Carl approached adolescence the battle was more often expressed in religious terms. Plate XIV, representing the angel of God casting Lucifer down to hell, is a good example of the spirit of tragedy which prevailed in these paintings. Carl produced the picture at the age of fourteen, shortly before his discharge from Wiltwyck School.

He had selected a large black sheet of paper on which he painted the figures in white, the angel's flaming sword being the only spot of color. Although the space is divided evenly between the two figures, there is a strong feeling of motion. The angel's person completely fills his side of the surface, conveying a sense of total command and stability. By contrast, Lucifer's smaller figure is set against empty black space which dramatizes his impending fall. The spectator's eye, which is first attracted by the flaming sword, is led toward Lucifer's person as it is balanced before his disappearance into the pit, his arms spread in what seems to be a gesture both of warding off the blow and attempting to regain balance. It is a moment of suspense which forces upon us an intense awareness of Lucifer's doom. We cannot doubt the angel's superior power, but we are made to feel compassion for the rebel's tragedy. Thus the painting conveys to us the inner division of its creator.

5. Carl and his work have been described in "Kings, Prisoners and Monsters," *Art Therapy in a Children's Community.*

Carl was talented in both music and art, and enjoyed exercising his faculties. His aspirations for a dignified life, removed from violence and delinquency and given to cultural pursuits, were genuine. Yet he felt himself menaced both from within and from the outside. He was given to rare but dangerous outbursts of violence, and he felt that, being Negro and coming from a delinquent background, he was doomed to failure. Unlike Larry, Carl never assumed a false front of white middle-class morality. Instead, he was earnestly searching for ideals within his own race and culture. He did not, like Leon, project all of his troubles outward, or blame society for all that had gone wrong with him. Although he was not always able to abide by the commands of his conscience, his superego was neither as cruel nor as unreliable as Larry's. Nevertheless, Carl had to pay dearly for his controls and his maturity.

Although we must not take his painting of Lucifer as an image of his total personality, the tragedy it depicts and the depressed mood which emanates from its darkness were decisive elements of Carl's character. His severe superego aggressively compelled the ego to exert controls. Since he had remained both impulsive and aggressive, the ego exhausted itself in keeping aggression within bounds, and the struggle reduced his vitality. Thus the tenor of Carl's art remained muted, his joy of life subdued.

I had a glimpse of the potential strength of Carl's submerged vitality when, for reasons unknown to me, his depression lifted and he produced a picture expressive of a healthy elation. The speedboat (Pl. XV) was painted when he was thirteen years old. The red boat is coming directly toward us. Behind it the sun rises, partly hidden by clouds through which its rays are bursting forth. The painting is unlike anything Carl had done before or was to do again as long as I knew him.

Even when controls are established slowly and when substitute gratifications are available, the price of becoming civilized, so it seems, is often a latent depression. We cannot tell whether the promise of spiritual liberation which Carl's speedboat painting contained would ever be fulfilled, or whether, having become a conscientious member of society, Carl would have to pay for it with the permanent dampening of his vitality.

AMBIVALENCE

Throughout this chapter I have presented work which exemplified various forms that aggression may take on in childhood. The forces that were active during the making of these works were not limited to raw aggression. Otherwise there would have been little else but torn paper, spilled paint, or broken heads. Evidently the practicing art therapist encounters a good deal of such unmitigated destructiveness, but its management is a disciplinary problem rather than one that concerns art therapy in particular. In handling it, the therapist must try to establish the minimum of order and serenity necessary for creative work and at the same time avoid excessively constricting discipline that would stifle expression. In any instance where work is successfully completed we can surmise, no matter how aggressive its content may be, that neutralized energy was available for creating form. Furthermore, we frequently find that the meaning of such art is not as hostile as it seems; it constitutes rather a mixture of positive and negative feelings.

Ambivalence and Identification with the Aggressor

Content was most explicitly hostile in those examples that embodied the child's identification with the aggressor. We noted, however, that this identification was born of mixed feelings of anger, anxiety, and admiration rather than of hostility alone. Since every child is inclined to perceive as aggressor anyone who interferes with his pleasures and desires, the aggressor is, more often than not, a parent or parent-substitute whom he also loves and admires. The object of identification is in this case invested with mixed feelings from the outset. When identification is established, the internalized image of the aggressor becomes part of the child's valuable arsenal of defenses and is invested with *narcissistic love*. If the authority figures whom the child internalizes are intrinsically benign, identification has a beneficial effect. It facilitates the child's reconciliation with those who exert control in real life, and it paves the way for the establishment of a benign superego and viable ego ideals. In such a situation ambivalence, though not eliminated entirely, does not exceed the child's tolerance and decreases in the course of maturation.

Identification, however, may occur not only when the aggressor is in reality benign but also when he is objectively deserving of the child's hostility. Indeed, since identification effectively binds anxiety, the very fear which such an individual inspires increases the child's need for identification. This sinister mechanism whereby a malignant external force is internalized and narcissistically invested can be observed frequently in children who grow up in the care of sadistic adults, or who for some reason or other experience the punitive aspects of their environment more keenly than the benign and protective one.

The saga of "the Cobra" (p. 133) is a good example. The little boys who feared and admired their evil counselor protected themselves against their anxiety by identifying with him and became thereby still more helplessly enthralled by his malign charms. I encountered the same phenomenon in the late 'thirties, when I was working with children who were refugees from Nazi Germany. Their representations of Hitler left no doubt that he had become for them both the incarnation of evil and a symbol of power and success which they secretly admired and with whom they identified.

It is evident that such identifications entail enormous danger. The child who internalizes a cruelly hostile power and invests it with narcissistic love while he is at the same time suffering from this power's sadistic attacks is divided within himself. The intense ambivalence generated by his situation exerts a distorting influence not only during the phase of primitive identification but beyond it into his subsequent ego and superego development.

We have encountered a variety of such distortions in this chapter.

Willie remained permanently fixed upon identification with the aggressor, developing a paranoid image of the world. Michael's excessive inner aggressions made it impossible for him to perceive the benign aspects of his environment, and he too remained largely fixed upon identification with the aggressor. Insofar as he developed inner controls, these became murderously self-destructive.

Larry's identification with a cruel authority forced his personality into a sado-masochistic mold. His later identification with benign personalities did not suffice to undo this fatal linkage.

Frank, whose identifications were also charged with more than ordinary ambivalence, established a viable balance between love and hate when his relationship to his parents improved, partly because the mother's behavior toward him changed for the better.

We noted that these children, whose work expressed identification with the aggressor, often produced powerful art which, however, lacked depth and variety. Their central theme remained the reiteration of threats and demonstrations of preparedness. Positive feelings were expressed mainly in the loving execution of their work. This corresponded to their narcissistic investment of the image of the aggressor.

In those children who did not remain fixed upon this initial primitive mechanism, we could observe the continuing influence of excessive ambivalence: Larry endeavored in his later work to present only that which he thought was acceptable by conventional moral standards. However, his repressed aggression reduced his efforts to an unconvincing display of good intentions. We have encountered examples of the same mechanism in Helen's art (p. 124) and in Ann's work (p. 130). These girls' professed intentions carried no conviction because their repressed hostility interfered with their artistic production.

When both the libidinal and the aggressive components of

the personality are expressed, art attains greater depth. We have seen two examples of paintings that contained ambivalent feelings in all their complexity—Walter's young gangster (Fig. 36, p. 173) and Carl's Lucifer (Pl. XIV, p. 191). Each of these paintings conveyed the child's divided feelings about his own person. Walter's picture shows his foreboding of a fate that seems both alluring and inescapable. The sense of doom in Carl's work concerns an inner change whereby not only the evil in him but also much of his vitality and healthy rebellion may be cast into oblivion.

Both Carl and Walter had grown beyond simple identification with the aggressor. They had established ego ideals and (at least rudimentary) superegos. Walter's values had remained tied to his early delinquency, while Carl had adopted middle-class morality. There was evidence that both these children had in the course of their lives internalized authority figures who, although not entirely evil, had been more punitive than benign, and that they had strong ambivalent feelings toward them. Just how their character formation evolved we cannot tell. We know that Carl emerged at fourteen burdened with considerable masochism and a propensity to depression, while Walter remained volatile, given to a paranoid interpretation of reality.

Gordon (ambivalent relationships): The art of the children whom we have described so far expressed ambivalence toward themselves and toward the internalized images that were part of them. Although we can surmise that their relationships to others were also ambivalent, their art tells us nothing about this.

We have already encountered one child whose work expressed intense ambivalence not only toward himself but also toward the most important person in his life. In the passage describing Gordon's painting of Moby Dick (Pl. VI, p. 84), we had clear evidence of the painter's ambivalent feelings toward his mother, for the picture was produced while he and another boy exchanged mutual insults about their mothers' love lives. We recognized the painting as a composite symbol both of Gordon's own sexuality and of the sexual aspect of his mother's person, perceived as at once dangerous and attractive.

In *Art Therapy in a Children's Community,* I described Gordon's ambivalent relationship toward his mother in all its tragic complexity. Devoted to her son but withdrawn and cold, intelligent but emotionally disturbed, attractive but elusive, she dominated the boy's life. The mixture of attraction and revulsion, desire and fear, love and hate which he felt for her filled him so completely that there was little room for other relationships.

His sinister cast of mind made Gordon the undisputed master of evil expressions at Wiltwyck (Moby Dick's sneer is a good example). His skill in producing these expressions was so much greater than mine that I used to call on him whenever a child needed help in drawing a particularly sinister countenance. It must be noted, however, that even if Gordon's dark feelings had their origin in his relationship to his mother, he confined the representation of absolute evil to figures that ordinarily symbolize devouring aggression, such as whales, lions, wolves, or bears. Although his women looked dangerous, they never appeared to be entirely malign.

Typical for the mixture of attractive and dangerous qualities Gordon gave to his women was an Egyptian princess (Fig. 44), painted when he was twelve years old. The princess is holding a knife in her hand (Gordon explained that she was prepared to kill her lover). Her strong shoulders and arms are distinctly masculine, and the shape of her red loincloth resembles that of a penis.

A detail (Fig. 45) shows a surprisingly human face unlike anything Gordon could have found in conventional stereotyped representations of vampirelike females. The face is his own creation. Evidently the fantasy which is expressed in the paintings is woven around a genuine relationship. This is unusual. Boys who are inclined to paint pictures of murderous but alluring women are rarely able to make them look attractive no matter how hard they try. (We are all familiar with the indefinably monstrous cast of many supposedly seductive women in the art of pre-adolescents and adolescents who harbor strong, repressed hostility against their mothers.)

Gordon really loved his mother. It was the strength of his

FIGURE 44. *Gordon*:
Egyptian Princess (24" x 36")

FIGURE 45. *Gordon*:
Egyptian Princess, detail

love that made him able to express rather than to betray his ambivalence. The genuine warmth which was at the core of his relationship, in spite of all frustration and bitterness, showed even in those of Gordon's paintings that, like Moby Dick, expressed his darkest feelings about his mother's person and sexuality. None of them was commonplace or entirely devoid of poetry.

I recall only one product that expressed total hostility to women. He had spent the whole art session unable to settle down to work, and had begun a number of paintings and torn each of them up. Finally in a towering rage he produced Figure 46. Handing it to me with murder in his eyes, he pronounced: "This is Cyclops." It was evident that he knew as well as I that he had transformed a drawing started as a picture of Cyclops into a gigantic vulva.

Coming from a Wiltwyck boy, such a gesture would in itself be neither very unusual nor particularly instructive, for references to sexual organs are so commonly used for insult that they lose their meaning. Most such offerings, however, are conventionally stylized. Gordon's painting is more realistic. It shows that he fully imagined this part of the female anatomy while painting it. Remembering the story of the blinding of the Cyclops Polyphemus by Odysseus, we can assume that the idea of viciously destructive rape is included in the painting. Such feelings were evidently connected with his idea of womanhood. Usually, however, they remained in abeyance. The love he bore for his mother counteracted his hostility. Most of his paintings therefore conveyed a feeling of tension, such as we see in Moby Dick (Pl. VI) or in his princess (Fig. 44), rather than plain horror.

This balance, however, could not endure. Inner divisions that can be borne in childhood and pre-adolescence become untenable with the increased pressures of adolescence. Unless the hostile component of Gordon's relationship to his mother could be reduced, it was bound to gain ascendancy as he grew older. Since the sexual aspect of the relationship was aggressively cruel, Gordon's developing masculinity was in danger of being cast in this

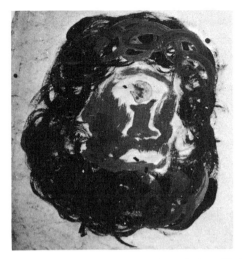

Figure 46. *Gordon*: Cyclops (18″ x 18″)

Figure 47. *Gordon*: Mexican Rider (24″ x 36″)

same mold. A Mexican Rider (Fig. 47), one of Gordon's last paintings at the school, produced when he was fourteen, shows manhood identified with florid narcissistic cruelty.

It is a terrible painting both from the artistic point of view and as an indication of the trend of Gordon's psychosexual development. The composition is weak, the style fragmented and overly ornate. The man's expression is cruel. The whip in his hand, symbol of masculine power, dangles weakly near the edge of the page.

When Gordon painted Figure 47 he was marking time. At fourteen, he had outgrown Wiltwyck School, which was equipped only to serve children between the ages of eight and twelve. But there was no place for him at home or in any other institution. In his bitterness and boredom Gordon was in no condition to work on himself or on his art. Thus the worst trends in his divided personality gained ascendancy, while the positive elements were at least for the time being submerged.

Ambivalence and Form

Gordon's last picture not only idealizes an unsympathetic person (which is his artistic right), but, as we said before, it is also a bad painting. Particularly irritating is the fussy ornamentation which destroys the picture's unity, accentuating the inept organization of the whole and the weakness of the central figure. It seems as if hostility had infiltrated the creative process, destroying the picture in the guise of loving attention to detail.

Such invasions of unsublimated aggression can take many forms. A picture may be worked to death by oversolicitude; hesitation and doubt may kill the freshness of the artist's perceptions; aggression may show in a lack of sensitivity to the medium, so that the artist seems driven to cruelly force it beyond its limitations or seems unable to perceive its potentialities. These and similiar manifestations have in common that the mixture of libido and aggression blinds the artist so that he cannot tell when he is improving his work and when he is damaging it.

The art therapist who works with children is fortunate in not having to contend with this particular phenomenon very often. He is more apt to see an oscillation of doing and undoing than to encounter work that expresses both tendencies at once. The latter is seldom possible before adolescence, and we note that Gordon was fourteen when he painted Figure 47.

Ambivalent Feelings toward the Product

There is, however, another kind of ambivalence of which children become victims just as easily as adults. It is, in a sense, the reverse of the ambivalent love that makes the artist blind to the destruction which he wreaks when trying to improve his work. I mean blindness to the merits of one's own work, and the inclination to deride or destroy it. This occurs among both children and adults, artists and amateurs, and what is most surprising, these negative feelings are just as apt to arise when the artist enjoys what he is doing as when he finds himself in difficulties. A child is engrossed, seemingly content, knowing just what to do next. The expression on his face tells of his pleasure in his work, which is reaching completion. Suddenly, without warning, he discards it or attacks it savagely. Or, in a less extreme case, all goes well until the work is finished, but when the child looks at it later, he declares that it is no good. His pleasure is gone, and he destroys his work or abandons it.

What has happened? Sublimation was evidently undisturbed, for there is nothing wrong with the work itself. The trouble lies elsewhere, in the realm of self-esteem. Sometimes the difficulty is caused by conflicting standards. The child has produced according to the dictates of his creative urge and finds himself confronted with work that does not measure up to his ideas of what art should be like. However, unless these standards are actively upheld by parents or other important persons in the child's life, children soon learn to accept the art therapist's judgment, and this particular difficulty is overcome.

Children who have had to swallow much derision and harsh

criticism sometimes protect themselves by turning passivity into activity. Taking the function of the hostile authority upon themselves, they win a Pyrrhic victory over those who would criticize them. To children who feel this way, praise alone is often aggravating rather than encouraging. The therapist must be ready to go to considerable trouble in mending broken sculpture or torn pictures, and must be willing to fight with the child over work she wants to rescue from his self-destructive attacks. Such actions permit him to discharge some of his pent-up bitterness and anger and prove to him at the same time that the art therapist is not merely being polite or "therapeutic" when she praises his work.

It is often important to allow such a bitter child to criticize the art therapist's work severely, or to handle some work she has done for him without respect. We have encountered one such example in Christopher's story (pp. 73 ff.). He habitually destroyed the clay models that I made in order to inform him about the shapes of wild animals. The same thing can happen if one makes a drawing to show a child various ways of solving a pictorial problem that has given him difficulty.

In this situation, as in others, the therapist offers the child some of her ego strength. Permitting hostile acts against the work of her hands, she proves that her self-esteem can survive such attacks, and that her willingness to help is not diminished by them. Of course the therapist must not allow a situation to arise where the child can obtain sadistic gratification by hurting her feelings. The message that should be conveyed is neither of a saintly willingness to suffer all injuries nor of total invulnerability, but of inner security that is not easily shaken, for this is the quality we hope the child will acquire.

It is very difficult to help a child who cannot accept his own work because of unconscious feelings of guilt. When an irrational and cruel superego punishes him for all pleasures, even those which came about through sublimation, art therapy alone cannot bring about a change. At best the therapist can hope to diminish the hostile superego's powers by offering rationally constructive criticism as an alternative to the superego's destructive attacks.

Such measures, however, can rarely effect the structural changes that would be necessary for establishing a relationship between ego and superego that would permit the child to fully enjoy the fruits of his creative efforts.

LIMITATIONS OF ART THERAPY

In several cases we followed a child's development until it reached an impasse where his existing mechanisms for dealing with aggression had become grossly inadequate and no new ways of reducing or transforming it could be found. When this happened, the child's art, which previously had served him well as a means of expressing and relieving psychic pressures, no longer fulfilled this function. The child either lost interest or his work became defensive rather than expressive.

No child is likely to maintain a high level of artistic production when psychic development has become stagnant. Art is compatible with a great deal of disturbance. As long as there is movement, either for better or for worse, art can contain and express much that is terrible or terrifying, but it cannot prevail against a protracted state of emotional deadlock.

Billy: Sometimes we see a child fighting a last-ditch battle against some impending disaster in art, probably because the medium permits *symbolic* action at a point where there is no longer any possibility of change in real life. I recall two such instances: Billy (see p. 57), one of a group of children at Jacobi Hospital who have frequently figured in this book, had until the age of six maintained a tenuous hold on reality. When his mother became pregnant once again, this seemed to precipitate a floridly psychotic episode. At this time, when the rest of the hospital staff reported ominously inappropriate behavior, grimacing, and other signs of his worsening condition, Billy was doing unusually well in art.

While he was ordinarily given to sterile, stereotyped work, he had suddenly begun to create a series of clay dogs. Starting with a tiny one, he proceeded to make a somewhat larger dog during each subsequent art session. He was pleasurably excited at seeing these animals grow under his hands, and painted each of them a different color, maintaining controlled and purposeful behavior throughout. It seemed clear that Billy was imagining the growth of the new baby and experiencing relief through actively reproducing a process which was, in real life, beyond his control.

This constructive mood lasted until the baby's birth. Then Billy's behavior changed. In the session following the event he began to destroy any protruding part of his clay objects. His face set in a fixed grin, he broke the tail of each of his dogs, the handle of each pot, the ears and noses of all clay faces. In short, anything remotely resembling a phallus was removed.

From this time on, his behavior in the art room was just as psychotic as on the ward. He endlessly made and unmade clay objects that became increasingly unrecognizable and disorganized. It seemed as if Billy's clay dogs had been a last attempt at mastering an unbearable event by turning a passive experience into an active one. When the baby which was to displace him in his mother's affection had been born, symbolic action no longer sufficed to protect him from the full impact of the blow, and so his art became as disorganized as his life.

Billy's sad story shows the strength of his psychosis rather than the weakness of art as therapy. The same kind of symbolic expression which only gave a moment's respite to Billy could have effectively helped a healthier child to come to terms with an occurrence which most children survive without psychotic breakdown.

Barry: My next story is of a child's attempt to restore a lost object through art in response to a situation that would have been devastating even to the healthiest child. Barry had been placed at Wiltwyck School because he ran away, and while away from home maintained himself by picking pockets. While he was at the school his mother slowly but inexorably disengaged herself from whatever emotional ties to him she had previously maintained. Barry was aware of this and did his best to make her take notice of his claims on her. The mother herself told his social worker of one of Barry's most ingenious devices. Before going back to the school after a home visit, he put his life-sized teddy bear into his bed, covering him up neatly as if he were a sleeping child. The mother said that it gave her a jolt each time she passed the bed, "it looked so much like Barry."

In spite of Barry's symbolic actions and the social worker's efforts, the mother proceeded to make for herself a life in which there was no place for her delinquent son. After a visit with her and a new stepfather, during which the mother had openly declared that she had no intention of ever taking him back, Barry returned to the school utterly crushed.

During his art session he told me about his mother's decision. Then he asked for a very large, strong sheet of paper. On a 24" x 36" cardboard he painted a huge bouquet of red roses against a pink background, working harder and more purposefully than I had seen him work before or was ever to see him work again. The picture seemed to be a last attempt at restitution, symbolizing mother, family life, all the good things he had lost. He kept it in his portfolio until his discharge to another institution. Then he left it with me.

I promptly lost this unusual and valuable demonstration piece by leaving it on a train. It seemed that I had to get rid of a picture that not only embodied tragedy but evoked my guilt. I knew only too well that I was pleased to take home what was evidence of an interesting psychic phenomenon but that I would have been just as unready as Barry's mother to give a home to this very difficult and rather sinister little boy.

My last two examples bear a certain resemblance to the "creative spells" of adult psychotics as analyzed by Ernst Kris.[6] They are unlike them inasmuch as neither of the two children had tried actually to negate reality by creating a new world through art. The ultimate fate of the two kinds of attempts at coming to terms with some unbearable aspects of reality is similar: they were eventually abandoned. Art, it seems, needs to be

6. *Psychoanalytic Explorations in Art.*

fed by living experience. When a child is left stranded because his psychic equipment is too inadequate or because the circumstances of his family life are too hopeless, or for other reasons beyond his control, his art eventually loses its vitality and meaning.

AGGRESSION CHANNELED, REDUCED, AND TRANSFORMED

The examples presented in this chapter have amply demonstrated the power of art to relieve pressures or to contain what is unbearable. We also have witnessed partial transformation of raw aggression into constructive energy as we saw the technical skill, the enthusiasm, and respect for art materials which many of the children developed while producing work that was loaded with aggression. We have seen art therapy contributing to temporary alleviation or partial remission of pathology.

We would like to know of examples where art therapy played a decisive role in the substantial reduction of aggression and in enduring positive changes in the child's personality.

One impressive example of such a development has been Christopher. In him we saw the gradual transition from preoccupation with self-defense to inner security and a broadening of his personality and his artistic powers.

The story testified to the necessity of teamwork. Without the sustained efforts of teachers and principal and without the help of psychotherapy, Christopher's art would probably have never gone beyond the reiteration of aggressive self-assertion. His talent alone could not have given him the self-confidence he needed; nor could the discipline of creative work have instilled in him the self-discipline he lacked. But when education and psychotherapy brought about changes, art became an organizing force that helped to make each of his gains more gratifying and more secure.

Christopher's relationship to his foster family, for instance, had at the time of his admission to the Guild School reached an impasse where exasperation and despair caused all parties to show their very worst sides to one another. His destructiveness and boasting called forth punishments and derision, which in turn made him more frantically belligerent and suspicious. Consequently, the first clay sculptures he brought home were thrown away as "junk." As his behavior improved, the mother's affection for her foster son was rekindled and she was able to understand how much his sculptures meant to him. His rhinoceros was therefore given a permanent place in the garden. By the time of his discharge from the Guild School, his blue heron, adorning the front lawn, was a source of pride to the whole family. The foster mother declared that Christopher had magic in his hands and hoped that he would have the opportunity to develop his talent further.

Oscar: The transition from belligerence born of anger and fear to inner strength signifying security sometimes occurs imperceptibly. We are surprised when a child's art proves to us that without our knowledge the step has been taken.

Oscar was a somewhat fearful boy who admired his stronger schoolmates and made great efforts to emulate them. He much admired the work of Hal, an excellent artist who was given to painting fear-inspiring creatures. When Hal produced a green man-monster whose arms were raised above its head in a threatening gesture, Oscar was greatly impressed. Thereupon Hal gave him the picture as a present. Weeks later, Oscar, at a loss for subject matter, rummaged through his portfolio and came upon Hal's picture. He declared that he would copy it. Tacking the picture up on the wall, he installed himself on a table before it and went to work.

Since Oscar seemed perfectly content with what he was doing, I paid him no further attention. At the end of the session I went to look at his "copy" and found to my surprise that he had imitated only the human outlines of the monster and had made it into a light-skinned Negro champion standing beside a table that held a trophy, his hands raised in greeting. Thus the monster had turned into a man; lawless aggression had become sportsmanlike competition; threat was turned into triumphant greeting.

All this had occurred without my intervention and without conscious decisions on Oscar's part. He had not criticized Hal's picture or *decided* to change it; it had changed because Oscar himself was at this time changing. He was ready for discharge. His former truculence had given way to serene dignity. Though he had once been a green monster like Hal, he had become a man, and therefore he no longer had any use for monsters in his art.

Martin: We conclude this chapter with another case history in which milieu therapy, psychotherapy, and art therapy complemented one another to bring about profound beneficial change. Martin has figured in this book already on two occasions: I told of an incident in his treatment exemplifying the pitfalls of transference and counter-transference (p. 41), and later I described his development from dependency to independence (p. 112).[7]

Martin was admitted to Wiltwyck School at the age of ten and a half upon his mother's petition. He was an only child. The family had been living for the past two years in a one-room apartment. The mother was both the main breadwinner and disciplinarian in the family, while the father, a passive man who worked only intermittently, did not concern himself much with his son's upbringing. Martin, a habitual truant from school, had been involved in a number of minor delinquent escapades. At home the relationship between him and his mother had gradually deteriorated into an endlessly repeated sequence: provocative behavior on his part, followed by cruel beatings administered by her, ending in short-lived reconciliations that were soon followed by new provocations. Feeling unable to go on like this, the mother had sought placement in an institution for her child.

Martin's behavior on my first encounter with him was typical. He eagerly entered the art room and quickly became engrossed in painting a picture representing a small tropical island surrounded by a dark green sea. When he had finished it, he collected a number of machinist's aprons belonging in the art room and hung them around his neck. So attired he ran to the middle

7. Martin's case has been described from a different point of view in *Art Therapy in a Children's Community.*

of the school's grassy yard and began a whirling dance with the aprons swinging dramatically around him. Finally he let go of each apron separately, scattering them widely, and ran off. He could not be induced to collect the aprons at this time, but before the day was over he had voluntarily returned them and apologized for his behavior—mainly, it seemed, to make sure that he would be allowed to come back.

Though his first painting gave no indication of the extent of his talent, its subject matter told of Martin's isolation and his preoccupation with faraway places. His dance showed both his exhibitionism and a keen sense for theatrical effects. The final conciliatory gesture showed that Martin was ready to placate the people whom he provoked and that he wished to maintain relationships in spite of his antagonistic behavior. From then on, he spent a great deal of time in the studio and proved to be one of Wiltwyck's most original and talented artists. He was attracted to all the arts, also taking part eagerly in drama and music sessions.

Martin soon became one of Wiltwyck's most troublesome children, not because of extreme behavior, but because of the exhibitionism which made him prefer punishment to anonymity. He was entirely recalcitrant toward male counselors, and alternatingly provocative and placating toward women.

In the arts, where his needs could be channeled into performance, he was difficult but not insufferable. He could be induced to work hard on learning a part for a play, practicing a song, or completing a picture, but in everyday matters he was unable to conform and endlessly provocative. Consequently, among both staff and children, those who enjoyed the arts could, with some difficulty, get along with Martin; the others found him unbearable. Thus Martin maintained himself at Wiltwyck School chiefly by virtue of his artistic talent. He haunted the art and music rooms and did his best to get parts in all of the school's plays.

In the beginning, Martin's art expressed much anger, bitterness, and sexual excitement. For example, his first Christmas at

Wiltwyck gave rise to a caricature of Santa Claus mercilessly whipping his reindeer who were careening madly downward, seemingly headed into a seething, fiery mess (Pl. XVI). The picture had begun tamely enough with Martin drawing Santa Claus's sleigh. Then he had difficulties drawing the reindeer and commanded me to draw them for him. When I refused and instead offered my help, telling him that he was a good enough artist to draw his own reindeer, he angrily exclaimed: "I will show you that I cannot draw." Then with lightning speed he produced his bitter denunciation of Santa Claus and all he stands for.

Holidays are hard on institutionalized children, and many of them feel betrayed, bitter, and rebellious in the face of conventional Christmas cheer. Usually these sentiments emerge in difficult behavior, while art becomes particularly dull and conventional at holiday time. Martin is the only child I know who had the talent and courage to produce a picture that ridiculed Christmas and yet remained an excellent work of art.

Martin's brush drawings of burlesque dancers also showed his capacity for retaining control over brush and paint even while in the throes of intense emotion. When he produced Figure 48, he was singing obscene songs and jumping up and down in nearly uncontrollable excitement. Nevertheless the picture is evocative rather than pornographic. The wavy lines of the background and the pointed shapes denoting the footlights convey a feeling of sexual excitement. The dancer's left arm is decidedly phallic. The two merging faces can be seen both as expressing motion and as indication of the dancer's ambiguous character. On the whole, the picture tells of sexual overstimulation, of sexual confusion, and of women conceived as obscenely seductive. None of this is surprising in a boy who had shared his parents' bedroom for years, whose mother dominated the marriage and maintained a sado-masochistic relationship to her son.

These emotions, however, were only one side of Martin's feelings toward his mother. He also idealized her and produced many pictures where she appeared as an exalted figure, her high po-

FIGURE 48. *Martin*: Burlesque Dancer (18″ x 24″)

sition usually somehow connected with her Ethiopian ancestry or the Coptic religion. Although both of Martin's parents were born in the United States, they continued to cherish the cultural and religious traditions of their forefathers. The mother had instilled this reverence in her son and had thereby given him a sense of pride in his race and color which was, in the early 'fifties, still unusual among blacks.

However, when he attempted pictures with positive content, he encountered greater difficulties than when he produced caricatures. During Easter, for example, Martin conceived of a large painting in the manner of an ancient stained-glass window in which the center was to be occupied by a black madonna with child. His first attempt ended with his obliterating the two figures with black paint. When I rescued the picture by pasting a fresh piece of brown paper over the mess, he succeeded the second time in producing a beautiful and tender painting.

Although such victories were possible even during the time of his acute disturbance, it was evident that Martin could not be rehabilitated solely through the arts and that removal from his mother had not substantially altered his feelings toward her. She remained the center of his life, and he transferred the pattern of his relationship to her onto all other women he liked. He continued to act out her fantasies and fight her battles: she had, besides conveying to him a commendable pride in his family's traditions, also instilled in him her own arrogant disdain and antagonism toward the ordinary American Negro. The glory of Ethiopia she had, on the other hand, exalted beyond the fact. Martin's Quixotic attempts at representing his glory both in his art and in his behavior at Wiltwyck had earned him much hostility and derision. Moreover, his mother kept the sado-masochistic pattern of their relationship alive with frequent letters abounding in recriminations and admonitions and devoid of tenderness.

For these reasons, psychotherapy was initiated six months after Martin's admission to the school. The therapist, a widely traveled, middle-aged woman, soon established a good working relationship with Martin. She did not encourage communications via drawing or play with this eleven-year-old, particularly because art therapy was also available. She found that he could sustain a more adult kind of verbal therapy.

One of the first therapeutic gains was Martin's realization that his bragging and exhibitionistic behavior actually prevented his schoolmates from admiring his painting and that greater modesty and a willingness to help them in their work would bring him the recognition he so ardently desired. Indeed, when he became helpful rather than critical, emulating me as "assistant art teacher," the other children began to appreciate his skill. He found disciples among the more gifted younger children, and his aggressive exhibitionism became transformed into constructive ambition. Somehow he succeeded in unraveling fact from fantasy about Ethiopia, and here also his pride became less aggressive.

The therapist succeeded in communicating to the child-care staff her understanding of the compulsive nature of Martin's provocative behavior, and this brought about a concerted effort to avoid feeding into his pathology by punishing him harshly. This strategy succeeded in diminishing his sado-masochistic behavior. Making everyday life easier, these gains helped prepare the way for more profound therapy.

When Martin was twelve, a dramatic session marked a turning point. I learned of it at first indirectly when one spring morning I found Martin waiting at the art room door with a gleam in his eye. He declared that he had a very important picture in mind which he had to begin right away: it was to be an apple, painted so that one could see all the little lines of different reds and yellows on it. It was to be the very best apple ever painted at the school. He installed himself at a table and, on an 18″ x 24″ paper, he began painting a life-sized apple. The picture grew into a close-up of an apple tree—leaves, branches, and apples forming an intricate pattern. In the middle there was a bird's nest, with a mother bird feeding her baby.

Since his work seemed extremely pressing and important to Martin, I arranged for him to be excused from school and allowed to stay in the studio. He stayed all day. With time out for meals, he worked nearly seven hours, an enormous feat of endurance for a twelve-year-old. Next morning he returned to his picture to view it from a distance. He discovered that the strong blue which he had used for the sky between the leaves did not contrast sufficiently with the brown-and-red mother robin. Therefore he changed the sky around her to a lighter blue. The completed painting looked like magnificently intricate embroidery.

The picture completed, Martin declared that it was first to be exhibited in the dining room, where the children's work was on constant display, but that he intended it for his counselor, Mr. Frank. This was a radical departure, for up to now Martin had ignored all the men at the school. The counselor was duly impressed, and cherished the picture both for its beauty and as a gift of love. (For this reason I am unable to furnish a reproduction of the painting, which went with Mr. Frank when he left Wiltwyck.)

At the time Martin painted the picture, I knew only that it was enormously important to him and that it was up to me to do everything in my power to make it possible for him to complete it while the spirit was upon him. Only later did the therapist's story shed light on the full meaning of the work.

The day before, he had walked with her through the woods (treatment was often conducted outdoors). The trees being full of new birds' nests, he had spoken of his wish to raise a baby bird in a cage. This led to a discussion about the feelings of a bird that would find itself robbed of its freedom. Martin declared that he would procure a kite string, which could be attached to the bird's leg and would allow it to fly around. The conversation now turned toward the bird's feelings when it was pulled back at a person's will. Finally, Martin decided to give his hypothetical bird full freedom. After this act of empathy had led to renunciation of possessiveness, he suddenly declared: "This is exactly what my mother does to me. She keeps me on a string." This insight led to a long conversation about the relationship between a mother and her son, how a child is not part of his mother, the way her arm or leg is part of her, but is a person in his own right with independent feelings and will. Martin understood, and the session marked a profound change in his relationship to the mother.

The insight into the pathological aspects of the relationship between them was possible only after he had recognized himself in the bird and renounced the temptation of treating the bird the way he had himself been treated. This meant that Martin also gave up the sado-masochistic gratifications which he obtained through his continuous wranglings with his mother, and this freed him from the compulsion of repeating the same pattern with other people. It lessened his identification with her and made identification with father-figures possible. Of this we have seen the first indication in Martin's gift to his counselor.

There is no doubt that Martin's painting somehow related to this important event in his therapy. But we are surprised that, instead of celebrating his newly won freedom, he depicts a mother feeding a helpless fledgling. How can we understand this contradiction? We recall that Martin had tried painting similar subjects before (for instance, a madonna and child). Each time he had been driven to wreck his picture and had completed it only with my support. This last picture, on the other hand, had grown without difficulties or hesitations.

We know that ambivalence disturbs relationships. Although Martin pursued his mother with the ardor born of unfulfilled longings, he could not create an image of motherly love while he was bound to her by intensely contradictory feelings.

When Martin renounced the substitute gratifications which he had obtained in his sado-masochistic relationships, his unfulfilled infantile needs re-emerged. The picture of the apple tree and birds seems to be an act of restitution. In the making of it, Martin remains mature and masculine, displaying unusual skill, concentration, and endurance. The content, on the other hand, gratifies his infantile longings. Motherhood appears both directly in the bird and symbolically in the profusion of apples. The gratification of the baby's needs also appears directly in the feeding scene, and indirectly in the close-up which depicts the world from the viewpoint of the infant, who is completely surrounded by a gratifying, protective environment. Form and content tell the same story.

It seemed as if the restitution which he had procured for himself in painting the picture gave Martin the strength to make the next step, to turn toward a father-figure, for he chose this very painting as an offering for the counselor who represented fatherly authority.

His subsequent pictures did not repeat this tender scene. Instead there were a number of paintings of proud Africans, and many realistic sketches of buildings and of people. The last drawing before his discharge represents Martin's street (Fig. 49). We see him, a tiny figure on a roof, flying a kite. Thus he asserts his masculinity in a realistic manner, rather than in grandiose fabrications. At the time of his discharge, Martin had won the admiration and affection of many children and adults who had

FIGURE 49. *Martin*: City Street (6" x 8")

found him insufferable when he first came to the school. His fame as an artist endured long after he had left Wiltwyck.

Martin's story shows the rehabilitation of a child who, in spite of his unusual artistic gifts, would probably have perished without the aid of both art therapy and psychotherapy. In the beginning, art therapy constituted a means of survival. It became a container for rebellion and bitter feelings and provided a way to gratify intense exhibitionistic needs in a constructive or at least tolerable manner. This beginning resembles many of our previous stories, where art therapy also constituted a way of making positive experiences available to disturbed children who were hard to approach by any other means.

When psychotherapy was initiated, Martin's emotional gains found expression in art before they showed themselves in changed behavior. Later his improvement in daily life made it possible for him to gain a deserved recognition for his art. A reduction of raw aggression made enormous energies available for creative work, and in one heroic effort he succeeded in symbolically restoring the early relationship between mother and infant without regressing himself.

The story is reminiscent of Christopher's creation of the Spring Tree (Fig. 9, p. 75). In both incidents, creating an image of infantile bliss led to a developmental spurt toward independence and masculinity. We see in the story of the apple tree art's power for symbolically restoring a lost object. I believe that such restitutions are usually only possible if the child has somewhere in his life experienced some measure of gratification. Martin's mother, though domineering and at times cruel, had given her son a certain amount of warmth, and had also given him pride. In restoring the image of the good mother, he could draw upon these experiences. The same is true for Christopher, whose foster mother had also given him good motherly care in his infancy. When these children later encountered other warm and understanding people and also received assistance in coming to terms with the emotional conflicts that centered around the original love objects, they could in their art create symbols of the positive aspects of these early experiences. Thus they could overcome some of the damage suffered at the time when the initially positive relationship to the mother had deteriorated. To attain such profound influence on their emotional life, art had to become an absorbing passion to which the boys gave much of their time and energy.

This, I believe, is essential in working with aggressive children in general. Rather than catering to their restlessness by offering distraction, one must give them substance. Interest, once awakened, must be allowed to build up to great intensity, so that the child can experience the organizing force of constructive action carried out with passionate feeling.

CLOSING REMARKS

Throughout this book I have tried to demonstrate that the art therapist must understand the relationship between the formal qualities of the products he encounters and the psychological processes which are active when they are made.

Our investigation was focused on the work of disturbed children, but the processes we have observed are not confined to childhood. Some of the ideas that we have formulated hold true for art therapy in general—some of them touch upon the mystery of art at large.

We recognized that art has the power to bind and contain drive energies through a form of sublimation which does not demand their full neutralization. Instead, sublimation is attained when forms are created that successfully contain and embody experience, even if the subject matter tells of anger, anxiety, or pain. Therefore immature, impulse-ridden children can often be productive in art, even though they are unable to achieve those forms of sublimation where more complete neutralization of instinctive energy is necessary.

As sources of pleasure that are linked to ego functions rather than to purely impulsive acts become available, the child experiences the integrative powers of his ego, which extends its domain over areas of the mind that otherwise remain elusive or dangerously disruptive. Although art cannot remove the cause of tension or directly help resolve conflict, it serves as a *model of ego functioning*. It becomes a sanctuary where new attitudes and feelings can be expressed and tried out, even before such changes can take place in daily life.

I hope to have shown in this book that art fulfills for the disturbed child the function which it has for all men: to create a realm of symbolic living, which allows experimentation with ideas and feelings; to make apparent the complexities and contradictions of human life; to demonstrate man's capacity to transcend conflict and create order out of chaos; and finally to give pleasure.

Although our examples were taken mainly from work with children who need institutional treatment, I believe that the most important field for art therapy lies outside of institutions. Art therapy is needed and can be successful in work with children, adolescents, and adults who are endangered yet still able to live in the community, and with those who are returning to it after a period of institutional care.

The methods of art therapy can be brought to neighborhood houses, clubs, halfway houses, and the schools. We have noted at the beginning that even the most enlightened methods of art teaching seem inadequate in work with children whose lives are burdened with extraordinary pressures, because these methods presuppose a certain measure of self-confidence, an openness to the world and to new suggestions.

When working with children who live in a world that has denied them the opportunity to develop self-esteem and the capacity to act constructively, the teacher has to give support far beyond that which is ordinarily needed. Although he must *accept* much that is banal and empty, seeing that the children have good reason to ward off confrontation with their feelings of insignificance or with their chaotic fantasy lives, he must not be willing to *settle for* empty production. Even when the work remains at first incoherent and unformed, he must encourage art that tells of the conflict, anger, anxiety, and sexual excitement that fill the children's lives.

How far he can go in this and how difficult the task will be depends of course on the situation in which he carries out his work. Large classrooms are less suitable for therapeutic art than small classes or voluntary afternoon programs. Much depends on the extent of the children's disturbances.

Often the teacher will find a reservoir of resilience and vitality which makes it possible even for children who live under unfavorable circumstances to learn to take in what the world has to offer. In such situations a good deal of energy can be devoted to nourishing a healthy need for new experiences that carry the child beyond his immediate preoccupations. We have spoken of this important aspect of art as therapy mainly in the chapter on sublimation, but it has not been stressed. More could have been said about the widening horizon, the increasing interest in the world, and the richer, more varied art which become possible as children become less disturbed.[8]

We have concentrated on showing how the art of children who labor under severe emotional pressures must be either perfunctory or empty except when it is expressive of their pathology. Art therapy was most effective when it helped them to create art out of the very material that disrupted their lives. Creative work then engaged them in an intense struggle, focusing on subject matter that had taken on overwhelming importance. The emotional climate was akin to the dedicated artist's single-minded concentration rather than to the normal child's more casual enjoyment of art.

We have seen that work produced under such pressures can, within the limitations of the child's endowment and maturity, attain the aesthetic quality of art in the full sense. However, to enable a troubled child to reach such expression, the art therapist must struggle with him like Jacob with the Angel, but must (unlike Jacob) be willing to accept defeat time and again.

When products of therapeutic creative activities attain the aesthetic qualities of art, this fact is too often neglected in psychological evaluation. Sometimes this is because art has been relegated to a vague field of cultural interest or is thought of as just another hobby, beyond the realm of therapeutic concern. At other times the attitude seems to be an unfortunate consequence of recognizing that much that is made of art materials in therapy is not art. The recognition is accurate, but to imply that there must be a sharp division between therapeutic creative activities and art is mistaken.

The range of the art of disturbed individuals is, as a rule,

8. For a description of this kind of change, see *Art Therapy in a Children's Community*, pp. 109–25.

narrow, bounded by their pathological preoccupations. Their work is in the main self-contained, and offers little to others. The artist's creative impulse stems from similar sources, but his art transcends his personal concerns and becomes a gift to the world. However, the psychological processes that are active in both types of production have so much in common, and transitions between them are so subtle, that there is little justification for viewing them as essentially different.

We have distinguished various products of art therapy which fall short of art in the full sense, but none of them is alien to art. Art derives emotional impact from the same primitive energies that find direct expression in the impulsive manipulation of art materials. But the artist imposes form upon these raw expressions of feeling, and when he does so, his work is linked to the same mechanisms of defense that are active in stereotyped art. However, whereas the painter of stereotypes employs established techniques, symbols, and conventions to ward off and deny conflict, the very same means are used by the artist to contain and express conflict. Finally, there are in most works of art traces of personal meaning that can be understood only through uncovering techniques such as free association. Thus art is also linked to the simpler pictograph, but while pictographs mainly satisfy the need to state a private meaning, in the work of art any element that contains private meaning is so integrated that it contributes to the universal message. Thus instinctual drives, defense mechanisms, and unconscious symbolism combine with each other in many different ways.

Complete unity of form and content, of private and universal meaning, cannot always be attained. The moment when scribble, stereotype, or pictograph may turn into art can never be predicted. In educational and in therapeutic practice it would often be futile to distinguish rigidly between the various kinds of products. Some kinds of therapeutic applications, however, are almost of necessity inimical to art.

For example, whenever pictorial expression is used primarily for communication in psychotherapy, it is unlikely that the product will be art. Insofar as psychotherapy seeks to uncover the hidden core of the individual's behavior, it is opposed to that aspect of the artistic process which leads from the private to the universal. Pictorial communication in psychotherapy has served its purpose when meaning is understood by patient and therapist. Often the most abortive pictorial signs serve this purpose best.

When manipulation of art materials is encouraged mainly to help break down rigid defenses and permit the emergence of pent-up emotion, the result will usually remain too disorganized to become art.

Finally, when therapy is limited to strengthening defenses, the patient may use art activity chiefly to negate some unbearable truth. Even if his products are the antithesis of art, the therapist may have good reason not to intervene.

Therapeutic situations favorable to art are those designed to provide areas of symbolic living that help develop a more economically organized personality. Since the artistic value of the work produced is a sign of successful sublimation, the quality of the work becomes a measure (though not the only measure) of therapeutic success.

Epilogue

Since "Art as Therapy with Children" was first published, more than twenty years have gone by. The children whose work served to illustrate the ideas presented are now adults. We wonder what became of them. Often we have no way of knowing. In other instances our information cannot be published. This epilogue tells of the fate of two children whose production and personality figure largely in this book.

WALTER

The inner division which Walter's two paintings, Figs. 36A and 36B, embodied never healed. It determined the course of his short and tragic life.

After his discharge from Wiltwyck School at age thirteen-and-a-half Walter soon engaged in delinquent acts. At age twenty-one he stabbed two men to death during a heated argument. While serving a sentence for double murder he escaped, but was again arrested in conjunction with a bank robbery.

While serving a sentence at Leavenworth penitentiary for this offense Walter began to participate in an educational program. This opportunity brought about a change of heart. Walter's superior intelligence and his capacity for passionate pursuit of a chosen goal, which in his school days had mainly centered on art, re-emerged. He became a model student earning a bachelor's degree at the University of Kansas. He received a Phi Beta Kappa membership and was at that time the first prisoner in the United States so honored. From this vantage point he embarked on studies for a master's degree in Sociology. Walter so greatly impressed his teachers with his ardor, intelligence (and charm) that several of them wrote letters of recommendation to the parole commission urging speedy parole.

Walter's academic achievements brought him publicity within the Black press. He began corresponding with some of his former counselors from Wiltwyck School and with myself. He also corresponded with his son, whom he had never met and who was at that time also serving a prison sentence. He declared that the good years at Wiltwyck had saved him from becoming 'entirely evil.' He made plans someday, after he had earned his doctorate, to found a school such as Wiltwyck, but one that would keep the boys sheltered from the city streets until they were adults.

Buoyed by his successes he seemed oblivious of the fact that he had never finished serving time for the double-murder. When he was denied parole he was devastated and ceased corresponding.

Released from prison in due time, he made contact with a white young man whom he had befriended while the latter had served a brief sentence. According to this youth, Walter had saved him both physically and spiritually. He now reciprocated by helping Walter to find good employment as a computer expert. All seemed set for a better future. However, Walter soon found himself once more behind bars. He attempted an escape with the help of his woman friend, who managed to enter the prison hospital to provide him with a gun. When the two of them found themselves cornered by a sizeable police force, Walter, unable to shoot his way out, used his last bullets to shoot his woman friend and himself. His life ended at age forty-five.

We cannot fathom whether Walter's life and the life of his victims would have been spared if psychotherapy as well as educational opportunities had been available to him. All we know is that both aspects of Walter's personality were active to the end. He could be a friend and inspire friendship, he could work constructively, and he could be murderous.

Walter's painting Fig. 36A testifies to the power of art. Created at age thirteen-and-a-half, this impressive work embodies the impending tragedy. In restrospect, my description written 12 years before his death attains an almost predictive significance.

ANGEL

We left Angel (pgs. 135-138) at ten years of age still poised between illusory ego-ideals fashioned in the image of superman, and more realistic ones founded on his substantial artistic and intellectual gifts. With the exception of a brief interlude in a foster home, Angel spent his childhood at a Catholic home for dependent children. Later on, while attending the High School of Art and Design, he lived in a group home.

When I discussed his fate with Angel at age 16 he declared that his hospitalization had been a blessing in disguise. Had he remained at home, no one would have been interested in his school work or in his art, and his gifts "would have gone down the drain."

When he was 21 years old I asked Angel's permission to publish an autobiography[1] which he had written and illustrated with my assistance at 10 years of age. He readily consented.

In his letter he declared:

It was very interesting and very revealing to read about my past in detail. . . . It came at a very opportune time and I needed to read that in order for me to open some doors in my head that were closed at the time.

He also enclosed the following exquisite poem, apparently inspired by the look into his past afforded by reading my comments and his own story about his early years:

Nothing but the Light

By the time he could kick
he was constant motion
legs pumping piston-fast
accelerating over all obstacles—
in fact he was so fast
he could outrun the wind

No matter what, he would go his way oblivious to all
that was captured inside that little head of his

---

1. *Art Therapy Viewpoints*, pgs. 253-266. Elinor Ulman and Claire A. Levy (Eds.), 1980, Schocken Books, NY.

But when he sat down
to recollect himself,
visions of his past pleasure
floated by so quickly
all he could see
was the tail-end of his future
running toward a star
at the end of the sky
Before he could think
he was up chasing
what he would hope to find ahead

Calling upon that little extra
he thought he must've used years ago,
he pumped—
pumped so hard
he was nothing more
than a blur
and when
he was
a grasp
away
He just plain fizzled out.

Could his capacity to tell of his driven state in poetry have contributed to his ability to make a life for himself in the real world?

Angel joined the Navy at age twenty-two and has made a successful career of it up to date. In 1993 he is a married man with a teenaged daughter and a little son. He continues to draw and paint, taking his art materials along when he goes on missions. He states that making art to please himself is more important to him than attaining fame. However, he does exhibit his work, has won a measure of recognition and plans to devote more time to his art in the future. His identity as an artist constitutes an essential element of his sense of self.

Bibliography

Alschuler, R. H., and Hattwick, L. W. *Painting and Personality: A Study of Young Children.* Chicago: University of Chicago Press, 1947.

Bender, Lauretta. *Child Psychiatric Techniques.* Springfield, Ill.: Charles C Thomas, 1952.

Bernard, W. Viola; Ottenberg, Perry; Redl, Fritz. "Dehumanization: A Composite Psychological Defense in Relation to Modern War," in *Behavioral Science and Human Survival,* ed. Milton Schwebel. Palo Alto, Calif.: Science & Behavior Books, 1965.

Bernfeld, Siegfrid. "Zur Sublimierungstheorie," *Imago,* XVII (1931), 339.

————. "Bemerkungen über Sublimierung," *Imago,* VIII (1922), 333.

Betensky, Mala. "Case Study: Four Years of Art Therapy with a Schizoid Boy," *American Journal of Art Therapy,* IX, No. 2 (1970).

Bettelheim, Bruno. *Love is Not Enough.* New York: Free Press, 1950.

————. *Truants from Life: The Rehabilitation of Emotionally Disturbed Children.* New York: Free Press, 1955.

Bloom, Leonard. "Aspects of the Use of Art in the Treatment of Maladjusted Children," *Bulletin of Art Therapy,* IV, No. 2 (1963).

Bornstein, Berta. 'On Latency," in Ruth S. Eissler, Vol. VI (1951).

————. "Masturbation in the Latency Period," *ibid.,* Vol. VIII (1953).

Brown, Claude. *Manchild in the Promised Land.* New York: Macmillan, 1965.

Burlingham, Dorothy. "Developmental Considerations in the Occupations of the Blind," in Ruth S. Eissler, Vol. XX (1967).

Cane, Florence. *The Artist in Each of Us.* New York: Pantheon, 1951.

Cižek, Franz. *Children's Colored Paper Work.* New York: G. E. Stechert and Hafner, 1927.

Cole, Natalie R. *The Arts in the Classroom.* New York: John Day, 1940.

Crane, Rebecca. "An Experiment Dealing with Color and Emotion," *Bulletin of Art Therapy,* I, No. 2 (1962).

Crawford, James. "Art for the Mentally Retarded: Directed or Creative," *Bulletin of Art Therapy,* II, No. 2 (1962).

Dewdny, Selwyn. "The Role of Art Activities in Canadian Mental Hospitals," *Bulletin of Art Therapy,* VIII, No. 2 (1969).

Eckstein, Rudolf; Wallerstein, Judith; Mandelbaum, Arthur. "Counter-Transference in a Residential Treatment Home," in Ruth S. Eissler, Vol. XIV (1959).

Eissler, Kurt. *Leonardo da Vinci: Psychoanalytic Notes on the Enigma.* New York: International Universities Press, 1961.

————. *Goethe: A Psychoanalytic Study.* Detroit: Wayne State University Press, 1963.

Eissler, Ruth S.; Freud, Anna; Hartmann, Heinz; Lustman, Seymour; Kris, Marianne, eds. *The Psychoanalytic Study of the Child.* 24 vols. New York: International Universities Press, 1945–69.

Fraiberg, Selma. "Enlightenment and Confusion," in Ruth S. Eissler, Vol. VI (1951).

Freud, Anna. *The Ego and the Mechanisms of Defense.* New York: International Universities Press, 1946.

————. "Indications for Child Analysis," in Ruth S. Eissler, Vol. I (1945).

————. *Normality and Pathology in Childhood.* New York: International Universities Press, 1965.

Freud, Sigmund. The following selections are taken from the *Complete Psychological Works,* Standard Edition, 24 vols., translated by Alix Strachey and Alan Tyson. London: Hogarth Press and Institute of Psychoanalysis, 1951.

Delusion and Dream, 1909.

The Ego and the Id, 1923.

Formulations on the Two Principles of Mental Functioning, 1911.

The Infantile Genital Organisation and the Libido, 1925.

Inhibitions, Symptoms and Anxiety, 1926.

Leonardo da Vinci and a Memory of His Childhood, 1910.

A Neurosis of Demoniacal Possession in the Seventeenth Century, 1923.

The Relation of the Poet to Day Dreaming, 1909.

The Unconscious, 1915.

Gitter, Lena L. "The Montessori View of Art Education," *Bulletin of Art Therapy*, II, No. 1 (1962).

———. "Art in a Class for Mentally Retarded Children," *ibid.*, III, No. 3 (1964).

Goldstone, Stephen E., ed. *Concepts of Community Psychiatry.* Washington, D.C.: National Institute of Mental Health, 1964.

Goodenough, F. L. *Children's Drawings: A Handbook of Child Psychology.* Worcester, Mass.: Clark University Press, 1931.

Greenacre, Phyllis. "The Childhood of the Artist: Libidinal Phase Development and Giftedness," in Ruth S. Eissler, Vol. XII (1957).

———. "Play in Relation to Creative Imagination," *ibid.*, Vol. XIV (1959).

Hammer, Emanuel F. *Clinical Application of Projective Drawings.* Springfield, Ill.: Charles C Thomas, 1958, 1967.

Hartmann, Heinz. "Notes on the Theory of Sublimation," in Ruth S. Eissler, Vol. X (1955).

———; Kris, Ernst; Loewenstein, Rudolph. "Comments on the Formulation of Psychic Structure," *ibid.*, Vol. II (1946).

Kramer, Edith. "Art and Craft," *Bulletin of Art Therapy*, V, No. 4 (1966).

———. "Art and Emptiness," *ibid.*, I, No. 1 (1961).

———. "Art Education and Emptiness," *ibid.*, I, No. 3 (1962).

———. "Art Therapy and the Severely Disturbed Gifted Child," *ibid.*, V, No. 1 (1965).

———. *Art Therapy in a Children's Community: A Study of the Function of Art Therapy in the Treatment Program of Wiltwyck School for Boys.* Springfield, Ill.: Charles C Thomas, 1958.

———. "Autobiography of a Ten-Year-Old," *Bulletin of Art Therapy*, VII, No. 3 (1968).

———. "A Critique of Kurt Eissler's *Leonardo da Vinci*," *ibid.*, IV, No. 1 (1964).

———. *Kunsttherapie mit Kindern: Handbuch der Kinderpsychotherapie.* Munich: Gerd Biermann-Ernst Reinhardt Verlag, 1969.

———. "The Problem of Quality in Art," *Bulletin of Art Therapy*, III, No. 1 (1963).

———. "Stereotypes," *ibid.*, VI, No. 4 (1967).

Kris, Ernst. "Neutralization and Sublimation," in Ruth S. Eissler, Vol. X (1955).

———. *Psychoanalytic Explorations in Art.* New York: International Universities Press, 1952; Schocken Books, 1964.

Kubie, Lawrence. *Neurotic Distortion of the Creative Process.* Lawrence, Kan.: University of Kansas Press, 1959.

Kwiatkowska, Hanna Yaxa. "Family Art Therapy: Experiments with a New Technique," *Bulletin of Art Therapy,* I, No. 3 (1962).

——. "The Psychiatric Patient and His 'Well' Sibling," *ibid.,* II, No. 2 (1962).

——. "The Uses of Families' Art Productions for Psychiatric Evaluation," *ibid.,* VI, No. 2 (1967).

Langer, Susanne. *Feeling and Form.* New York: Charles Scribner's Sons, 1953.

——. *Philosophy in a New Key.* New York: Mentor Books, 1948.

Levick, Myra; Goldman, Morris; Fink, Paul Jay. "Training for Art Therapists," *Bulletin of Art Therapy,* VI, No. 3 (1967).

Lorenz, Konrad. *On Aggression.* New York: Harcourt Brace Jovanovich, 1966.

——. *Über tierisches und menschliches Verhalten: Gesammelte Abhandlungen.* 2 vols. Munich: R. Piper Verlag, 1966.

Lowenfeld, H. "Psychic Trauma and Productive Experience in the Artist," *Psychoanalytic Review,* I (1941), 116.

Lowenfeld, Viktor. *The Nature of Creative Activity.* London: Routledge & Kegan Paul, 1952.

——, and Brittain, W. L. *Creative and Mental Growth.* New York: Macmillan, 1957.

Machover, Karen. *Personality Projection in the Drawing of the Human Figure.* Springfield, Ill.: Charles C Thomas, 1952.

Mahler, Margaret. *On Human Symbiosis and the Vicissitudes of Individuation.* New York: International Universities Press, 1968.

Manzella, David. *Educationists and the Evisceration of the Visual Arts.* Scranton, Pa.: International Textbook Co., 1963.

Marshall, Sybil. *An Experiment in Education.* New York: Cambridge University Press, 1963.

Meares, Ainslie. *The Door of Serenity: A Study in the Therapeutic Use of Symbolic Painting.* Springfield, Ill.: Charles C Thomas, 1958.

——. *Shapes of Sanity.* Springfield, Ill.: Charles C Thomas, 1960.

Münz, L., and Lowenfeld, Viktor. *Plastische Arbeiten Blinder.* Brünn: Verlag Rudolf M. Rohrer, 1934.

Naumburg, Margaret. *Dynamically Oriented Art Therapy: Its Principles and Practice.* New York: Grune & Stratton, 1966.

——. *Schizophrenic Art: Its Meaning in Psychotherapy.* New York: Grune & Stratton, 1950.

——. *Studies of the Free Art Expression of Behavior Problem Children and Adolescents.* New York: Grune & Stratton, 1947.

Olden, Christine. "Notes on the Development of Empathy," in Ruth S. Eissler, Vol. XIII (1958).

———. "On Adult Empathy with Children," *ibid.*, Vol. VIII (1953).

Orbis Statini Židovske Muzeum. *Children's Drawings and Poetry from Terezin.* Prague, 1962.

Paneth, Marie. *Branch Street.* London: George Allen and Unwin, 1947.

Pattison, E. Mansell. "The Relationship of Adjunctive and Therapeutic Recreation Services to Community Mental Health Programs," *American Journal of Art Therapy*, IX, No. 1 (1969).

Peller, Lilli. "Daydreams and Children's Favorite Books," in Ruth S. Eissler, Vol. XIV (1959).

———. "Libidinal Phases, Ego Development and Play," *ibid.*, Vol. IX (1954).

———. "The School's Role in Promoting Sublimation," *ibid.*, Vol. XI (1956).

Plank, Emma. "Leg Amputation in a Four-Year-Old: Reactions of the Child, Her Family and the Staff," in Ruth S. Eissler, Vol. XVI (1961).

———. *Working with Children in Hospitals: A Guide for the Professional Team.* Cleveland: Western Reserve University Press, 1962.

Prinzhorn, H. *Bildnerei der Geisteskranken.* Berlin: Springer Verlag, 1923.

Redl, Fritz, and Wineman, David. *Children Who Hate: The Disorganization and Breakdown of Behavior Controls.* New York: Free Press, 1951.

———. *Controls from Within.* New York: Free Press, 1952.

Refsnes, Carolyn. "Art Therapy as Adjunct to Long Term Psychotherapy," *Bulletin of Art Therapy*, VII, No. 2 (1968).

———. "Recovery, Repression and Art," *ibid.*, VI, No. 3 (1967).

Reich, Annie. "Structure of the Grotesque-Comic Sublimation," *Bulletin of the Menninger Clinic*, XIII, No. 5 (1949).

———. "Further Notes on Countertransference," *International Journal of Psychoanalysis*, XLI (1960).

———. "On Countertransference," *ibid.*, XXXII (1951).

Sachs, Hanns. *The Creative Unconscious.* Cambridge, Mass.: Sic-Art Publishers, 1942.

Schaefer-Simmern, Henry. *The Unfolding of Artistic Activity.* Berkeley: University of California Press, 1948.

Schmidt-Waener, T. "Formal Criteria for the Analysis of Children's Drawings," *American Orthopsychiatric Journal,* XII (1952), 95.

Silver, Rawley, A. "Art and the Deaf," *American Journal of Art Therapy,* IX, No. 2 (1970)*.*

Site, Myer. "Art and the Slow Learner," *Bulletin of Art Therapy,* IV, No. 1 (1964).

Stern, Max M. "Trauma, Projective Technique and Analytic Profile," *Psychoanalytic Review,* XXII (1953).

Themal, Joachim H. "Children's Work as Art," *Bulletin of Art Therapy,* II, No. 1 (1962).

Tinbergen, N. *The Study of Instinct.* London: Oxford University Press, 1958.

Ulman, Elinor. "Art Therapy: Problems of Definition," *Bulletin of Art Therapy,* I, No. 2 (1961).

———. "A New Use of Art in Psychiatric Diagnosis," *ibid.,* IV, No. 3 (1965).

———. "Psychotherapy and the Arts at Withymead Center," *ibid.,* II, No. 4 (1964).

———. "Therapy Is Not Enough," *ibid.,* VI, No. 1 (1966).

———. "The War Between Therapese and English," *ibid.,* II, Nos. 2 and 4 (1964).

Vaessen, M. L. J. "Art or Expression: A Discussion of the Creative Activities of Mental Patients," *Bulletin of Art Therapy,* II, No. 1 (1962).

Zierer, Edith; Steinberg, David; Finn, Regina; Farmer, Mark. "Family Creative Analysis," *Bulletin of Art Therapy,* V, Nos. 2 and 3 (1966).

Index

Adolescence, 10, 22, 44, 72, 117–18, 121, 148, 156–57, 175, 191, 197, 199, 202, 220

Adults, 10, 14, 27–28, 92, 109, 157, 194, 202, 220

Aesthetics, 5, 22, 52, 76, 90–91, 221

Age, chronological, 8; mental, 7

Aggression, 81, 87, 89, 106, 146, 152, 158–223; and control, 162–71; dammed-up, 160–62; intraspecific, 159, 167; neutralized, 158, 183–84; oral, 165; unsublimated, 201

Aggressor, 145, 168. *See also* Identification with the aggressor

Alice, 161, fig. 33

Allan, 38, 103–5, 108, fig. 14

Ambivalence, 57, 66, 86-87, 89, 105, 144, 146, 159, 174, 193–204, 216

Andrew, 116, VII, VIII

Angel, 65, 115, 134–39, 145–46, figs. 6, 21, 22, 23, 24, 25

Ann, 130–31, 144, 146, 195, fig. 19

Art, anti-, 2–3, 13, 92, 125; children's, 3, 6–8; evocative power of, 8, 50, 53, 67, 87–88, 150; folk, 1, 3–4; inner consistency of, 50, 53, 67, 87; naïve, 123;

pseudo-, 5, 12–14, 122; quality in, 47–67, 76; teaching of, 6–9, 14, 23, 123–27, 220–21

Barry, 205–6

Behavior, symptomatic, 56, 73, 76, 89, 92

Bernard, 35–36

Billy, 55, 57–59, 66, 204–5

Bob, 30, fig. 2

Body-image, 79, 97, 116

Brian, 38

Cane, Florence, 4, 6, 8–11

Carl, 191–93, 196, XIV, XV

Castration, 52, 59, 70, 165, 168, 177–78

Catharsis, 110

Chaos. *See* Stereotyped chaos

Children, atypical, 7, 163–68; borderline, 45, 54; brain-damaged, 45–46, 147; psychotic, 147–48; underprivileged, spoiled, 15–21, 23

Christopher, 73–80, 93–97, 100, 109, 113–14, 129, 203, 207–8, 218, figs. 9, 10, 11

Cižek, Franz, 6

Clyde, 34–38, 103–8, 167, fig. 15

Cobra, 133–34, 144–45, 194

Compulsion, 33, 38, 46, 56–59, 64, 66, 132

Confrontation, 29–33, 220
Control, 162–77, 187–88
Counter-transference, 38–43, 112
Crafts, 26, 33–34, 43

Danny, 71–72, 89
David, 162–63
Deadlock, 133–34, 143–45, 149, 204
Defense, 8, 14–15, 17–20, 46, 49, 54, 56–59, 64, 70, 83, 88, 105, 119, 120–57, 160, 165, 187, 190, 194, 204, 222–23; compulsive, *see* Compulsion; mechanisms of, 19, 89–90, 122–23, 134, 157, 222
Delinquency, 17, 45, 112, 134, 150–54, 171–74, 179–86, 192, 196, 206, 209–18
Denial, 18, 79, 123
Dependency, 16, 111–14
Depression, 192, 196
Discharge, chaotic, emotional, 54–57; direct, 87; impulsive, 68
Displacement, 70–74, 79, 100–101
Drive energies, 91, 162, 219
Drives, 13, 67–68, 89, 158, 160, 222

Eddie, 128
Ego, 68–70, 77, 81–82, 88–89, 93, 102, 156, 162, 171, 180, 191–92, 194, 204, 219; extension of, 40, 93–103; ideal, 138, 141, 144–45, 149–50, 154–56, 172–75, 194, 196; strength, 69, 102, 187, 203
Eissler, Kurt, 91
Elation, 192
Empathy, 39, 42, 96, 109, 120
Emptiness, 2, 9–15, 18–24, 49, 116, 147, 152, 220–21
Energy, neutralized, 193
Eric, 129

Ersatz, 16–17, 23, 69–70
Exhibitionism, 210, 213, 217
Experimentation, 45, 66
Expression, formed, *see* Formed expression; symbolic, 33, 83

Fantasy, 20, 29–30, 34, 46, 92, 94–98; delusional, 138, 145, 148; sexual, 64, 83, 85–86, 102
Formed expression, 54, 63–66
Fragmentation, 7, 29–30, 51, 130, 188, 201
Frank, 139–42, 145–46, 172, 195, IX, X, fig. 26
Free association, 9, 222
Freudian theory, 68, 147
Functioning, 37–38

Gordon, 84–90, 93, 196–202, VI, figs. 44, 45, 46, 47
Gratification, 32, 69–70, 75, 77, 203
Guilt, 154–55, 203

Hal, 208–9
Harry, 185–91, figs. 41, 42, 43
Helen, 124–27, 143–46, 195, figs. 16, 17
Henry, 39–40, 131–33, 144, fig. 20
Herman, 51–54, 177–78, 182–83, I, II, III

Id, 68–69, 102
Identification, 23, 30, 42, 104, 134, 155, 169, 171–72, 195, 215; with the aggressor, 133–34, 144–45, 168–70, 172–77, 193–201
Identity, 8, 29, 36, 40, 49, 132, 138, 149, 156–57, 179; loss of, 2, 18, 156
Image, projection of, 8, 10, 19–20, 116
Imagination, 20, 97, 185

Impulse, 48, 64–65, 81, 88, 171, 188, 192
Independence, 112–13
Individuation, 108, 164
Inhibition, 67–68
Instinct, 68–70, 222
Integration, 7, 96, 107
Internalization, 166, 170, 175, 177–78, 191, 194, 196
Interpretation, 25, 34, 36–38, 167
Isolation, 16, 29, 109, 140

Jerry, 110
John, 113
Johnny, 37
Judy, 36

Kenneth, 29–32, 97, fig. 1
Kramer, Edith, fig. 5
Kris, Ernst, 206

Larry, 149–57, 192, 195, figs. 27, 28, 29, 30, 31, 32
Latency, 22, 26, 72, 139
Leon, 178–85, 191, XIII, figs. 39, 40
Libido, 201
Lillian, 82–84, 88–90, 93, V
Lorenz, Konrad, 158–59
Lowenfeld, Viktor, 6, 8–9

Margaret, 165–68, 170, fig. 34
Mark, 37
Martha, 36
Martin, 41–43, 112–13, 209–18, XVI, figs. 48, 49
Mary, 80–82, 89–90, 93, IV
Masochism, 149–50, 196. *See also* Sado-masochism
Max, 53–54, fig. 3
Mervin, 115
Michael, 55–56, 64–66, 168–71, 177, 195, fig. 35
Milieu, therapeutic, 23–46
Milieu therapy, 24, 178, 209

Narcissism, 156, 170, 174, 194–95, 201
Naumburg, Margaret, 4–5, 25
Neurosis, 16, 73, 75, 80
Neutralization, 69, 88–89, 91, 193, 219

Obsession, 46, 74, 79, 86–87, 89, 97, 100, 145, 187, 190
Oedipal complex, 35, 77, 163
Oscar, 208–9

Paranoia, 37, 175, 177, 187, 195–96
Philip, 161
Pictograph, 47–50, 54, 59–62, 66, 90, 222
Play, 10, 26–28, 34, 43, 92, 164
Pre-adolescence, prepuberty, 10, 22, 26, 93, 102, 122, 157, 197, 199
Precursory activities, 54–55
Projection, 9, 29–33, 48, 59, 85, 123. *See also* Image, projection of
Psychoanalysis, psychoanalytic theory, 4–5, 9, 13, 17, 23, 32, 39, 67, 157–58, 160, 169–70
Psychology, 4–6
Psychosis, 54, 147–48, 179, 204–5
Psychotheraphy, 25–26, 32–33, 37, 40, 59, 73, 119, 164, 172, 207, 209, 213, 217, 222–23

Questioning, compulsive, obsessive, 74–75

Ralph, 128, fig. 18
Reality, 37–38
Regression, 13–14, 42, 96, 139, 147, 161
Renunciation, 69, 77
Repetition, 38, 127–30
Repression, 68, 70, 88, 102, 118, 146, 154

Restitution, 206, 216, 218
Robert, 55–58, 60, 62–64, 66, 163, figs. 4, 7, 8
Rose, 164–65

Sadism, 150
Sado-masochism, 41, 43, 105, 152, 195, 211, 213–16
Sam, 117
Schaefer-Simmern, Henry, 4
Schemata, 10, 127, 139–40, 142
Schizophrenia, 7, 48, 119, 187–88
Scribble, 10–12, 15, 19, 48, 50, 222
Seduction, 14, 16–17, 35, 42, 197, 211
Self-esteem, 33, 156, 203, 220
Self-representation, 19, 154, 162, 172, 175–77
Shirley, 163–64
Smith, Mrs., 161–62, XI
Stanley, 103, 105–8, fig. 15
Stereotype, 8–10, 12, 15, 17–18, 47–50, 57, 59, 90, 98, 122, 124–25, 127–49, 175, 197, 204, 222
Stereotyped chaos, 11–15, 19, 23, 143

Sublimation, 42, 67–121, 129, 152, 158, 162, 189, 202–3, 219, 223
Substitution, 70–72, 88, 132
Superego, 68, 81, 93, 192, 194, 196, 203–4
Support, 111–14
Symbolism, 28, 33, 45, 50, 83, 85–87, 89–90, 144, 219, 223
Symptom, 73–79, 129, 187

Talent, 7, 80, 103–10, 117, 125, 134–35, 138–39, 144, 149–57, 174, 185, 192, 207, 210
Tinbergen, N., 158
Tom, 55
Tommy, 37
Tonio, 97–103, 109, figs. 12, 13
Transference, 25, 38–43, 112, 209

Unconscious, 13, 23, 25, 35–36, 46, 49, 60, 80, 83, 91, 123, 170, 203, 222

Walter, 110, 172–75, 196, fig. 36
Willie, 175–77, 195, XII, figs. 37, 38